Colonial Identities

Records of Our History

Colonial Identities

Canada from 1760 to 1815

Bruce G. Wilson

National Archives of Canada / Archives nationales du Canada

Available in Canada through
associated bookstores
and other booksellers

Cat. No.: SA2-129/3-1988-E
ISBN: 0-660-12666-4
Canada: $34.95
Other countries: $41.95

Canadian Cataloguing in Publication Data

Wilson, Bruce G., 1946–
Colonial identities: Canada from 1760 to 1815

(Records of our History)
Issued also in French under title:
Identités coloniales.
DSS cat. no. SA2-129/3-1988-E (bound)
DSS cat. no. SA2-129/3-1988-1E (pbk.)
ISBN 0-660-12666-4 (bound): $34.95 ($41.95, foreign)
ISBN 0-660-12721-0 (pbk.): $24.95 ($29.95, foreign)
1. Canada—History—1763–1791—Sources.
2. Canada—History—1760–1763—Sources.
3. Canada—History—1791–1841—Sources.
I. National Archives of Canada. II. Title. III. Series.
FC410.W54 1988 971.02 C88-099000-7
F1032.W54 1988

Table of Contents

Economy
113

Religion
153

Society and Culture
167

Social Conditions
185

Native Peoples
197

War of 1812
211

Index
231

Foreword

Colonial Identities is the third volume of a National Archives series entitled *Records of Our History*. The series is based on the premise that Canada's past has a future: that Canadians can come to a better understanding of themselves through an appreciation of their collective memory — their archival heritage. The book can be used by scholars and the general public both as a reference tool and as a general history. It consists of reproductions of 113 archival documents — manuscripts, maps, works of documentary art and rare printed items. Almost all are contemporary to the period. Some have the stature and significance to make them national treasures, while others, once part of everyday life, are now made rare and precious by the fact of their survival. All are drawn from the extensive collections of the National Archives of Canada.

The documents have been arranged by broad theme with a commentary to describe each item, fit it into the theme and explain the significance of such material in understanding our past. The book is designed to allow readers to browse through it or to read it from cover to cover, and refer to the records that illustrate, support and explain the text.

I trust that many people will have the opportunity to read *Colonial Identities*. It is my hope that the wealth of records it contains will make Canadian history more alive and meaningful. This, after all, is the objective of the National Archives of Canada.

Jean-Pierre Wallot
National Archivist

Introduction and Acknowledgments

Between the years 1760 and 1815, Canada as we know it today did not exist. In the scattered colonies and territories of the half of North America that would one day become the Canadian nation, people went about their daily routines in ways that now seem exotic and quaint. In retrospect, the period was one of limited colonial identities.

No other period in the history of Canada, however, incorporates more events and developments as basic to the understanding of present-day Canada as that between the Conquest and the end of the War of 1812. In that period, a coherent geographical outline of Canada was pieced together for the first time. The previously unexplored parts of the Prairies, the western mountains and the Pacific slope all became known to Europeans. Only the far north remained little known, except to its own inhabitants.

Like our own days, this period was one of wars and uncertainties. Its conflicts shaped modern Canada. The Conquest established a basic reality of Canadian existence: the continuing presence of the French and English cultures within a single political entity. Both language groups then established patterns of confrontation and conciliation within which they still co-exist today. Other ethnic groups at the time adapted to this pattern, some finding advantages in a mixed-culture society, others, like Canada's native peoples, having to struggle to maintain their distinctiveness.

A second conflict, the American Revolution, coming less than twenty years after the Conquest, shattered dreams of a British empire that would encompass most of North America and, almost by default, define Canada's modern boundaries. The Revolution brought to Canada a population, refugees from the old Thirteen Colonies, who would be both attracted and repelled by their former homeland. The War of 1812, thirty years later, gave the British American colonies a sharp awareness of the might of their southern neighbour, but also marked their firm rejection of absorption into the republic. International events, like the French Revolution and the Napoleonic Wars, did much to shape emerging patterns of politics, ideology and economic development.

The period was one of growth and increasing sophistication. In the beginning, the economy was based primarily on furs and fish. Well before 1815, the colonists became successful hewers of wood, processors, manufacturers, grain exporters, shipbuilders, entrepreneurs and international traders. The growth of Canadian culture often seemed fragile, but it began to blossom with the publication of British North America's first novel, poetry and plays in both languages, substantial travel and religious writings, and a distinctive style of French Canadian painting. All the existing colonies that would some day make up Canada experienced their regional variations as each looked to solve its distinctive political and social concerns, yet all shared the common experience of contending with the imperial government to establish a space in which to be themselves.

It may be helpful to clarify some geographical areas. "Canada," in the period before 1791, meant the province of Quebec and much of what is now Ontario. "British North America" seems a preferable term to cover the other colonies and regions with which we are concerned, and this term will be used throughout, even though before the American Revolution it could be taken to include what is now the United States of America.

I hope this book will give its readers as much pleasure as its compilation has given me.

Many people have aided in the preparation of this book. For their substantial contributions, I wish especially to thank my colleagues, Jim Burant, Terry Cook, Ed Dahl, Patricia Kennedy, Gilles Langelier, Lise Perron-Croteau and Dawn Monroe. Many thanks to all those in the Historical Resources, Conservation and Public Programs Branches who have contributed to it. Stephen Willis of the Music Division, National Library, was generous with his knowledge of the Ste. Foy volume of religious music (Item 74), while Bernard Pothier of the Canadian War Museum and Richard Wright of the University of New Brunswick shared their knowledge of the Micmac catechism and grammar (Item 90).

The items in this book were displayed in an exhibition at the National Archives of Canada.

Bruce G. Wilson

I

Exploration and Surveying

The period 1760 to 1815 saw Canada quite literally "put on the map." Exploration, mapping and charting of the Canadian West and the Pacific Coast by Europeans proceeded at a remarkable rate. Native peoples, who had for generations known their particular territories, provided vital aid and guidance to white explorers. Driven by economic forces as well as imperial rivalries, explorers and traders surveyed the Prairies and penetrated through the mountain barriers to the ocean. Others sailed up the Pacific Coast. Two explorers journeyed northward overland to touch the Arctic coast at two different points. In the East, extensive charting of the Atlantic coastline and more comprehensive land surveys yielded an increasingly detailed and complex picture of the land and its surrounding waters. By 1815, only the western Arctic coastline and islands remained largely unknown territory. The geographical jigsaw puzzle for the half continent that was to become Canada had otherwise been pieced together.

I

A Contemporary Account of Little-Known Spanish Voyages Along the Pacific Coast, 1774–1792

It is not well known that the first European explorers of Canada's West Coast were Spanish. Reacting to the beginnings of Russian penetration from the north, the Spanish in 1774 sent Juan José Pérez (circa 1725–1775) from Monterey, California, to explore the unknown coast to the north. Pérez reached as far as the northwest corner of the Queen Charlotte Islands. A second Spanish voyage occurred the following year. Explorations continued at intervals until 1793. The Spanish penetrated up the coast well into Alaska, but withdrew from the Northwest Coast after 1795, and had no further direct influence on its history.

The book illustrated here describes the voyage of the *Sutil* and the *Mexicana*, two Spanish schooners that spent the summer of 1792 exploring the Strait of Georgia. The 167-page introduction describes all the Spanish voyages to 1792. The secrecy with which Spanish authorities cloaked the voyages makes this comprehensive review of great significance.

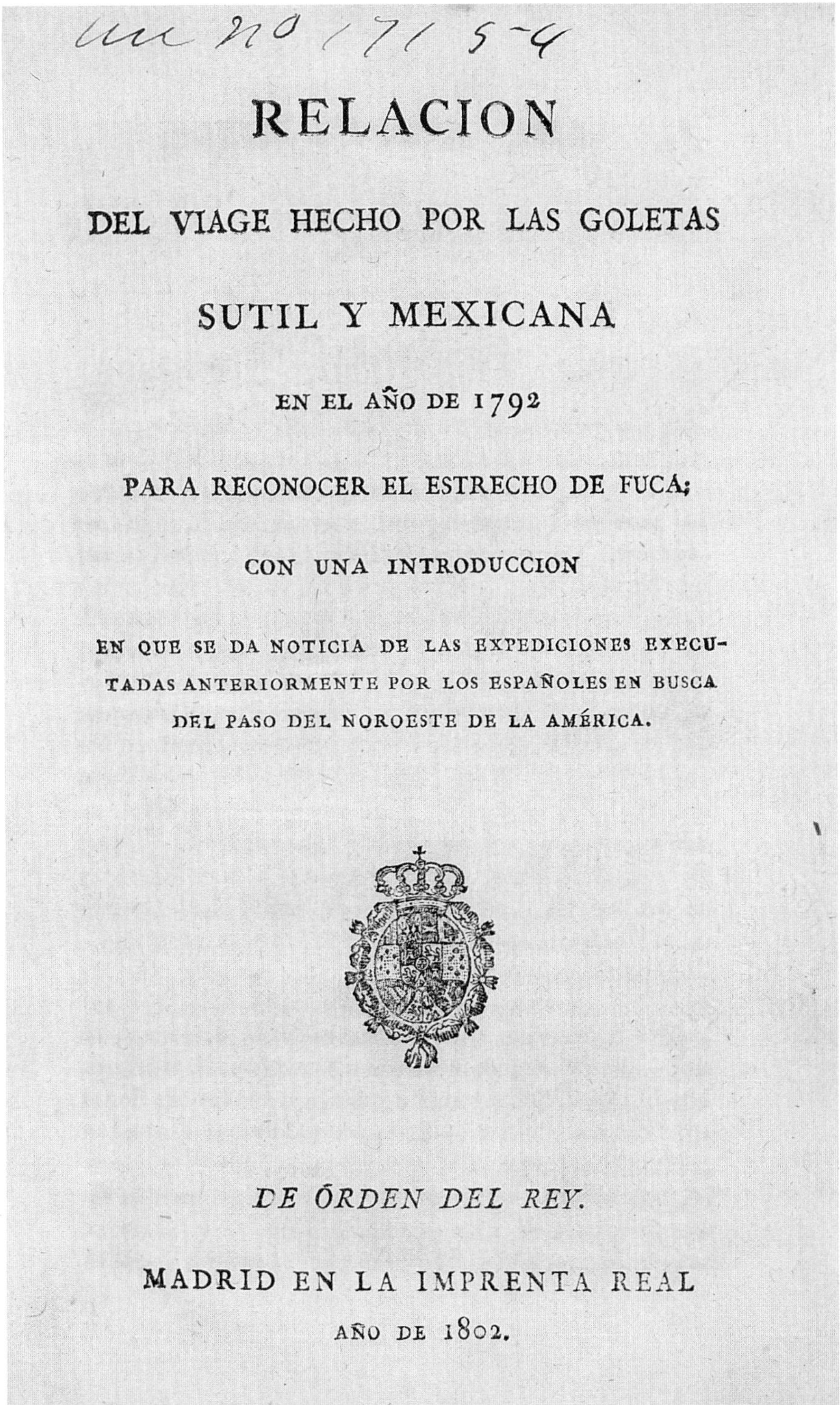

RELACION

DEL VIAGE HECHO POR LAS GOLETAS

SUTIL Y MEXICANA

EN EL AÑO DE 1792

PARA RECONOCER EL ESTRECHO DE FUCA;

CON UNA INTRODUCCION

EN QUE SE DA NOTICIA DE LAS EXPEDICIONES EXECUTADAS ANTERIORMENTE POR LOS ESPAÑOLES EN BUSCA DEL PASO DEL NOROESTE DE LA AMÉRICA.

DE ÓRDEN DEL REY.

MADRID EN LA IMPRENTA REAL

AÑO DE 1802.

Relacion del viage hecho por las goletas Sutil y Mexicana . . . . [Jose Espinosa y Tello], ed. Madrid en la Imprenta Real, 1802. Title page.

National Archives of Canada: Library (Negative no. C-130522).

A Native of Nootka Sound (Vancouver Island), 1778

The third voyage of the famous explorer and navigator, Captain James Cook (1728–1779), which he commenced in 1776, was intended as an assertion of British claims following reports of the first Spanish expeditions. Previous attempts had been made from the east to find a northern passage by water between the Atlantic and the Pacific oceans. With his extensive experience in the Pacific, Cook was instructed to try to find a passage from the west.

Cook arrived on the northwest coast in March 1778. His two vessels anchored at Nootka (now Resolution Cove, Nootka Sound, Vancouver Island) for a month to take on wood and water and to undertake repairs. The halt allowed Cook and his officers to make detailed observations of the local people.

This careful sketch of a native is one of twenty-nine extant drawings by John Webber (1751–1793) depicting Nootka Sound. The sketches constitute an important basis of our present understanding of Nootka culture at the time of first contact with Europeans. The man has dressed his hair and body with grease and paint. His face is painted with red ocher — a custom that was common everywhere on the northwest coast — perhaps as a protection against the sun. This man's addition of other paint was for aesthetic reasons. Ear ornaments were common, as were nose-rings cut from pieces of abalone shell or fashioned from copper. The fur-trimmed rain cape of woven cedar hints at the skill in basketry and weaving possessed by the Nootka.

John Webber, a professional portrait and landscape painter, was the official artist on Cook's third voyage. Sixty-one engravings were commissioned from his works to appear in James Cook's and James King's *A Voyage to the Pacific Ocean . . .* (3 vols., London, 1784). The National Archives holds six original Webber drawings from the expedition. This particular pastel was not the source of a published engraving and has seldom been seen by the public.

Man of Nootka Sound (Vancouver Island), April 1778. John Webber (1751–1793). Pastel with ink and grey wash, after 1778. 45.6×31.1 cm.

National Archives of Canada: Documentary Art and Photography Division (Negative no. C-13415).

I

Cook's Men Turn Back from Their Search for a Northwest Passage, 1778

Bad weather forced Cook's vessels out to sea as they left Nootka. They did not sight land again until they had moved beyond the boundaries of present-day Canada and into Alaskan waters. There the grim reality of polar navigation soon emerged as the expedition was driven back by a massive wall of ice blocking its progress eastward.

In this sketch, also by Webber, Cook's ships, the *Resolution* and the *Discovery*, can be seen in the background, and behind them the mountains of ice that had blocked their progress. Walrus were not generally eaten, but occasionally those on board Cook's ships welcomed a respite from the ever-present salted meat.

Cook's ships retreated through the Bering Strait to winter in the Sandwich (Hawaiian) Islands, where Cook met his death. A second attempt by his crew to find a Northwest Passage was equally unsuccessful. Despite the fact that the expedition had failed in what it considered its primary objective, the real significance of the voyage was that the northwest coast of America was known to Europeans at last. Unlike the Spaniards, Cook and his officers revealed to the world — through narratives, maps and drawings like this one — where they had been and what they had seen.

This is a relatively finished drawing probably done after the voyage as an intermediary step between an on-the-spot-sketch and a finished engraving. The National Archives of Canada holds another version of this sketch of the scene, probably made on the spot.

Cook's Men Shooting Walrus,
19 August 1778. John Webber (1751–1793). Pencil, ink, and grey wash, after 1778. 16.3 × 30.1 cm.

National Archives of Canada: Documentary Art and Photography Division (Negative no. C-2621).

The Log of a Spanish Ship that Almost Started a War, 1789

The Spaniard Esteban José Martínez (circa 1742–1798) wrote in the log of his ship *Princesa* a list of all ships that he believed had visited Nootka Sound up to and including his visit in 1789. The list included names of explorers such as the Spaniard Pérez, the Englishman Cook and the Frenchman Lapérouse. The majority of the names, however — Cooper, Colnett, Dickson, Meares and others — were those of English and American merchants trading for highly profitable sea otter skins.

On their way home to England, Captain Cook's crews called at Canton for supplies. There they discovered that furs for which they had bartered trinkets on the northwest coast could be sold at fantastically high prices. Their profits did not go unnoticed, and for a short period sparked a trade in sea otter fur by British and American vessels. These trading expeditions, too, added to the knowledge of the coast and its inhabitants.

Increased commercial activity led the Spanish to send Martínez to Nootka to bolster his nation's claim to sovereignty. Martínez seized a small fort built by the Englishman John Meares and two of Meares's ships, the *Argonaut* and the *Princess Royal*, both of which appear on Martínez's list.

It was a period of international tension, and the incident brought England and Spain to the brink of war. The French Revolution, however, intervened, and the protagonists came together to sign the Nootka Sound Convention of 1790, which stated that the fisheries and navigation of the Pacific Ocean would be open to British subjects except within ten leagues of coasts occupied by Spain.

The log of the *Princesa* is a clerical copy of the original, which was lost shortly thereafter when the ship sank. The last page of this copy contains a certification signed on 6 December 1789 by Martínez, that this is a faithful copy of the original log made at anchor off San Blas, Mexico.

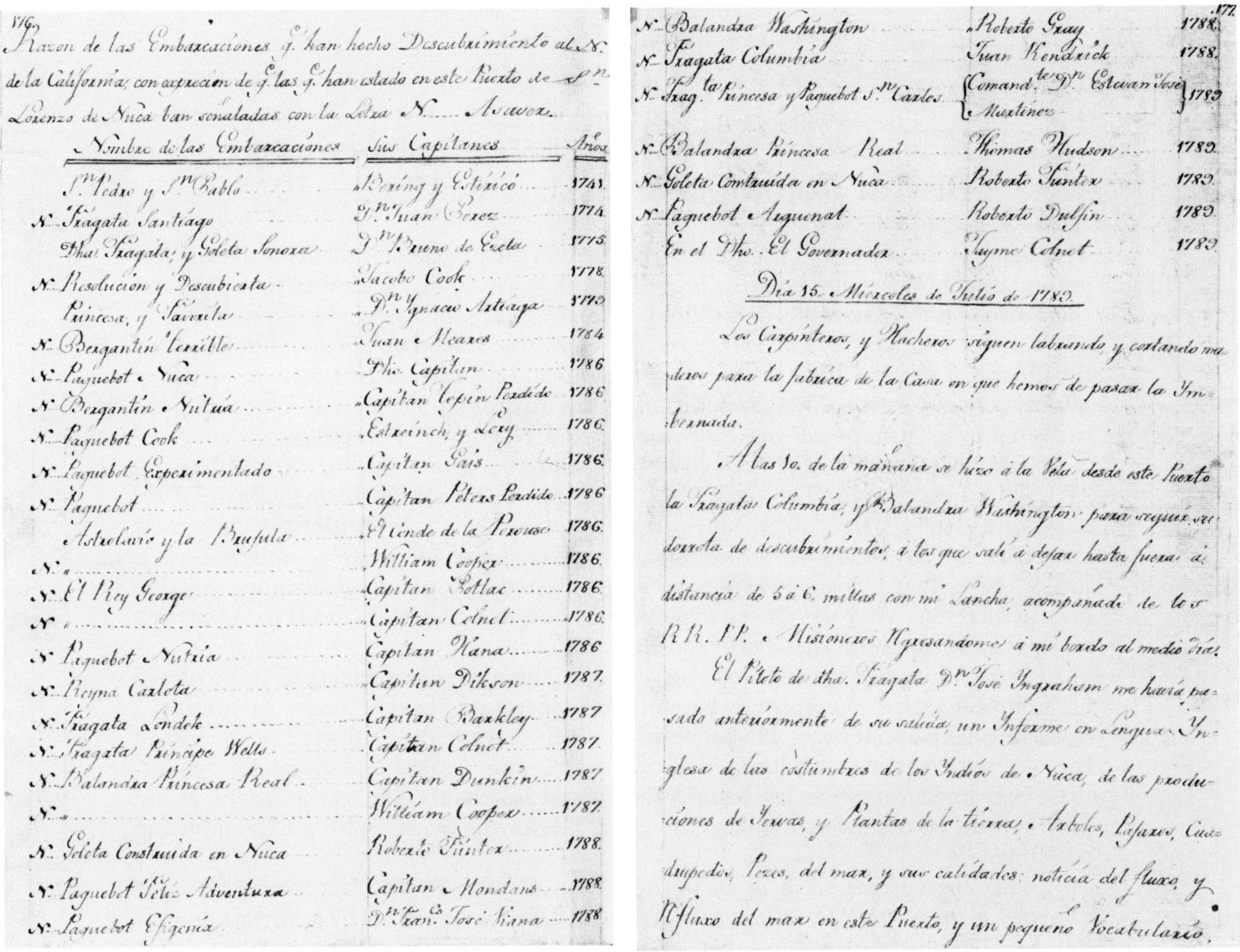

176

Razon de las Embarcaciones q. han hecho Descubrimiento al N. de la California; con expresion de q.e las q.e han estado en este Puerto de S.n Lorenzo de Nuca van señaladas con la Letra N.... A saver.

Nombre de las Embarcaciones	Sus Capitanes	Años
S.n Pedro y S.n Pablo	Bering y Estirico	1741.
N. Fragata Santiago	D.n Juan Perez	1774.
Dha. Fragata, y Goleta Sonora	D.n Bruno de Ezeta	1775.
N. Resolucion y Descubierta	Jacobo Cook	1778.
Princesa, y Favorita	D.n y D.n Ygnacio Arteaga	1779.
N. Bergantin Terrible	Juan Meares	1784
N. Paquebot Nuca	Dho. Capitan	1786
N. Bergantin Nutria	Capitan Tepin Perdido	1786
N. Paquebot Cook	Estreinch, y Lory	1786.
N. Paquebot Experimentado	Capitan Gais	1786.
N. Paquebot	Capitan Peters Perdido	1786
Astrolavio y la Brujula	El Conde de la Perouse	1786.
N. "	William Cooper	1786.
N. El Rey George	Capitan Potlac	1786.
N. "	Capitan Colnet	1786.
N. Paquebot Nutria	Capitan Hana	1786
N. Reyna Carlota	Capitan Dikson	1787.
N. Fragata Londek	Capitan Barkley	1787
N. Fragata Principe Wells	Capitan Colnet	1787.
N. Balandra Princesa Real	Capitan Dunkin	1787
N. "	William Cooper	1787.
N. Goleta Construida en Nuca	Roberto Funter	1788.
N. Paquebot Feliz Adventura	Capitan Mondans	1788.
N. Paquebot Efigenia	D.n Fran.co José Viana	1788

177.

N. Balandra Washington	Roberto Gray	1788.
N. Fragata Columbia	Juan Kendrick	1788.
N. Frag.ta Princesa y Paquebot S.n Carlos	Comand.te D.n Estevan José Martinez	1783
N. Balandra Princesa Real	Thomas Hudson	1783.
N. Goleta Construida en Nuca	Roberto Funter	1783.
N. Paquebot Arguenat	Roberto Dulfin	1783.
En el Dho. El Governador	Jayme Colnet	1783.

Día 15. Miércoles de Julio de 1783.

Los Carpinteros, y Hacheros siguen labrando y cortando maderos para la fabrica de la Casa en que hemos de pasar la Ymbernada.

A las 10. de la mañana se hizo á la Vela desde este Puerto la Fragata Columbia, y Balandra Washington para seguir su derrota de descubrimientos, á los que salí á dejar hasta fuera á distancia de 5 á 6. millas con mi Lancha, acompañado de los RR. PP. Misioneros regresandome á mi bordo al medio día.

El Piloto de dha. Fragata D.n José Ingraham me havía pasado anteriormente de su salida, un Informe en Lengua Ynglesa de las costumbres de los Indios de Nuca, de las producciones de Yervas, y Plantas de la tierra, Arboles, Pajaros, Quadrupedos, Pezes, del mar, y sus calidades; noticia del fluxo, y Refluxo del mar en este Puerto, y un pequeño Vocabulario.

Log of the *Princesa* [clerical copy].
Esteban José Martínez Fernandez y Martínez de la Sierra (circa 1742–1798).
Manuscript log, 1789.

National Archives of Canada:
Manuscript Division, MG 23, J 12,
pp. 176–177.

I

Vancouver Traces the Coastline of Modern British Columbia and Alaska, 1792–1794

The Spanish concessions encouraged the British to undertake an extensive hydrographic survey of the north Pacific in 1792, both to encourage trade and to consolidate their own claims. The skills and thorough work of Captain George Vancouver (1757–1798) made him an obvious choice for the expedition. He had spent more than half his life at sea and had been trained in surveying and navigation by Cook and William Wales, a noted astronomer. In addition to the hydrographic survey, Vancouver was to search again for a water network leading to a Northwest Passage.

The chart shown here was compiled from the data collected on Vancouver's 1792–1794 expedition. The track of his ships can be traced on the map. Many place names he assigned are still in use, a tribute to the wide currency of his charts. As the chart notes, Vancouver relied on Spanish accounts for areas he did not visit; indeed he assigned Spanish names to places visited by Spanish navigators, notably on this chart between the Queen Charlotte Islands and the mainland (Hecate Strait), and north of the same islands (Dixon Entrance).

With Vancouver's meticulous surveys, a whole new region emerged to be placed on European maps. Vancouver's careful work shattered the last hopes of finding a transcontinental waterway. He provided the definitive eighteenth-century survey of the western coastline of Canada, and his charts were copied and recopied. As yet, little was known of what lay behind the coastal headlands, but earlier maps would now have to be redrawn to replace the great "Sea of the West" with a new unbroken coastline.

This chart is the sixth in an untitled atlas accompanying Vancouver's *Voyage of Discovery to the North Pacific Ocean* . . . (3 vols., London, 1798). The atlas was quickly followed by other editions in other languages. The Archives holds the 1798 English edition and the 1799 French edition.

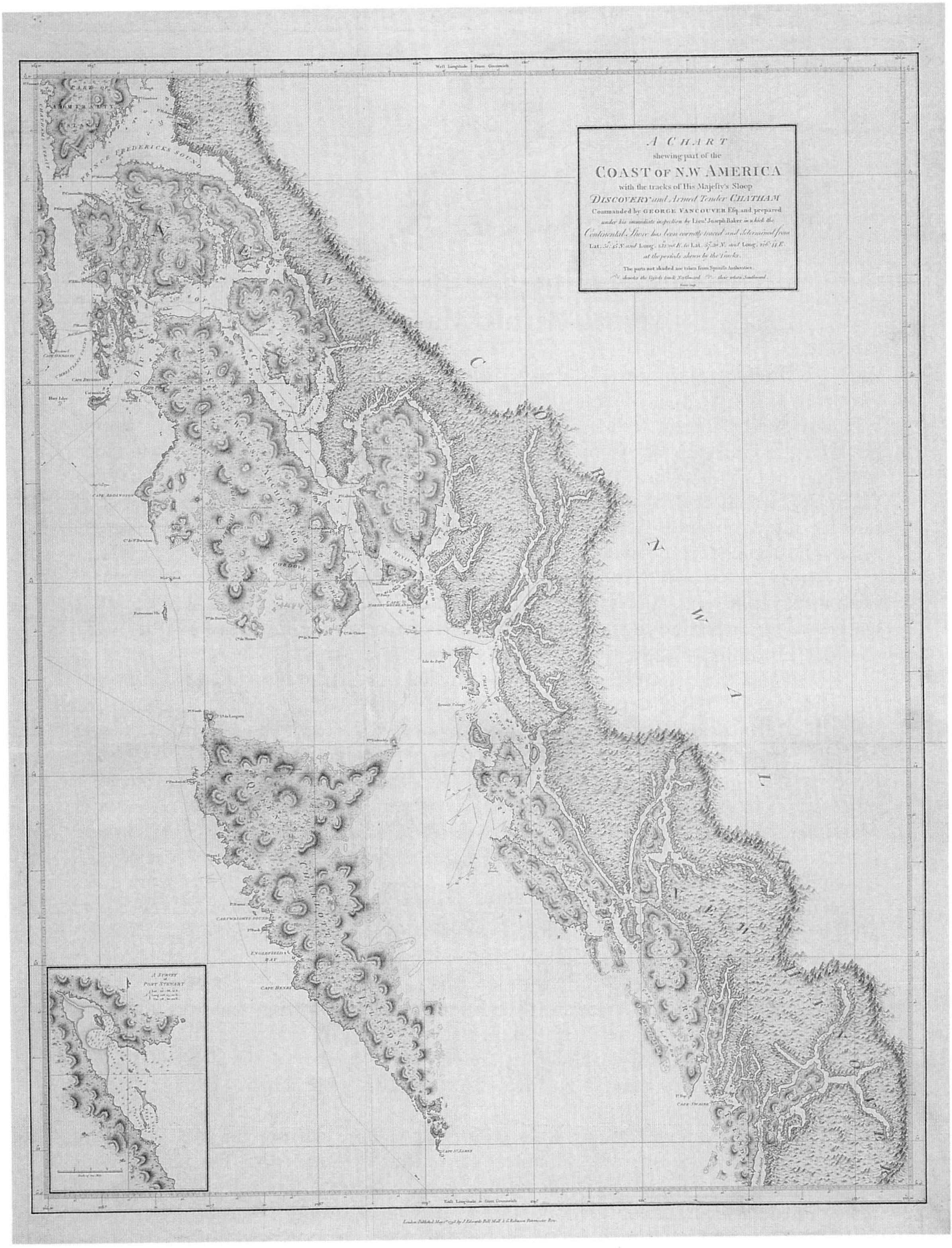

A Chart shewing part of the Coast of N.W. America . . . . [Insert of Port Stewart], George Vancouver (1757–1798) and Joseph Baker. Etching by Warner. Map: engraved, 74.2 × 60.0 cm.

In Atlas to accompany George Vancouver. *Voyage of Discovery to the North Pacific Ocean and Round the World.* 3 vols., London: J. Edwards and G. Robinson, 1798.

National Archives of Canada: Cartographic and Architectural Archives Division (NMC 18923).

The Western Interior Begins to Emerge: Arrowsmith's Map of 1795

At the beginning of the British regime, the far western interior of the continent was almost as unknown to whites as the Pacific Coast until the impetus for exploration was provided by the fur trade. That trade was locked in a great commercial struggle between the Hudson's Bay Company (operating through the rivers flowing into Hudson Bay) and the Montreal fur companies (dominated eventually by the North West Company, which entered the West via the Great Lakes). Their race for dominance of new fur supply grounds pushed the companies westward into the Athabasca Country, across the Rockies, and finally to the Pacific.

Searching for a western passage to the markets of the Orient, Samuel Hearne, a Hudson's Bay Company servant, journeyed down the Coppermine River with a Chipewyan Indian band to the shores of the Arctic Ocean, becoming on 17 July 1771 the first European to sight the continent's northern coastline.

The most extensive explorations were carried out by the North West Company. In 1778, one of its partners, Peter Pond, pushed decisively westward. Crossing the western end of Lake Superior, Pond tracked northwest across the height of land at Methye Portage and into the fur-rich Athabasca region. He had crossed the watershed dividing the Hudson Bay and the Arctic Ocean drainage basins, taking Europeans a large step closer to the mountains and the Pacific. Pond's associate, Alexander Mackenzie, set out in 1789 from Lake Athabasca to follow a river (the Mackenzie River) that he thought would lead to the Pacific, only to discover it led to the Arctic. Undaunted, Mackenzie tried again in 1793, following the Peace River from Lake Athabasca into the Rockies, and the Fraser and Bella Coola Rivers to the coast. Mackenzie had become the first white man to cross the Canadian Rockies.

This map by Aaron Arrowsmith (1750–1833) depicts Hearne's and Mackenzie's journeys to the Arctic Sea — although information on Hearne's journey of 1771 was apparently unavailable to Arrowsmith at the time of publication and was added on a small slip pasted in sometime after the sheet had been printed. The Athabasca country explored by Pond is shown, as are the lower reaches of the Peace River out of Lake Athabasca, but there is no hint of Mackenzie's great journey by that river in 1793 on his way to the Pacific.

Vital as these explorations were, they traced only narrow trails through the wilderness; the lands between remained unknown. If the men of the North West Company made the more spectacular discoveries, it was the Hudson's Bay Company that trained surveyors of considerable skill — men such as Philip Turnor, Peter Fidler and David Thompson — who, aided by Indian guides, mapped the waterways of the fur country. The surveys of Philip Turnor from York Factory to Lake Athabasca in 1791 are faithfully recorded on the map, as is the latest information on the Saskatchewan River system, based principally on Peter Fidler's travels.

The maps of the Arrowsmith firm are among the most important sources of information on western exploration. This map, of which only the centre sheet of three is reproduced, is Arrowsmith's first American compilation. Before Arrowsmith's map was published, little was known about western Canada. Previous maps were generalized and frequently inaccurate.

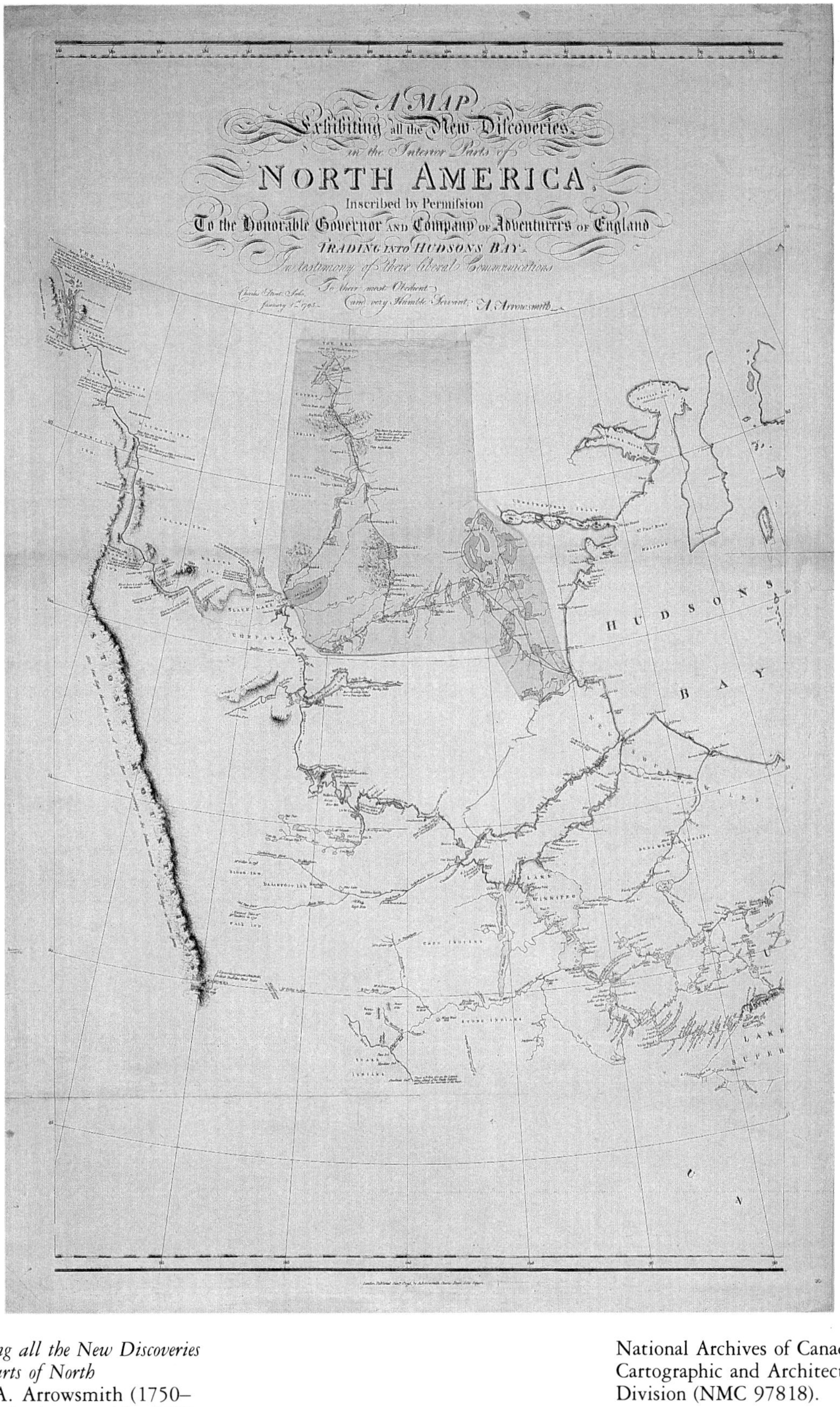

A Map Exhibiting all the New Discoveries in the Interior Parts of North America . . . . A. Arrowsmith (1750–1833). London: A. Arrowsmith, 1795. Map: hand-coloured, engraved, 88.4 × 57.5 cm. Middle sheet of three only.

National Archives of Canada: Cartographic and Architectural Archives Division (NMC 97818).

I

The Interior Emerges: Arrowsmith's Map of North America, 1814

A comparison of the 1795 and 1814 versions of Arrowsmith's map graphically demonstrates the rapidly developing knowledge of the Canadian interior.

Much of Arrowsmith's information on the Canadian interior came from his firm's position as unofficial map-maker to the Hudson's Bay Company, which gave him access to information and manuscript maps sent to London by servants of the Company. Arrowsmith had little access to information on North West Company discoveries and surveys. He could use published accounts for Mackenzie's route to the Pacific. There is nothing on Arrowsmith's 1814 map, however, of Simon Fraser's journey in 1808 to the Pacific down the river that was to bear his name. The portrayal of the Columbia River drainage is based on information from the American Lewis and Clarke Expedition rather than on the work of David Thompson. It is also unlikely that Arrowsmith had access to Thompson's extensive surveys of areas east of the Rockies.

Still, the numerous editions of Arrowsmith's map of North America are the best documents for the study of the evolving cartographic knowledge of the Canadian West and North from 1795 to 1850. The map went through more than twenty revisions. The Archives holds six versions, dated 1795 (centre sheet of three only), 1796, 1802, 1814, 1821 and 1833 (with manuscript additions to 1838).

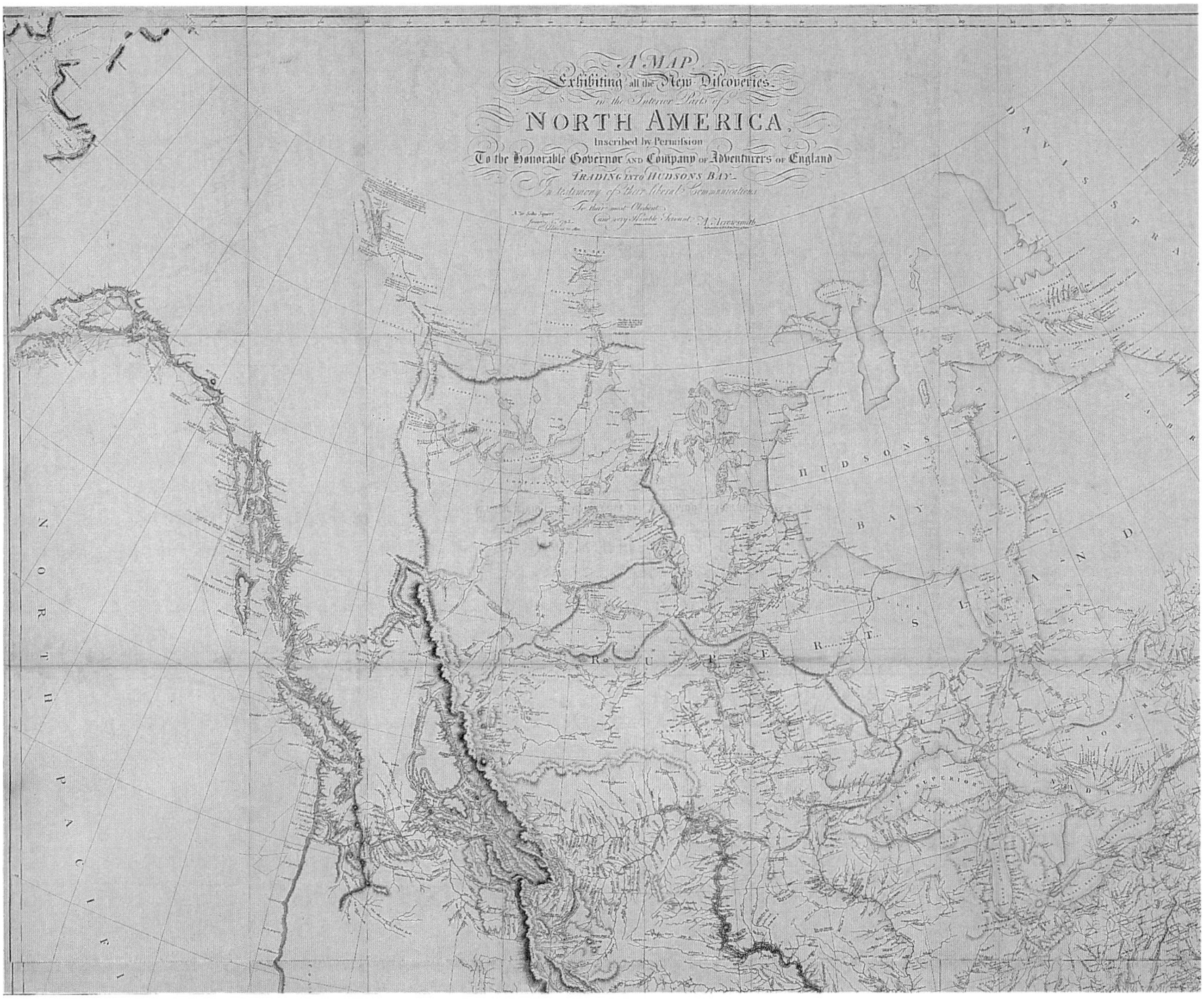

A Map Exhibiting all the New Discoveries in the Interior Parts of North America . . . . Additions to June 1814
A. Arrowsmith (1750–1833). Engraved by Puke. London: Arrowsmith, 1795.
Map: hand-coloured, engraved, 124.0 × 145.0 cm.

National Archives of Canada: Cartographic and Architectural Archives Division (NMC 48909).

I

A Landmark of Eighteenth-Century Surveying: *The Atlantic Neptune*, 1775–1781

Surveying in Western Canada and on the Pacific coast was matched by work on the Atlantic coast. With her victory over France in 1763, Britain found herself in possession of a vast new American empire, the eastern coasts of which were only sketchily charted. To prepare for increased settlement and trade, better surveys were urgently required. The need was filled beginning in 1763–1764 by three junior officers who had served in previous military campaigns.

Before his Pacific voyages, James Cook (1728–1779) surveyed the deeply indented coast of Newfoundland with such accuracy that he still earned the admiration of surveyors a century later. His charts were published privately in London. Samuel Holland (1728–1801), named Surveyor General of the Northern District of America, commenced a decade of surveys of Prince Edward Island, the shores of the Gulf of St. Lawrence, Cape Breton and the Atlantic coastal lands from the Saint John River to New York City. Joseph Frederick Wallet DesBarres (1722–1824) undertook the more laborious surveys around Nova Scotia.

The need for improved charts for the impending American war led the British Admiralty to commission DesBarres in 1774 to undertake the publication of his survey and those of other officers working on the Atlantic coast. The project took ten years, and at its height DesBarres employed twenty engravers, printers and colourists.

The map of Saint John Harbour illustrates the excellence of the surveyors' and the cartographers' work. The harbour has ample soundings; the coastline is depicted in great detail. Various degrees of shading and ink-cover assist perspective and the perception of distance. So skilled is the work that it conveys the impression of an aerial photograph.

The high quality of DesBarres's charts meant a high sale price, and they were never widely used for commercial shipping, although they were extensively copied by other early chart-makers. However, there were doubts about many of the soundings, which were confirmed by the re-survey work of the following century. In spite of its flaws, *The Atlantic Neptune* remains a monument to the energy and ambition of its creator.

The National Archives holds more than seven hundred sheets from the various revisions of *The Atlantic Neptune*, as well as thirty of the sixty-four surviving copperplates used to produce the charts. The personal copy belonging to Jeffrey, Lord Amherst, military Commander-in-Chief in North America, was presented to the Archives by his descendants. The National Archives holds original DesBarres papers as well as transcripts, photocopies and microfilm copies.

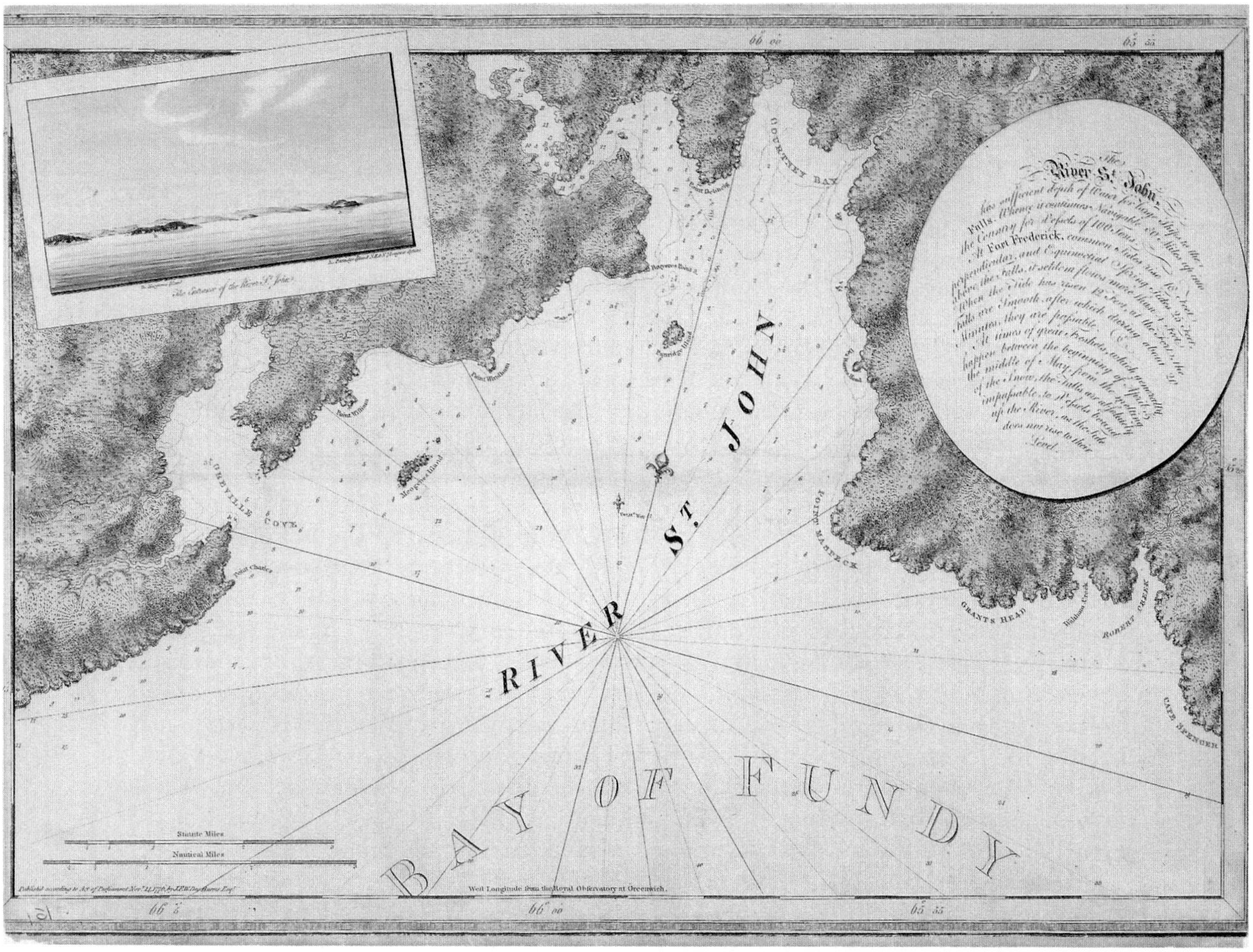

A Chart of the Mouth and Harbour of the Saint John River. J.F.W. DesBarres (1722–1824). London: J.F.W. DesBarres, 1776. Map: hand-coloured, engraved, 49.8 × 74.2 cm.

In J.F.W. DesBarres. *Surveys of North America Entitled The Atlantic Neptune . . . .* London: J.F.W. DesBarres, 1775–1781.

National Archives of Canada: Cartographic and Architectural Archives Division (NMC 27969).

A Small Portion of Murray's Gigantic Map of the Province of Quebec, 1761

This depiction of Montreal Island and its environs is a detail from an extraordinary manuscript map. In its full extent, the map is 13.5 by 10.8 metres. It encompasses an area on both sides of the St. Lawrence River from Les Cèdres, upstream from Montreal, to Île aux Coudres in the vicinity of Baie St. Paul. Undertaken just after the Conquest by a group of British military surveyors under the supervision of General James Murray (d. 1794), it is a work of exceptional craftsmanship, combining superior cartography with a thorough examination of the land and its people. It incorporates a census done as part of the project so that one can tell at a glance such details as ownership, population, location of mills, and history.

Most of the surveys for the map were done between February and November 1761. Seven copies were laboriously produced by hand between the fall of 1761 and the summer of 1763. Before the Peace of 1763, the possibility of Canada being ceded back to France motivated the British to collect as much information as possible in the event that a future military conflict necessitated an attempt to retake the colony. If Quebec stayed British, the map could prove a useful tool in suppressing civil unrest or resisting future French invasion. Military concerns are evident in such details as the recording of the numbers of men capable of bearing arms. The map is particularly notable for its attempt to show the extent of farm land in the St. Lawrence Valley. The survey was one of the biggest and most difficult undertaken anywhere by British map-makers up to that time. In scale and content, it far surpasses any maps of the French period, and it foreshadows the many land surveys, large and small, of Upper Canada (Ontario), Quebec and the Maritimes that would be undertaken before 1815.

Five originals of this map are known to exist today. The National Archives of Canada holds two of them. The sheet illustrated here is from the original, which is believed to have been made for General Murray himself. It was drawn on smaller sheets of paper than the others, and with a key sheet to make it both portable and an easy reference tool. This map has a greater amount of detail than any of the others, including the depiction of individual buildings in the major towns.

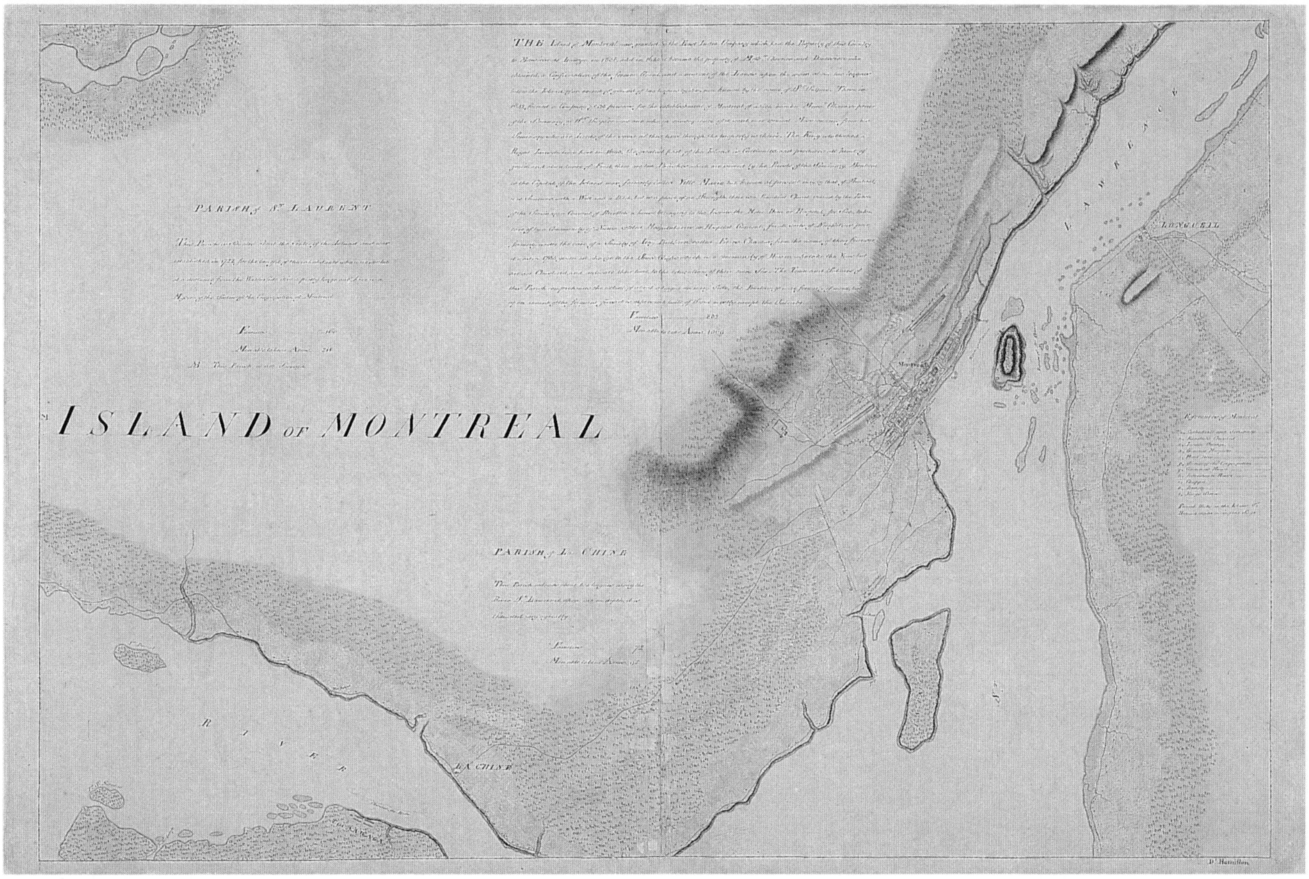

Portion of Montreal Island and Environs. Map: hand-coloured, manuscript, 62.2×95.5 cm. Sheet Mc(8).

Detail of "Plan of Canada or the Province of Quebec from the uppermost Settlements to the Island of Coudre as survey'd by order of His Excellency Governor Murray in the year 1760. 61 & 62 . . . ."

National Archives of Canada: Cartographic and Architectural Archives Division (NMC 10842).

II

After the Conquest

Louisbourg, the French guardian of the St. Lawrence, fell in 1758. Québec City capitulated to the British in 1759. Montreal remained French until 1760. The Peace of Paris of 1763 confirmed the victories of British arms.

These were the bare facts of the Conquest, but behind them were many questions and uncertainties. The inhabitants of the colony of New France did not know what to expect. Would they remain French? That hope lingered until 1763. Would they be allowed to keep their property? Their language? Their religion? Would they be deported? Would they be allowed to leave the country? Should they return to France?

The British victors, for their part, faced for the first time the necessity of governing a European-settled colony different in civilization and culture from their own. They would need to provide answers to the hard questions the Canadians were asking.

In the Maritimes their new and underpopulated possessions also posed problems for the British. Newfoundland remained as it had long been, a major fisheries centre, with no official recognition given to its needs as a permanent colony.

II

A New Dawn? The British Army Occupies Québec City, 1759

British soldiers drilling before the gates of Fort Saint-Louis (the former residence of the French governor) must have been a poignant sight for French Canadians. Behind the soldiers, other reminders of the French influence — the Recollet Church and Convent and, to the right, the Roman Catholic Cathedral — lie damaged. In front of the cathedral are the shattered houses along rue Sainte-Anne, the most important of which were restored and still stand today. Fort Saint-Louis and the Recollet Church and Convent have long since disappeared.

One third of the houses in Québec City were destroyed by British bombardment, and many more were so shattered that they had to be pulled down. Winter was coming, and many people had been impoverished by the long conflict. There were fears of plundering by the army. Most Canadians would have scoffed at the notion of a "new dawn" implied by the artist of this view in the sun rising behind the church.

The engraving is one of a set of twelve views of Québec City based on the on-the-spot drawings of Richard Short (fl. 1754–1766), a naval officer who had come with the British fleet in 1759. Short is near the beginning of the long tradition of British military topographers in Canada whose works are well represented in the collections of the National Archives of Canada.

The print reproduced here is remarkable for its condition and looks as fresh as if it had been pulled off the press yesterday. It is from the Coverdale (Manoir Richelieu) Collection, one of the most important collections of Canadian documentary art, the majority of which was acquired by the National Archives of Canada in 1970.

A View of the Cathedral, Jesuits College, and Recollect Friars Church, taken from the Gate of the Governors House. Richard Short (fl. 1754–1766). Etching by P. Canot. London: Thomas Jefferys, 1761. Engraving. 32.4×50.8 cm.

National Archives of Canada: Documentary Art and Photography Division (Negative no. C-361).

The British Commemorate Their Victories, 1758–1760

Weary of a long war that had stretched around the globe, the British were delighted with their victories in North America. This contemporary ballad and these commemorative medals suggest their enthusiasm.

The ballad was probably sung at the fashionable concerts at Vauxhall Gardens, London, where the composer, John Worgan, and the singer, Thomas Lowe, enjoyed much popular success. The lyricist, Mr. Lockman, demonstrates a sharp sense of the economic benefits of victory — especially in verses three and four. This song sheet was issued for general sale in London in 1760. The song also appeared in the *London Magazine* in 1760.

British victories in Canada occasioned a large number of medals, which ranged from expensive and finely crafted works of art for the rich and influential to cheap, mass-produced tokens. The medals depicted not only heroes and places associated with the Conquest, but also striking allegorical images contrasting Britain's glory to France's defeat.

The "Louisbourg Taken, 1758" medal (top) is an example of superior workmanship. Unlike most of the other medals shown here, which, after the convention of the time, were commemorative, it was a distinguished service medal to be conferred on selected recipients who took part in the capture. The obverse (front) is a large globe with a map of eastern North America. The globe is crushing a female figure (France) who casts away a fleur-de-lis. A British soldier and sailor stand to the left and right of the globe. The motto "Paritur in bello" (Equal in war) refers to their cooperation in the conflict.

Very different in quality and intended market is the Admiral Boscawen medal (top left). It was issued by Christopher Pinchbeck, a London clockmaker who had for some time worked in "pinchbeck" metal, a cheap alloy of copper and zinc that looked like gold but tarnished rapidly. "Pinchbeck" became slang for anything inferior. The design, which is crude, represents Admiral Edward Boscawen, naval commander at Louisburg, on the obverse. Medals like this were intended for sale to the London crowd as mementos of great events.

Also the work of Pinchbeck, the medal labelled on the reverse "I Surrender Prisoner, 1758" (centre) and struck in bronze, shows the French commander Drucour surrendering to Boscawen.

II

The following three medals, labelled on their reverse "Québec Taken, 1759" (top right), "Montreal Taken, 1760" (bottom left) and "Canada Subdued, 1760" (bottom right) would have been purchased by an affluent clientele. All are variations on the theme of France as a classically robed woman, captured or mourning, subdued by British might.

The last medal in this grouping, inscribed "Montreal" on its obverse (bottom), is the rarest, and the only one of those shown here that was made in North America. Struck in pewter, it is one of twenty-three medals distributed to Indian chiefs who had aided in the taking of Montreal. One of only seven now known to exist, it is inscribed "Tankalkel/MOHIGRANS" on the reverse. The medal was executed by Daniel Christian Fueter in New York City.

The Medal Collection of the National Archives contains 12,000 medals, decorations, tokens and medallic items relating to a wide range of organizations and events in Canadian history.

A SONG On the taking of MONT–REAL by General Amherſt.
Sung by Mr. Lowe. Set by Mr. Worgan. The Words by Mr. Lockman.
Preſented to His Royal Highneſs the Prince of Wales.

2
Thrô Woods, and o'er Lakes,
His progreſs he takes,
With Mont-real full in his Eye.
The French wou'd, in vain,
Or Indians, reſtrain
His Troops who to Victory fly.

3
Cape Breton our own,
Gallia's Fiſhery's o'erthrown,
Chief Nurſery of her Marine.
Invaſion, that Joke,
Will thence end in Smoke,
And Britain ſtill reign Ocean's Queen.

4
The Indians, and We,
Shall henceforth agree,
Thus our Manufactures advance.
Our Foes, to their coſt,
See Their rich Fur-Trade loſt,
Great Blow to the Commerce of France.

5
Triumphant, with Pride,
O'er Ocean we ride;
Not a ſingle Attempt now miſcarries.
To our raviſh'd Eyes,
Creſsy, Agincourt riſe,
And the Days of our Edwards & Harrys.

6
Juſt George! O for Thee
The Fates did decree,
A Reign will eternally ſhine.
The fam'd Conqueſts told,
In our Annals of old,
Are already equal'd in Thine.

7
O'erwhelm'd with ſad Fears,
See Gallia, in Tears,
The Loſs of Mont-real bemoan.
The French are undone;
And now Canada's won,
Britannia ſhall there fix Her Throne.

8
But hark! Heav'n–born Peace,
Bids War's Horrors ceaſe;
And lo! where the Goddeſs deſcends.
Her Charms all adore;
Human Blood ſtreams no more:
And Foes, long contending, are Friends.

A Song. On the taking of Mont-Real by General Amherst. Composed by Worgan. Lyrics by Lockman. London, 1760. Broadside.

National Archives of Canada: Manuscript Division, MG 18, 05.

Top: Obverse of "Louisbourg Taken, 1758" medal. Struck in bronze, 1758. Diameter 44 mm.

Top left: Obverse of Boscawen medal. Struck in pinchbeck metal, 1758. Diameter 37 mm.

Bottom left: Reverse of "Montreal Taken, 1760" medal. Struck in bronze, 1760. Diameter 41 mm.

Centre: Reverse of Boscawen medal, inscribed "I Surrender Prisoner, 1758." Struck in bronze. Diameter 26 mm.

Top right: Reverse of "Quebec Taken, 1759" medal. Struck in bronze, 1759. Diameter 40 mm.

Bottom right: Reverse of "Canada Subdued, 1760" medal. Struck in bronze, 1760. Diameter 26 mm.

Bottom: Obverse of Montreal medal. Struck in pewter, 1760. Diameter 45 mm.

National Archives of Canada: Documentary Art and Photography Division.

II

Some French and French-Canadians Leave

After the fall of New France, the British did not expel any former French subjects, but allowed those who wished to depart to do so. About four to five thousand (six to seven percent of the population) left, not enough to substantially alter the composition of French-Canadian society.

This French poster of 1791 enumerates the seigneurs, the civil and military officials, and their families — refugees and casualties of the Conquest — as well as Acadians expelled earlier from the Maritimes, who were then living in France and were eligible for French pensions.

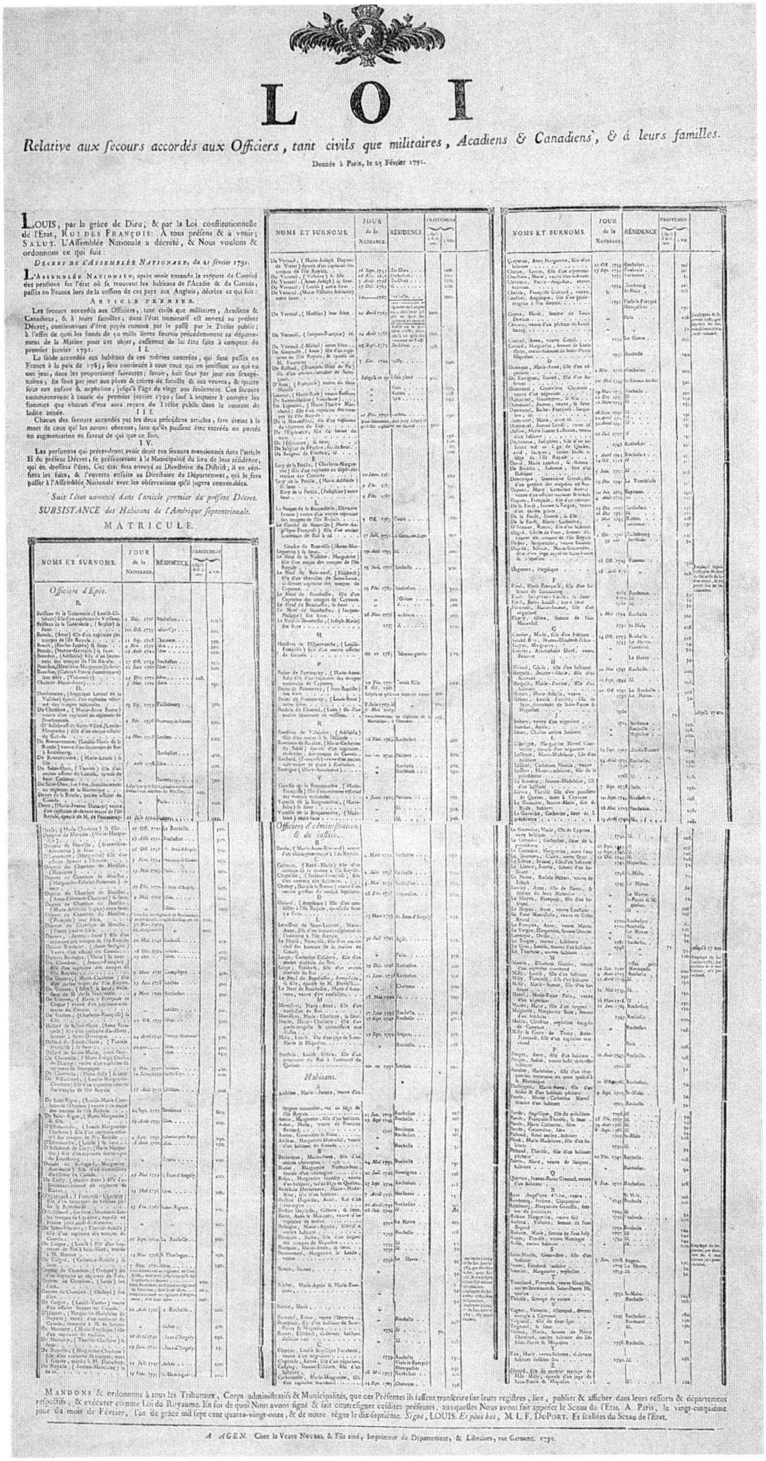

LOI

Relative aux secours accordés aux Officiers, tant civils que militaires, Acadiens & Canadiens, & à leurs familles.

Donnée à Paris, le 25 Février 1791.

Loi Relative aux secours accordés aux Officiers, tant civils que militaires, Acadiens & Canadiens . . . . Agen: Chez la Veuve Noubel et Fils, 1791. Broadside.

National Archives of Canada: Library (Negative no. C-121417).

II

A Few British Come

At the Conquest and in the years thereafter, only a handful of British subjects, including American colonials, were drawn to Quebec, mainly by the prospects of trade.

Alexander Henry the Elder (1739–1824), a native of New Jersey, was one of the first to arrive: he accompanied the British army to Canada as a supplier. Taking advantage of the newly established British control, he almost immediately launched himself into the western fur trade. Having travelled and traded as far west as the Saskatchewan River, he retired in 1776 and spent the rest of his long life in Montreal as a merchant and Customs officer. A man of limited formal education, he had a vigorous intellect. His vivid memoir, *Travels and Adventures in Canada and the Indian Territories* (1809), is a classic of Canadian travel literature. The Archives holds an original of the first edition. He was a cartographer as well; the map shown in the portrait was presented by Henry to Sir Guy Carleton (later Lord Dorchester) in 1776 and is now in the Library of Congress. Considerable artistic liberties have been taken in the depiction of the map.

Henry and the other merchants like him were ambitious, aggressive men. Although a tiny minority in the colony, they agitated powerfully for English commercial law, for trial by jury and especially for a parliamentary system.

This early nineteenth-century portrait of Henry by an anonymous artist, although heavily inpainted at a later date, remains a powerful representation of a talented man and his class.

13

Portrait of Alexander Henry (1739–1824). Artist unknown. Oil on canvas, late eighteenth century. 73.8×61.1 cm.

National Archives of Canada: Documentary Art and Photography Division (Negative no. C-103612).

The Proclamation of 1763: The British Set Out How They Will Govern Quebec

This proclamation of the British government declared:

— the Province of Quebec was to be reduced to a narrow parallelogram comprising only the settled areas along the St. Lawrence River;

— New France's rich fur trade hinterland in the West was to become an Indian preserve;

— British institutions were to be introduced, including representative government and British patterns of law and land ownership; and

— Roman Catholics were confirmed in their right to worship, but denied all political offices.

The proclamation was based on the false hope of a heavy influx of British immigrants into Quebec. Its provisions were never fully implemented. Governors stalled on the introduction of British institutions. Roman Catholics did hold office. Quebec's ties with the western fur trade remained strong.

The book illustrated here is a collection of capitulations and treaties, 1759–1783. Printed in Québec City in 1800, it is one of 50,000 rare books, broadsides and pamphlets held by the National Archives of Canada.

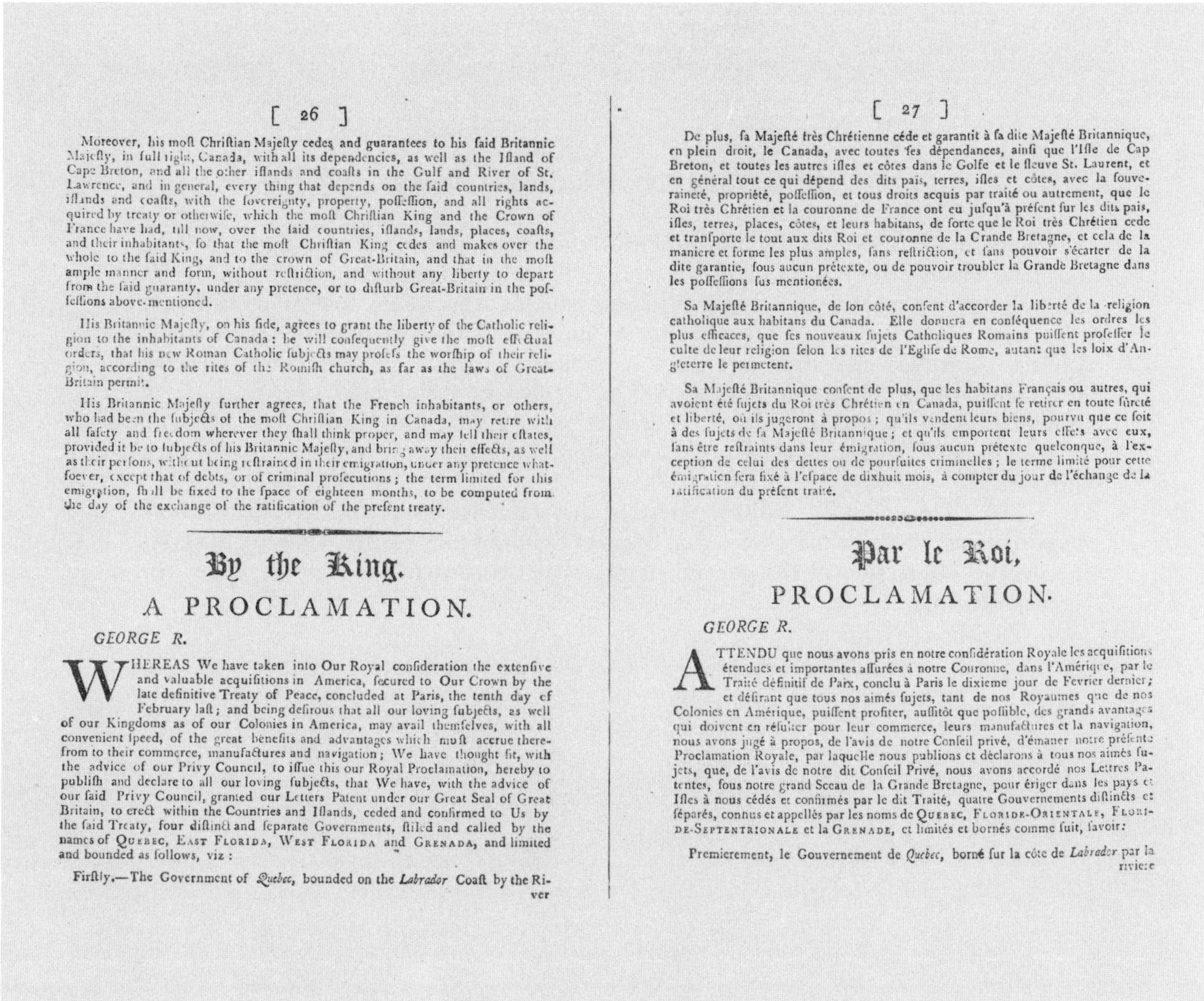

[26]

Moreover, his most Christian Majesty cedes and guarantees to his said Britannic Majesty, in full right, Canada, with all its dependencies, as well as the Island of Cape Breton, and all the other islands and coasts in the Gulf and River of St. Lawrence, and in general, every thing that depends on the said countries, lands, islands and coasts, with the sovereignty, property, possession, and all rights acquired by treaty or otherwise, which the most Christian King and the Crown of France have had, till now, over the said countries, islands, lands, places, coasts, and their inhabitants, so that the most Christian King cedes and makes over the whole to the said King, and to the crown of Great-Britain, and that in the most ample manner and form, without restriction, and without any liberty to depart from the said guaranty, under any pretence, or to disturb Great-Britain in the possessions above-mentioned.

His Britannic Majesty, on his side, agrees to grant the liberty of the Catholic religion to the inhabitants of Canada: he will consequently give the most effectual orders, that his new Roman Catholic subjects may profess the worship of their religion, according to the rites of the Romish church, as far as the laws of Great-Britain permit.

His Britannic Majesty further agrees, that the French inhabitants, or others, who had been the subjects of the most Christian King in Canada, may retire with all safety and freedom wherever they shall think proper, and may sell their estates, provided it be to subjects of his Britannic Majesty, and bring away their effects, as well as their persons, without being restrained in their emigration, under any pretence whatsoever, except that of debts, or of criminal prosecutions; the term limited for this emigration, shall be fixed to the space of eighteen months, to be computed from the day of the exchange of the ratification of the present treaty.

By the King.

A PROCLAMATION.

GEORGE R.

WHEREAS We have taken into Our Royal consideration the extensive and valuable acquisitions in America, secured to Our Crown by the late definitive Treaty of Peace, concluded at Paris, the tenth day of February last; and being desirous that all our loving subjects, as well of our Kingdoms as of our Colonies in America, may avail themselves, with all convenient speed, of the great benefits and advantages which must accrue therefrom to their commerce, manufactures and navigation; We have thought fit, with the advice of our Privy Council, to issue this our Royal Proclamation, hereby to publish and declare to all our loving subjects, that We have, with the advice of our said Privy Council, granted our Letters Patent under our Great Seal of Great Britain, to erect within the Countries and Islands, ceded and confirmed to Us by the said Treaty, four distinct and separate Governments, stiled and called by the names of QUEBEC, EAST FLORIDA, WEST FLORIDA and GRENADA, and limited and bounded as follows, viz:

Firstly.—The Government of *Quebec*, bounded on the *Labrador* Coast by the River

[27]

De plus, sa Majesté très Chrétienne céde et garantit à sa dite Majesté Britannique, en plein droit, le Canada, avec toutes ses dépendances, ainsi que l'Isle de Cap Breton, et toutes les autres isles et côtes dans le Golfe et le fleuve St. Laurent, et en général tout ce qui dépend des dits païs, terres, isles et côtes, avec la souveraineté, propriété, possession, et tous droits acquis par traité ou autrement, que le Roi très Chrétien et la couronne de France ont eu jusqu'à présent sur les dits païs, isles, terres, places, côtes, et leurs habitans, de sorte que le Roi très Chrétien cede et transporte le tout aux dits Roi et couronne de la Grande Bretagne, et cela de la maniere et forme les plus amples, sans restriction, et sans pouvoir s'écarter de la dite garantie, sous aucun prétexte, ou de pouvoir troubler la Grande Bretagne dans les possessions sus mentionées.

Sa Majesté Britannique, de son côté, consent d'accorder la liberté de la religion catholique aux habitans du Canada. Elle donnera en conséquence les ordres les plus efficaces, que ses nouveaux sujets Catholiques Romains puissent professer le culte de leur religion selon les rites de l'Eglise de Rome, autant que les loix d'Angleterre le permetent.

Sa Majesté Britannique consent de plus, que les habitans Français ou autres, qui avoient été sujets du Roi très Chrétien en Canada, puissent se retirer en toute sûreté et liberté, où ils jugeront à propos; qu'ils vendent leurs biens, pourvu que ce soit à des sujets de sa Majesté Britannique; et qu'ils emportent leurs effets avec eux, sans être restraints dans leur émigration, sous aucun prétexte quelconque, à l'exception de celui des dettes ou de poursuites criminelles; le terme limité pour cette émigration sera fixé à l'espace de dixhuit mois, à compter du jour de l'échange de la ratification du présent traité.

Par le Roi,

PROCLAMATION.

GEORGE R.

ATTENDU que nous avons pris en notre considération Royale les acquisitions étendues et importantes assurées à notre Couronne, dans l'Amérique, par le Traité définitif de Paix, conclu à Paris le dixieme jour de Fevrier dernier; et désirant que tous nos aimés sujets, tant de nos Royaumes que de nos Colonies en Amérique, puissent profiter, aussitôt que possible, des grands avantages qui doivent en résulter pour leur commerce, leurs manufactures et la navigation, nous avons jugé à propos, de l'avis de notre Conseil privé, d'émaner notre présente Proclamation Royale, par laquelle nous publions et déclarons à tous nos aimés sujets, que, de l'avis de notre dit Conseil Privé, nous avons accordé nos Lettres Patentes, sous notre grand Sceau de la Grande Bretagne, pour ériger dans les pays et Isles à nous cédés et confirmés par le dit Traité, quatre Gouvernements distincts et séparés, connus et appellés par les noms de QUEBEC, FLORIDE-ORIENTALE, FLORIDE-SEPTENTRIONALE et la GRENADE, et limités et bornés comme suit, savoir:

Premierement, le Gouvernement de *Quebec*, borné sur la côte de *Labrador* par la riviere

Capitulations and extracts of treaties relating to Canada: with His Majesty's Proclamation of 1763 . . . . / Capitulations et extraits des traités concernant le Canada; avec la Proclamation de sa Majesté, de 1763 . . . . Québec: P.E. Desbarats, 1800, pp. 26–27.

National Archives of Canada: Library (Negative no. C-130523).

II

The Church Faces a Crisis

Damage to its buildings was only one of the many problems facing the Roman Catholic Church after the Conquest. Under the colony's new Protestant rulers, the Church did not exist legally. The effects were evident everywhere: foreign recruitment of priests was virtually cut off, leaving the number in Quebec woefully inadequate; Church-controlled education lost its state support; it was even in question whether the appointment of a new Bishop of Quebec would be allowed. An attitude of conciliation on both sides allowed for resolution of most controversies, and although it remained weak and short of priests well into the nineteenth century, the Church survived.

The view, again by Richard Short, shows the interior of the Recollet Church seen in Item 10. It is the only visual record of the interior of that church and gives a valuable impression of the general decor of parish churches in Quebec under the French Regime.

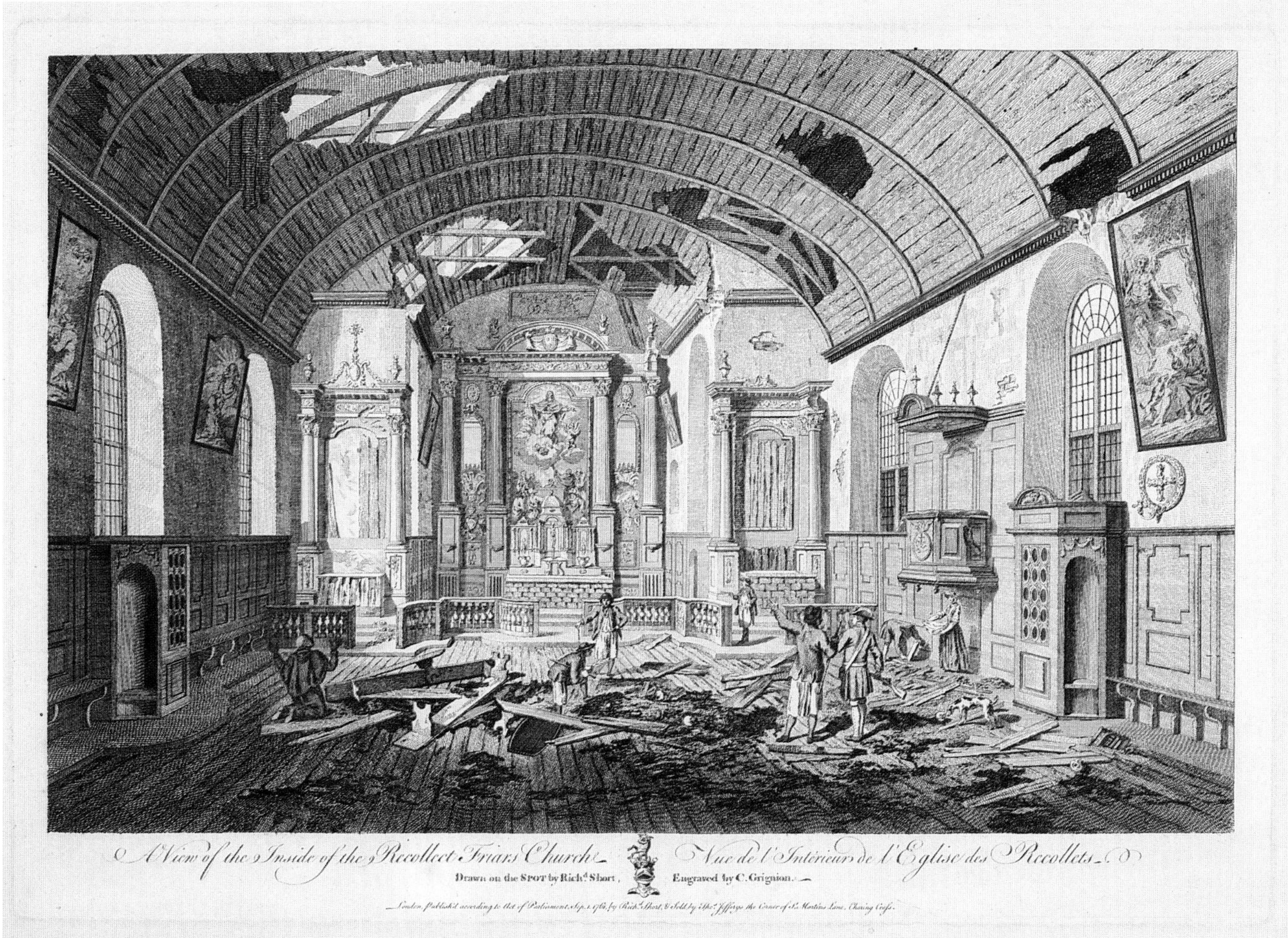

A View of the Inside of the Recollect Friars Church. Richard Short (fl. 1754–1766). Etching by C. Crignion. London: Thomas Jefferys, 1761. Engraving. 62.8 × 44.3 cm.

National Archives of Canada: Documentary Art and Photography Division (Negative no. C-353).

II

Life Goes On

In some ways what was most remarkable about the Conquest was how little immediate effect it had on most inhabitants of Quebec. Most Canadians stayed. Few British came. Many French institutions and customs continued, while the economy produced the same products in the same manner.

This idyllic view representing the Seigneury of Berthier approximately twenty years after the Conquest suggests the continuity of traditional Canadian society — except that the bridge in the background was constructed by the British army for defensive supply. Things were the same — but different.

The artist of this view, James Peachey (fl. 1773–1797), was, like Richard Short, associated with the military. A draughtsman, surveyor and army officer, he was one of the most prolific and significant artists of the period. The National Archives of Canada holds the largest extant group of his works: forty-two watercolours, etchings and aquatints.

A View of the Bridge Built Over the Berthier River in 1781. James Peachey (fl. 1773–1797). Watercolour, 1785. 32.1×48.9 cm.

National Archives of Canada: Documentary Art and Photography Division (Negative no. C-45559).

The British Revise the Rules: The Quebec Act of 1774

The Quebec Act was an attempt to provide Quebec with a government suited to its needs. One of its major provisions was a continuation of freedom of worship for Roman Catholics. Their payment of tithes to their church was made enforceable by law. The Act also restored the core of the old French western fur empire to Quebec.

This cartoon is a satirical comment on the religious implications of the Act. Four Anglican bishops directed by British political figures dance around the bill. A devil flies above, implying the source of inspiration for the bill. The cartoon, which appeared in the *London Magazine* of July 1774, is by an unidentified artist and is an early example from the Archives' collection of more than 10,000 satirical drawings and cartoons from the early eighteenth century to the present.

The increasingly rebellious colonies to the south were distressed that the Act cut off their access to the inland west and saw in it proof that the British were planning to force Quebec's mode of government and established Church on all Americans. The Quebec Act thus became one of the causes of the coming American Revolution.

According to other clauses of the Act:

— English criminal law was formally established, but the "Laws and Customs of Canada" were retained in civil law;

— the seigneurial system of land tenure was permitted to continue; and

— the colony was to be administered by a governor and appointed council rather than by an elected assembly.

The Mitred Minuet. Artist unknown.
Hand-coloured engraving.
10.7 × 17.2 cm.
In *London Magazine*, July 1774.

National Archives of Canada:
Documentary Art and Photography
Division (Negative no. C-38989).

Newfoundland: Britain's Greatest Ship, circa 1800

Newfoundland was viewed by the British government as a "great English ship Moored near the Banks" for the purpose of carrying on the fisheries. Permanent settlement was officially forbidden. The thinking was that Newfoundland should be a "nursery" for seamen who could be readily pressed into the navy if need be in time of war. In fact, the island had about 15,000 permanent residents in the 1770s, seven-eighths of whom lived along the coast of the peninsula between Trinity and Placentia Bays on the eastern tip of the island. Tensions between fact and official policy led to conflict.

In this anonymous watercolour, men can be seen emptying a net into a dory. On a fishing stage with a schooner anchored by it, cod are being set out. The two large containers on the stage, called "moutons," were used to press excess oil and salt out of the fish before it was dried in the sun.

Perhaps the most important feature of this view is the town itself, seen in the background. St. John's has always been the most important centre in Newfoundland because of its proximity to the fishing grounds. Like many others in the Archives' collection, this scene can be used to identify buildings and their exact construction, streetscapes, and many other details not available from any other documentary source.

A View of the Upper End of the Harbour, St. John's, Newfoundland. Artist unknown. Watercolour, late eighteenth century. 33.6 × 52.1 cm.

National Archives of Canada: Documentary Art and Photography Division (Negative no. C-3372).

II

Peopling the Maritimes: A Census of 1775

After the Conquest, the British authorities hoped to attract a substantial English-speaking population to Nova Scotia (which then included New Brunswick). This list of families in the province reveals their failure.

Halifax was the capital and major centre. Germans had been previously settled at Lunenburg. The end of French control brought an influx of 7,000 New England farmers and fishermen who, as the list notes, settled primarily along the coasts of the southern half of the peninsula and in the Annapolis Valley. More than 1,000 Yorkshiremen and many families from the north of Ireland settled on the Chignecto Isthmus. A few Scots, the beginning of a later influx, came to Nova Scotia and Cape Breton. (They are not included in this list.) Very limited settlements up the Saint John River Valley and on Passamaquoddy Bay in present-day New Brunswick are listed. Some of the French Acadians, who had been expelled by the British in 1755, returned, and pockets of them appear on the list. There was a total population of 17,000 to 20,000 in the colony, half of which was from New England. On the Island of St. John (Prince Edward Island) there was a population of only 1,300, largely immigrant Scots.

In the next decade, refugees fleeing the American Revolution would almost triple the existing population of the Maritimes.

William Legge, second Earl of Dartmouth (1731–1801), was the recipient of this census. As President of the Board of Trade (1765–1766) and Secretary of State for the American Department (1772–1775), he was heavily involved in North American affairs. Virtually all his papers relating to Canada were presented by his British descendants to the National Archives in 1926.

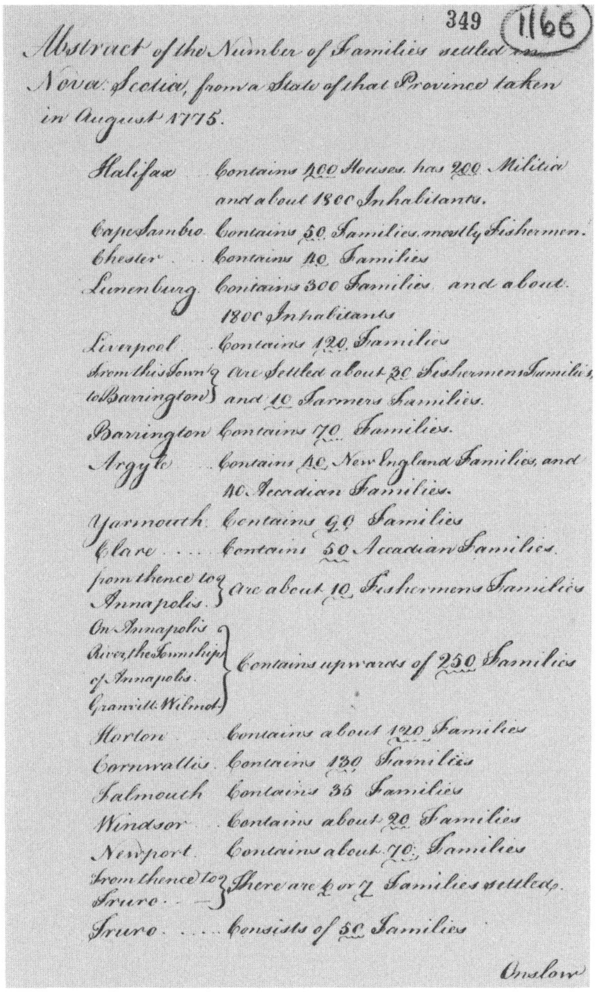

349 (1166)

Abstract of the Number of Families settled in Nova Scotia, from a State of that Province taken in August 1775.

Halifax	Contains 400 Houses, has 200 Militia and about 1800 Inhabitants.
Cape Sanbro	Contains 50 Families, mostly Fishermen.
Chester	Contains 40 Families
Lunenburg	Contains 300 Families and about 1800 Inhabitants
Liverpool	Contains 120 Families
from this Town to Barrington	Are settled about 30 Fishermens Families, and 10 Farmers Families.
Barrington	Contains 70 Families.
Argyle	Contains 40 New England Families, and 40 Accadian Families.
Yarmouth	Contains 90 Families
Clare	Contains 50 Accadian Families.
from thence to Annapolis	Are about 10 Fishermens Families
On Annapolis River, the Townships of Annapolis, Granville, Wilmot	Contains upwards of 250 Families
Horton	Contains about 120 Families
Cornwallis	Contains 130 Families
Falmouth	Contains 35 Families
Windsor	Contains about 20 Families
Newport	Contains about 70 Families
from thence to Truro	There are 6 or 7 Families settled.
Truro	Consists of 50 Families

Onslow

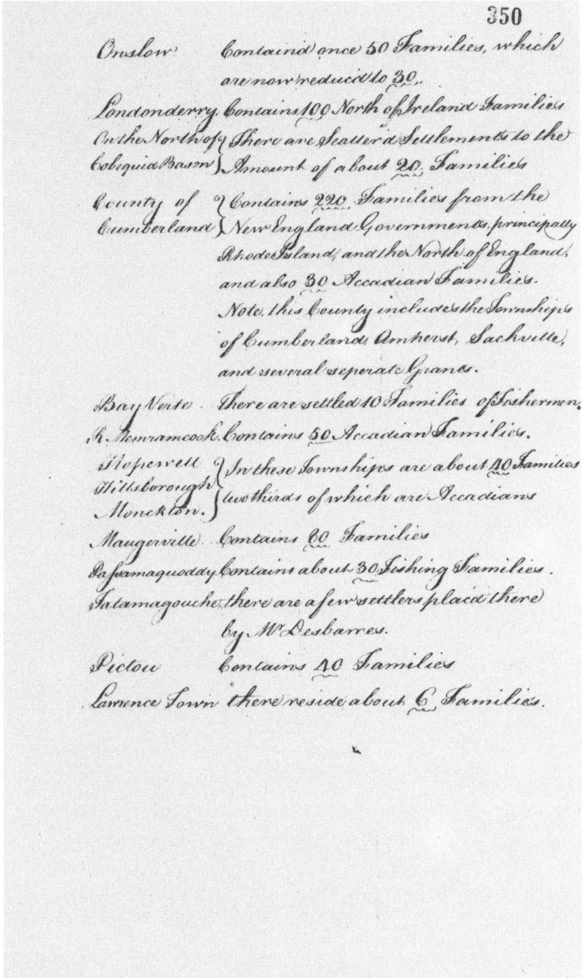

350

Onslow	Containd once 50 Families, which are now reduced to 30.
Londonderry	Contains 100 North of Ireland Families
On the North of Cobequid Bason	There are Scatter'd Settlements to the Amount of about 20 Families
County of Cumberland	Contains 220 Families from the New England Governments, principally Rhode Island, and the North of England, and also 30 Accadian Families. Note, this County includes the Townships of Cumberland, Amherst, Sackville, and several seperate Grants.
Bay Verte	There are settled 10 Families of Fishermen.
R. Memramcook	Contains 50 Accadian Families.
Hopewell, Hillsborough, Monckton.	In these Townships are about 40 Families two thirds of which are Accadians
Maugerville	Contains 60 Families
Passamaquoddy	Contains about 30 Fishing Families.
Tatamagouche	there are a few settlers placed there by Mr Desbarres.
Pictou	Contains 40 Families
Lawrence Town	there reside about 6 Families.

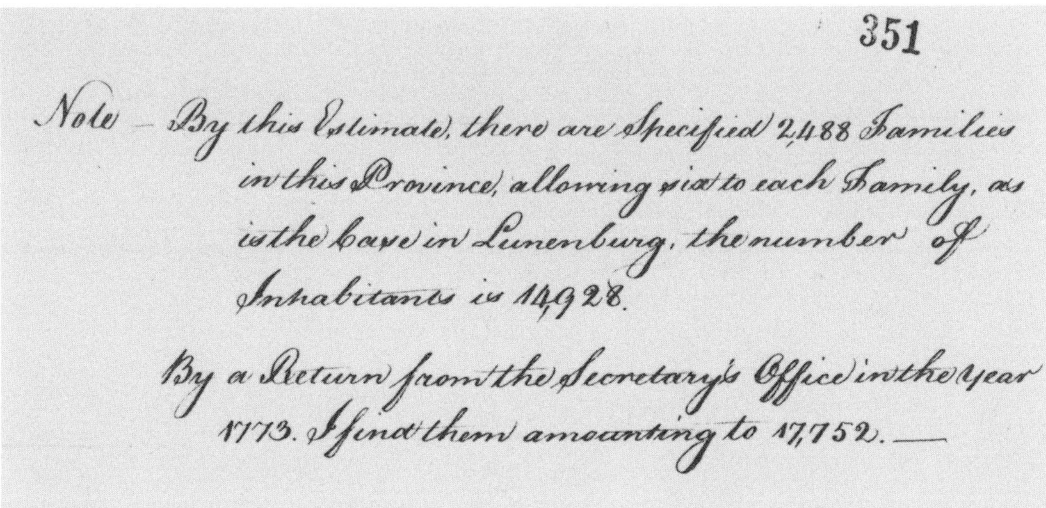

351

Note – By this Estimate, there are Specified 2,488 Families in this Province, allowing six to each Family, as is the Case in Lunenburg, the number of Inhabitants is 14928.

By a Return from the Secretary's Office in the Year 1773. I find them amounting to 17,752. —

"Abstract of the Number of Families settled in Nova Scotia . . . August 1775."

National Archives of Canada: Manuscript Division, Dartmouth papers, MG 23, A 1, vol. 1, pp. 349–351.

III

The American Revolution, 1775–1783

The American Revolution was often not so much a revolt against a distant king as a brutal civil war between those who supported the Crown and those who did not. Many had no strong reason to support the Revolution. Others, both in the Thirteen Colonies and in the colonies to the north, either rejected revolution or saw it as too radical a solution to existing problems.

Quebec suffered direct invasion by the rebels in 1775. The Maritimes provided an important British base for operations against the colonies in revolt. The most significant result of the Revolution for the northern colonies was the influx of Loyalist refugees — continuing supporters of the Crown — who provided the core of their non-French-speaking population.

The Rebel Appeal to French Canada, 1776

Signed by John Hancock as the President of the Second Continental Congress, this broadside announces the rebel march against Montreal and Québec in 1775–1776 and urges the Canadians to form a provincial congress to support the Revolution.

Those in Quebec to whom the American revolutionary ideals might have appealed, however, lacked leadership. The seigneurs and the Church supported the Crown. Many others, seeing no reason to involve themselves in the quarrel, maintained a pragmatic neutrality.

One of the printers of the broadside (a single sheet, printed on one side only), the Frenchman Fleury Mesplet (1734–1794), followed the American forces to Montreal. Ironically, he stayed on after their retreat to become the first printer west of Québec City. He produced eighty titles, including two periodicals, and printed in four languages: English, French, Latin and Mohawk. He published the first entirely French newspaper in Quebec and inaugurated the *Montreal Gazette/La Gazette de Montréal* (which still exists today as the *Gazette*).

AUX

HABITANTS

DE LA PROVINCE DU CANADA.

AMIS ET COMPATRIOTES;

NOTRE Précédente Adreſſe vous a démontré nos Droits, nos Griefs & les Moyens que nous avons en notre pouvoir, & dont nous ſommes autoriſés par les CONSTITUTIONS BRITANNIQUES, à faire uſage pour maintenir les uns, & obtenir juſtice des autres.

NOUS vous avons auſſi expliqué, que votre Liberté, votre Honneur & votre Bonheur, ſont eſſentiellement & néceſſairement liés à l'Affaire malheureuſe que nous avons été forcé d'entreprendre, pour le ſoutien de nos Priviléges.

NOUS voyons avec joie, combien vous avez été touché, par les remontrances juſtes & équitables de vos Amis & Compatriotes, qui n'ont d'autres vues que celles de fortifier & d'établir la cauſe de la Liberté: les ſervices que vous avez déjà rendus à cette cauſe commune, méritent notre reconnoiſſance; & nous ſentons l'obligation où nous ſommes, de vous rendre le reciproque.

LES meilleures cauſes ſont ſujettes aux événements, les contre-temps ſont inévitables, tel eſt le ſort de l'humanité; mais les ames genereuſes, qui ſont éclairées & échauffées par le feu ſacré de la Liberté, ne ſeront pas découragées par de tels échecs, & ſurmonteront tous les obſtacles qui pourront ſe trouver entr'eux & l'objet prétieux de leurs vœux.

NOUS ne vous laiſſerons pas expoſé à la fureur de vos ennemis & des nôtres; deux Bataillons ont reçu ordre de marcher au Canada, dont une partie eſt déjà en route; on leve ſix autres Bataillons dans les Colonies unies pour le même ſervice, qui partiront pour votre Province auſſi-tôt qu'il ſera poſſible; & probablement ils arriveront en Canada, avant que les Troupes du Miniſtere, ſous le Général Carleton, puiſſent recevoir des ſecours: en outre, nous avons fait expédier les ordres néceſſaires pour faire lever deux Bataillons chez vous. Votre aſſiſtance pour le ſoutien & la conſervation de la Liberté Amériquaine, nous cauſera la plus grande ſatisfaction; & nous nous flattons que vous ſaiſirez avec zèle & empreſſement l'inſtant favorable de co-opérer au ſuccès d'une entrepriſe auſſi glorieuſe. Si des forces plus conſidérables ſont requiſes, elles vous ſeront envoyées.

Apréſent, vous devez être convaincus, que rien n'eſt plus propre à aſſurer nos intérêts & nos libertés, que de prendre des méſures efficaces, pour combiner nos forces mutuelles, afin que par cette réunion de ſecours & de conſeils, nous puiſſions éviter les efforts & l'artifice d'un ennemi qui cherche à nous affoiblir en nous diviſant; pour cet effet, nous vous conſeillons & vous exhortons, d'établir chez vous des Aſſociations en vos différentes Paroiſſes, de la même nature que celles qui ont été ſi ſalutaires aux Colonies unies; d'élire des Députés pour former une Aſſemblée Provinciale chez vous, & que cette Aſſemblée nomme des Délegués, pour vous repréſenter en ce Congrès.

NOUS nous flattons de toucher à l'heureux moment, de voir diſparoître de deſſus cette terre, l'Etendard de la Tyrannie, & nous eſpérons qu'il ne trouvera aucune place en l'Amérique Septentrionalle.

Signé au Nom & par l'Ordre du Congrès: JOHN HANCOCK, *Préſident.*

A Philadelphie, le 24 Janvier 1776.

Aux Habitants de la Province du Canada.
John Hancock. Philadelphia: Fleury Mesplet and Charles Berger, 1776.
Broadside.

National Archives of Canada: Library (Negative no. C-111468).

III

A Loyalist Speaks His Mind, 1775

Many in the Thirteen Colonies were perplexed by the coming of the American Revolution. There is a sense of sincere dismay in this letter by Jonathan Sewell, Attorney-General of Massachusetts. Sewell wrote from Boston, the very centre of the Revolutionary movement.

Sewell was astonished that citizens who lived in one of the most fertile and expansive lands on earth — who enjoyed "the highest portion of civil and religious liberty that the nature of human society admits" and who were protected "by the only Power on Earth capable of affording that protection" — should "rush to arms with the ferocity of savages and with the fiery Zeal of Crusaders!" He believed that the Revolution was a scheme of ambitious and designing men working their wiles on a credulous population. His contention that armed rebellion was an over-reaction to the situation was shared by many. Some fled to Canada during or after the Revolution.

Jonathan Sewell, Sr., first fled to England in 1775, and then in 1778 settled at Halifax where he became Judge of the Vice-Admiralty Court of Nova Scotia and New Brunswick. His correspondent, Major-General Frederick Haldimand, became Governor of Quebec in 1777.

This letter is a draft retained in the Sewell papers. The National Archives of Canada holds extensive Sewell family papers, as well as hand transcripts and microfilm copies of the Haldimand papers, a basic source for the study of the American Revolutionary period in Quebec and what would later become Ontario.

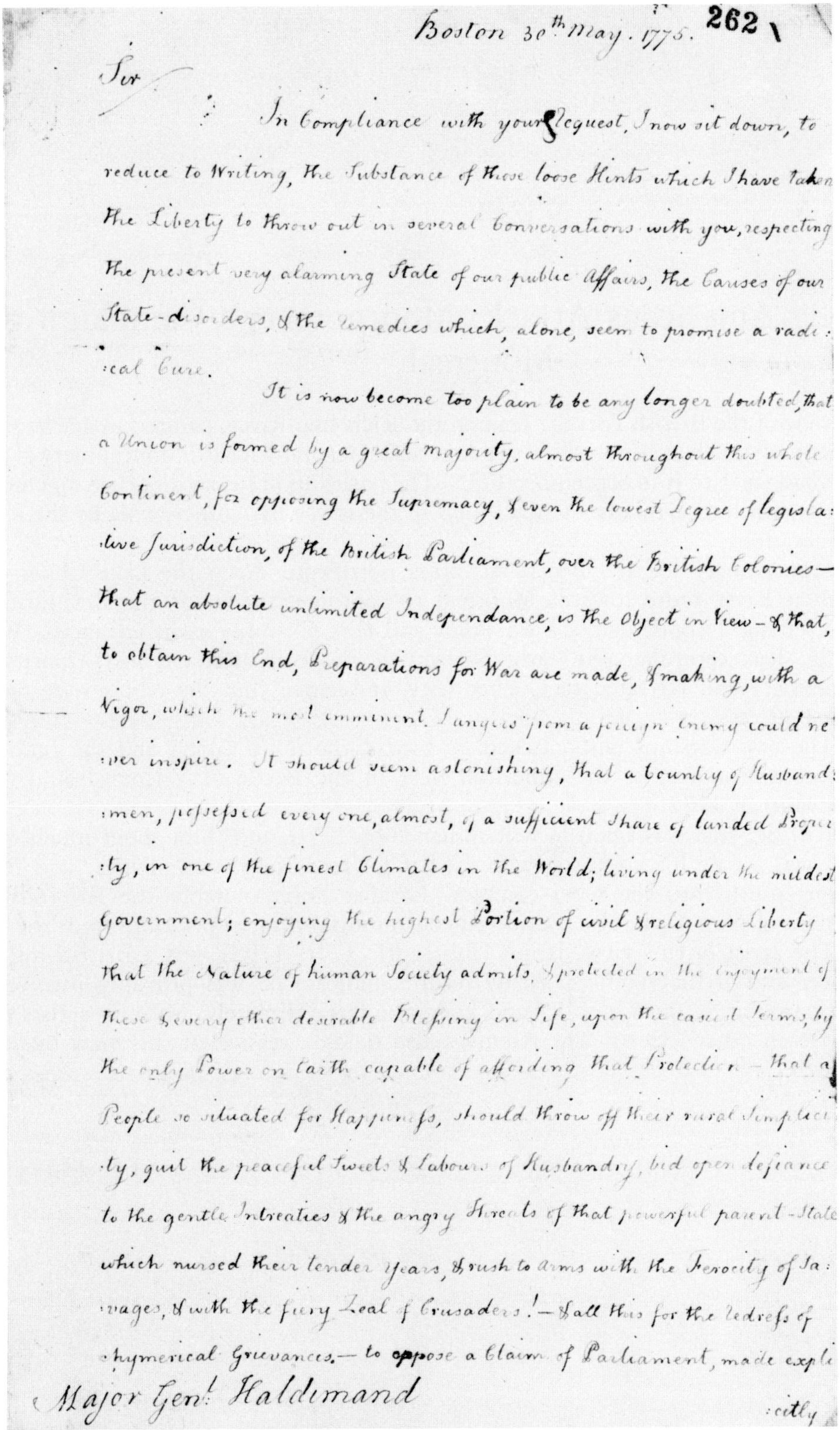

Boston 30th May. 1775. 262

Sir

In Compliance with your Request, I now sit down, to reduce to Writing, the Substance of those loose Hints which I have taken the Liberty to throw out in several Conversations with you, respecting the present very alarming State of our public Affairs, the Causes of our State-disorders, & the Remedies which, alone, seem to promise a radi:cal Cure.

It is now become too plain to be any longer doubted, that a Union is formed by a great majority, almost throughout this whole Continent, for opposing the Supremacy, & even the lowest Degree of legisla:tive Jurisdiction, of the British Parliament, over the British Colonies— that an absolute unlimited Independance, is the Object in View—& that, to obtain this End, Preparations for War are made, & making, with a Vigor, which the most imminent Dangers from a foreign Enemy could ne:ver inspire. It should seem astonishing, that a Country of Husband:men, possessed every one, almost, of a sufficient Share of landed Prope:rty, in one of the finest Climates in the World; living under the mildest Government; enjoying the highest Portion of civil & religious Liberty that the Nature of human Society admits, & protected in the Enjoyment of these & every other desirable Blessing in Life, upon the easiest Terms, by the only Power on Earth capable of affording that Protection — that a People so situated for Happiness, should throw off their rural Simplici:ty, quit the peaceful Sweets & Labours of Husbandry, bid open defiance to the gentle Intreaties & the angry Threats of that powerful parent-State which nursed their tender Years, & rush to Arms with the Ferocity of Sa:vages, & with the fiery Zeal of Crusaders!—& all this for the Redress of chymerical Grievances.— to oppose a Claim of Parliament, made expli:citly

Major Genl. Haldimand

Letter, Jonathan Sewell to Major-General Frederick Haldimand, Boston, 30 May 1775.

National Archives of Canada: Manuscript Division, Sewell papers, MG 23, G II 10, vol. 2, p. 262.

The Americans Attack: Montgomery's Campaign to Montreal, 1775

This view of the British Fort St. Jean on the Richelieu River, painted in 1779, shows the fort very much as it was when the American General Richard Montgomery (1736–1775) laid siege to it in September 1775. The positions of his artillery are ingeniously marked with bird symbols. A small map in the lower left corner explains the alphabetic notations.

Montgomery led the American forces northward down the Lake Champlain-Richelieu River route towards Montreal to capture Canada for the Revolutionary cause, seizing Ticonderoga, Crown Point and Fort Chambly as he advanced. When Fort St. Jean capitulated in early November, the British abandoned Montreal to Montgomery and retreated to Québec City. It seemed that the rebels were on the verge of success.

The two warships (also marked by birds), the *Royal George* and the *Inflexible*, were prominent against the American fleet in the Battle of Valcour Island (Lake Champlain) in 1777.

Fort St. Jean was again in British hands by 1776, and throughout much of the war it was a base for Loyalists, who used it for recruiting, surveillance, and rescue missions south into the rebel colonies. Loyalist units, notably the King's Royal Regiment of New York, also conducted continuing military operations from the fort.

The artist of this view, James Hunter (fl. 1776–1792), was a British military engineer and artillery officer. Army records indicate he was probably involved in construction at St. Jean in 1779 and knew the fort intimately. Military artists often copied each other's views. The Archives also holds a version of this view by James Peachey.

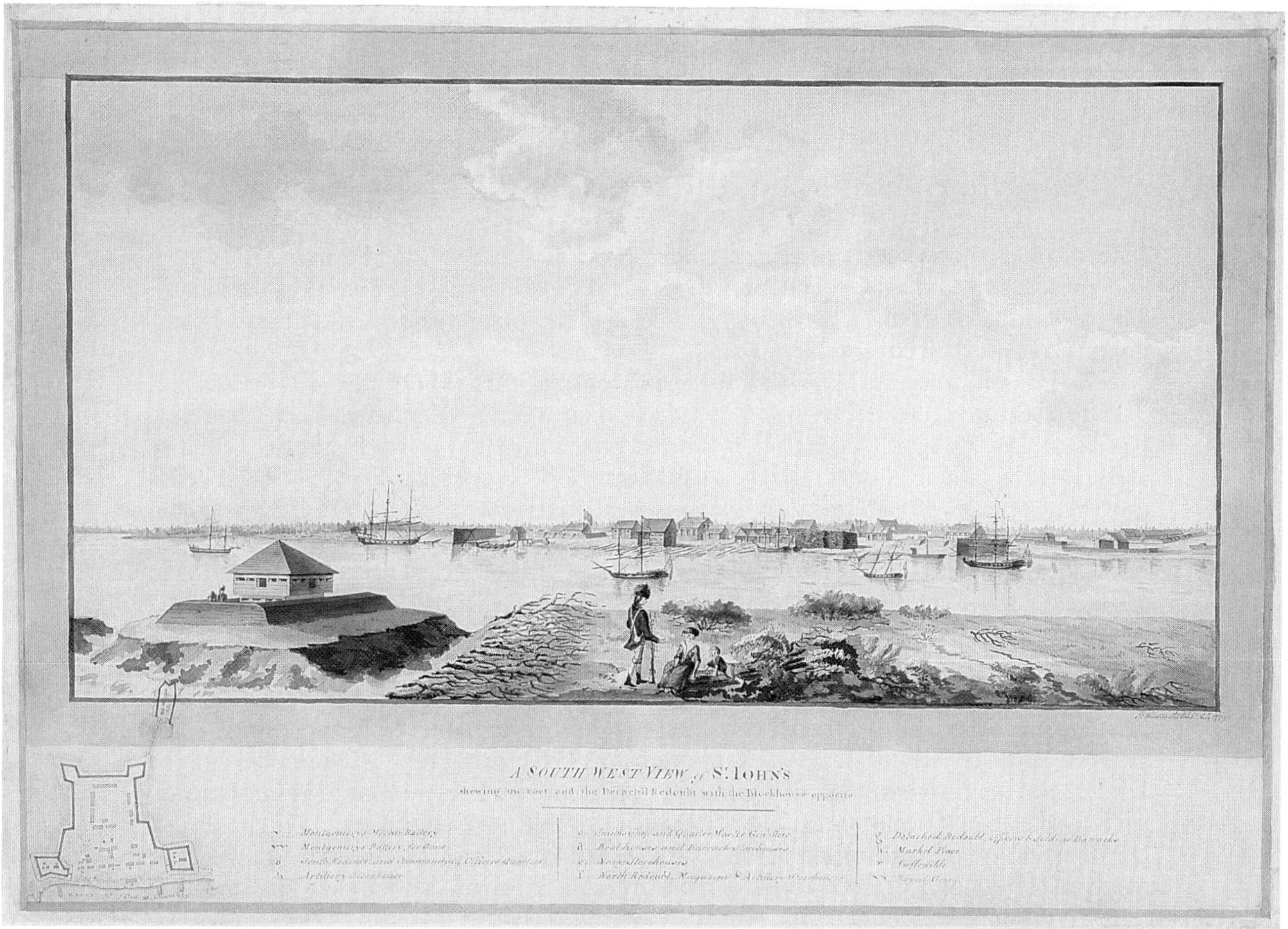

A South-West View of Fort St. Jean, Quebec, with Plan. James Hunter (fl. 1776–1792). Watercolour, 1779. 41.9 × 60.6 cm.

National Archives of Canada: Documentary Art and Photography Division (Negative no. C-1507).

Benedict Arnold Shells Québec City, 1775–1776

Jefferys' map shows the American artillery positions, indicating the number of guns and the deployment of General Benedict Arnold's troops on the Plains of Abraham. The fortifications of the city are delineated and the places where Arnold and Montgomery began their attack are marked.

While Montgomery advanced towards Montreal, Arnold (1742–1801) managed, despite hardships, to bring seven hundred men via the Kennebec and Chaudière Rivers to Québec City. Montgomery joined him with another three hundred men in early December 1775, and during a snowstorm on New Year's Eve they launched a desperate attack against the city. Arnold was driven back, while Montgomery and his leading officers were killed. The remaining besiegers were routed when the spring thaw allowed British reinforcements up the St. Lawrence. The rebels abandoned Montreal on 9 May. Quebec had repulsed the rebel onslaught.

Like the Arrowsmith firm, that of Thomas Jefferys (circa 1710–1771) was a pioneer in British map publishing concerning North America. Great Britain in this period did not have an official map or chart publishing office, and it was in the government's interest to support cartographic publishing firms of demonstrated competence such as that of Jefferys. Jefferys from 1761 had been "Geographer to the King," and his firm was thus in a favoured position to benefit from official information such as that being collected in North America by military engineers. William Faden (1750–1836), Jefferys' junior partner, succeeded to control of the firm on Jefferys' death in 1771, and became an even more influential cartographer than his master.

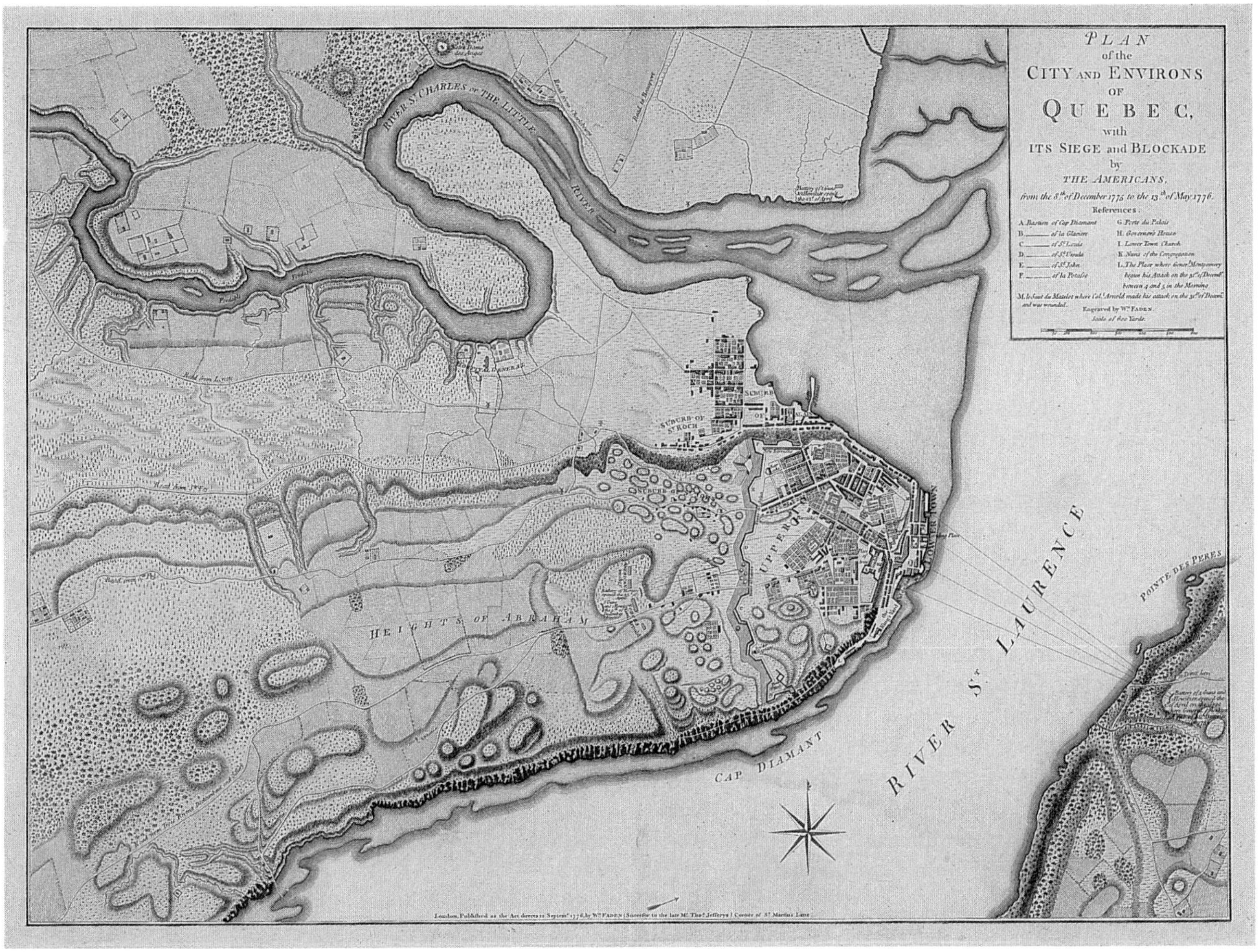

Plan of the City and Environs of Quebec with its seige and blockade by the Americans from the 8th of December 1775 to the 13th of May 1776. Engraved by William Faden (1750–1836). London: William Faden, 1776. Plan: hand-coloured, engraved, 44.1 × 61.4 cm.

National Archives of Canada: Cartographic and Architectural Archives Division (NMC 55019).

Halifax: Guardian of the North, 1781

Throughout the Revolutionary War, Halifax was a major harbour, supply centre and base for forces loyal to the King. As befitted a major base, it bristled with fortifications. By the war's end, the city had fourteen forts, barracks and blockhouses in and about the town proper, accommodating 2,800 troops.

This view was taken from one of the numerous small posts on Point Pleasant. Citadel Hill can be seen in the distance, crowned with a large octagonal blockhouse constructed at the beginning of the war, and a maze of trenches and earthworks. Below them is Fort Massey with its blockhouse, erected between 1776 and 1778.

A stream of military transports crossing the Atlantic touched at Halifax for orders and supplies before turning south. The British fleet came in at intervals. The little town was bursting at the seams. As the print shows, a tent city covered the slopes of Citadel Hill and spread out beyond.

A strong military presence and the activity of the British fleet helped discourage colonists in Nova Scotia who might have considered supporting the Revolution. From 1776, when British troops and Loyalists from Boston were evacuated to Halifax, the city attracted a growing refugee community. As the war wound down, this stream of refugees into Nova Scotia became a torrent.

The artist, Edward Hicks (fl. 1778–1782), was an officer of the 70th Regiment, stationed in Halifax in 1778. He executed sketches on which a series of four prints of Halifax were based. The prints are now extremely rare. The National Archives holds all four prints and a watercolour by Hicks.

"South aspect of Halifax Nova Scotia... in 1780...." Edward Hicks (fl. 1778–1782). London, 1781. Hand-coloured aquatint. 53.4×31.2 cm.

National Archives of Canada: Documentary Art and Photography Division (Negative no. C-11214).

III

The Loyalists Come: A Loyalist Provisioning List, 1786

The Loyalists enumerated in this list were part of the King's Royal Regiment of New York, which had fought with great success on the frontiers of New York and Pennsylvania (see also Item 22). They were being settled on the Bay of Quinte, Lake Ontario, near present-day Kingston, Ontario.

Resettlement was a tedious process and the government, as this list indicates, had to supply food to the Loyalists for some time before they could survive on their own crops.

The British government treated the Loyalists who came north extremely well, providing them with food, clothing, tools, seed, shelter, land and recompense for their war losses. It ultimately spent more than £30 million on the Loyalists.

The National Archives holds more than twenty original Loyalist provisioning lists for Upper Canada and several more for the Maritimes.

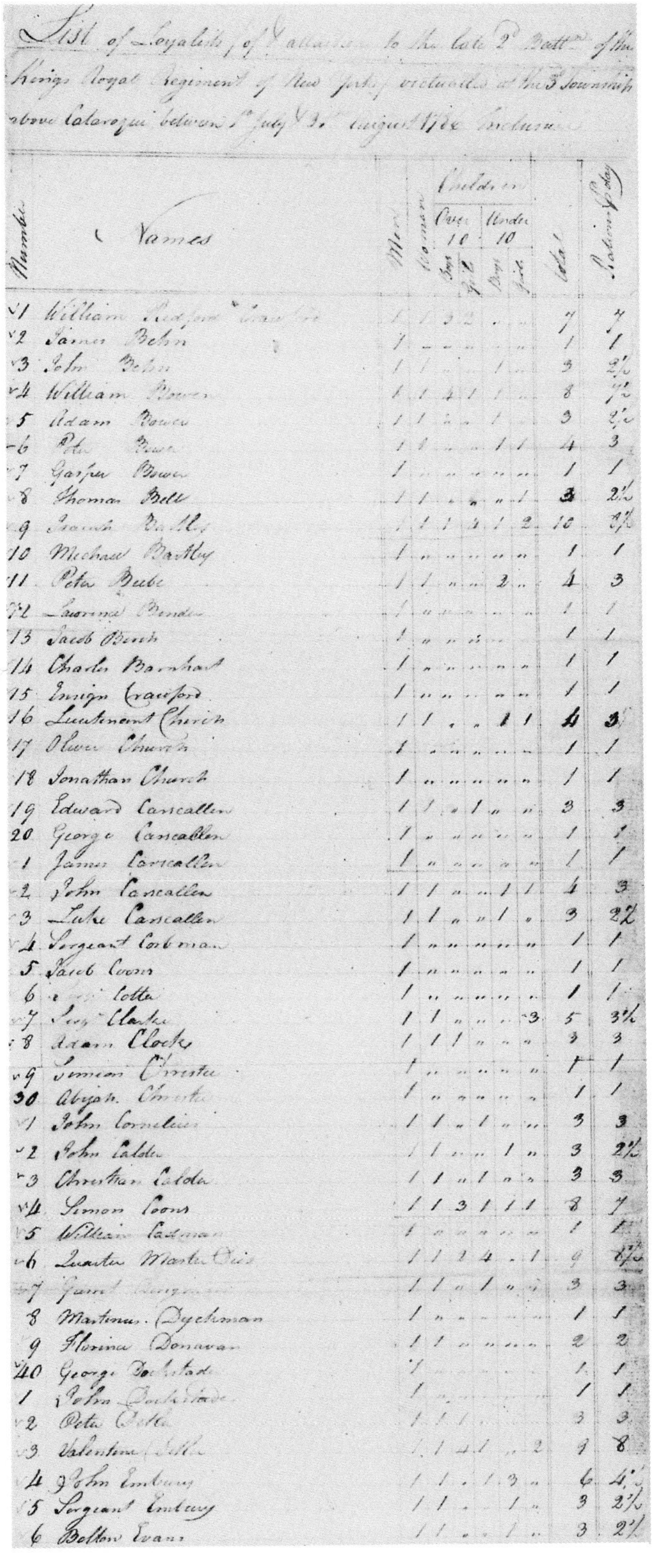

List of Loyalists of & attached to the late 2d Battn of the Kings Royal Regiment of New York victualled at the 3 Township above Cataroqui between 1st July & 31st August 1786 Inclusive

Number	Names	Men	Women	Children Over 10 Boys	Children Over 10 Girls	Children Under 10 Boys	Children Under 10 Girls	Total	Rations per day
1	William Redford Crawford	1	1	3	2	„	„	7	7
2	James Bohn	1	–	–	–	–	–	1	1
3	John Bohn	1	1	„	„	1	„	3	2½
4	William Bower	1	1	4	1	1	„	8	7½
5	Adam Bower	1	1	„	„	1	„	3	2½
6	Peter Bower	1	1	„	„	1	1	4	3
7	Gasper Bower	1	„	„	„	„	„	1	1
8	Thomas Bell	1	1	„	„	„	1	3	2½
9	Francis [illegible]	1	1	1	4	1	2	10	[illegible]
10	Michael Bartley	1	„	„	„	„	„	1	1
11	Peter Beebe	1	1	„	„	2	„	4	3
12	Lawrence Bender	1	„	„	„	„	„	1	1
13	Jacob [illegible]	1	„	„	„			1	1
14	Charles Barnhart	1	„	„	„	„	„	1	1
15	Ensign Crawford	1	„	„	„	„	„	1	1
16	Lieutenant Church	1	1	„	„	1	1	4	3
17	Oliver Church	1	„	„	„	„	„	1	1
18	Jonathan Church	1	„	„	„	„	„	1	1
19	Edward Cascallen	1	1	„	1	„	„	3	3
20	George Cascallen	1	„	„	„	„	„	1	1
1	James Cascallen	1	„	„	„	„	„	1	1
2	John Cascallen	1	1	„	„	1	1	4	3
3	Luke Cascallen	1	1	„	„	1	„	3	2½
4	Sergeant Corbman	1	„	„	„	„	„	1	1
5	Jacob Coons	1	„	„	„	„	„	1	1
6	[illegible] Cotter	1	„	„	„	„	„	1	1
7	Serg. Clarke	1	1	„	„	„	3	5	3½
8	Adam Clocks	1	1	1	„	„	„	3	3
9	Simeon Christie	1	„	„	„	„	„	1	1
30	Abijah Christie	1	„	„	„	„	„	1	1
1	John Cornelius	1	1	„	1	„	„	3	3
2	John Calder	1	1	„	„	1	„	3	2½
3	Christian Calder	1	1	„	1	„	„	3	3
4	Simon Coons	1	1	3	1	1	1	8	7
5	William Casman	1	„	„	„	„	„	1	1
6	Quarter Master [illegible]	1	1	1	4	„	1	9	8½
7	[illegible]	1	1	„	1	„	„	3	3
8	Martinus Dyckman	1	„	„	„	„	„	1	1
9	Florina Donavan	1	1	„	„	„	„	2	2
40	George Dockstader	1	„	„	„	„	„	1	1
1	John Dockstader	1	„	„	„	„	„	1	1
2	Peter [illegible]	1	1	1				3	3
3	Valentine [illegible]	1	1	4	1	„	2	9	8
4	John Embury	1	1	„	1	3	„	6	4½
5	Sergeant Embury	1	1	„	„	1	„	3	2½
6	Bolton Evans	1	1	„	„	1	„	3	2½

List of Loyalists of and attached to the Second Battalion of the Kings Royal Regiment of New York Victualled at the third township above Cataraqui between 1 July and 31 August 1786 (detail). George Singleton.

National Archives of Canada: Government Archives Division, Records of the Department of Finance, RG 19, E 4, vol. 4447, file 1, part 1, parcel 1, #4.

The Loyalist Boom Town of Shelburne, Nova Scotia, 1789

The framed houses and the masts of ships in Booth's 1789 sketch suggest the early prosperity of Shelburne. Indeed, with the Saint John River Valley, New Brunswick, it was the major area for first Loyalist settlement in the Maritimes. In only three years, it grew from nothing to a town of eight thousand inhabitants, complete with the amenities one would have expected of a major settlement: fine houses, taverns, a jeweller, a dancing instructor, a hairdresser, churches, schools, three newspapers, sawmills and shipyards. It threatened to rival Halifax.

The town's growth was short-lived, however; by the late 1780s, it had entered a sharp decline, and by 1815 the population was a mere six hundred. Its soil and timber were poor, inland communications primitive, whaling and fisheries disappointing. Although the town disappeared, most of its inhabitants settled elsewhere in the Maritimes.

William Booth, the artist (fl. 1785–1788), was a captain in the Royal Engineers. While stationed in Halifax, he travelled extensively in Nova Scotia, executing watercolour sketches. The National Archives also holds a watercolour sketch by Booth of a black Loyalist cutting wood at Shelburne.

26

Part of the Town of Shelburne, Nova Scotia, with the Barracks Opposite. William Booth (fl. 1785–1788). Pencil with wash, 1789. 29.2 × 54.6 cm.

National Archives of Canada: Documentary Art and Photography Division (Negative no. C-10548).

Origin of the Term "United Empire Loyalist," 1789

In 1789, Lord Dorchester, the Governor-in-Chief of British North America, proclaimed that the Loyalists and their children should be allowed to append "UE" to their names, "alluding to their great principle, the Unity of the Empire," hence the phrase "United Empire Loyalist," or UEL. The term originally applied to Quebec and Upper Canada (Ontario) alone; it was officially recognized in the Maritimes only in the twentieth century.

This Quebec document of 1789 is an order-in-council — or official decree — requiring the Land Boards, which assigned land to new settlers, to keep a registry of persons "who had adhered to the Unity of Empire." It had been reprinted in pamphlet form from the minutes of the Legislative Council for wider distribution to officials concerned in Quebec and what was soon to be Upper Canada.

At the Council Chamber at Quebec,

Monday 9th November 1789.

PRESENT,

His Excellency the Right Honble LORD DORCHESTER.

The Honble. WILLIAM SMITH, Eſquire, Chief Juſtice.

HUGH FINLAY,	GEORGE POWNALL,	Eſquires.
THOS. DUNN,	HENRY CALDWELL,	
EDWD. HARRISON,	WILLIAM GRANT,	
JOHN COLLINS,	FRANÇOIS BABY,	
ADAM MABANE,	CHARLES DE LANAUDIERE,	
J. G. C. DELERY,	LE CTE. DUPRE',	

HIS Lordſhip intimated to the Council, that it remained a Queſtion, upon the late Regulation for the Diſpoſition of the Waſte Lands of the Crown, whether the Boards, conſtituted for that Purpoſe, were authorized to make Locations to the Sons of Loyaliſts, on their coming to full Age and that it was his Wiſh to put a Mark of Honor upon the Families who had adhered to the Unity of the Empire, and joined the Royal Standard in America before the Treaty of Separation in the year 1783.

The Council concurring with His Lordſhip, it is accordingly ORDERED,

That the ſeveral Land Boards take Courſe for preſerving a Regiſtry of the

[2]

the Names of all Perſons, falling under the Deſcription aforementioned, to the End that their Poſterity may be diſcriminated, from future Settlers, in the Pariſh Regiſters and Rolls of the Militia, of their reſpective Diſtricts, and other Public Remembrancers of the Province, as proper Objects, by their perſevering in the Fidelity and Conduct, ſo honorable to their Anceſtors, for diſtinguiſhed Benefits and Privileges.

And it is alſo Ordered, that the ſaid Land Boards may, in every ſuch Caſe, provide not only for the *Sons* of thoſe Loyaliſts, as they arrive to full Age, but for their *Daughters* alſo, of that Age, or on their Marriage, aſſigning to each a Lot of Two Hundred Acres, more or leſs, provided nevertheleſs that they reſpectively comply with the general Regulations, and that it ſhall ſatisfactorily appear, that there has been no Default in the due Cultivation and Improvement of the Lands already aſſigned to the Head of the Family, of which they are Members.

QUEBEC: PRINTED BY S. NEILSON.

Quebec. Order-in-Council for Land Boards to preserve registry of persons "who had adhered to the Unity of Empire." Broadside, 1789.

National Archives of Canada: Library (Negative nos. C-130528 and C-130529).

The Embryo of Modern Canada, 1784

The political map of North America looked very different at the end of the American Revolution than at its beginning. With its conclusion, Britain lost most of her possessions in North America. By the Peace of Paris of 1783, she acknowledged American independence and recognized a boundary — marked in red on this map — running through the centre of the four northerly Great Lakes and from Lake of the Woods "due west" to the imagined location of the Mississippi's headwaters, then south along the Mississippi. For the moment, the fate of the far west remained undecided, but eventually the Americans would claim all the territory from the line passing above the Mississippi's headwaters west to the Pacific and south to Mexico. The French, allies of the new American nation, obtained fishing rights off Newfoundland, marked on the map in blue.

What was left of British North America consisted of Newfoundland and its fisheries, the small struggling settlements of the Maritimes, French Quebec — which Britain had even been somewhat reluctant to keep just twenty years before — and the wilderness of the "upper country" beyond Quebec. Few observers at the time would have held out much hope of major development on this seemingly unpromising base.

This map, published by William Faden in 1796, is a later version of a map first published in 1777. The depiction of British North America is based heavily on French cartography prior to the Conquest of 1760. For example, two of the islands appearing in Lake Superior on this map, Philipeaux and Pontchartrain, are fictitious. The mistake was based on a French misinterpretation of a native account that had first been incorporated into a French map of the 1730s. General maps of British North America (as opposed to more detailed ones of settled areas) would continue for some time to rely upon the cartography of the French Regime.

The United States of North America with the British Territories and those of Spain according to the Treaty of 1784. Engraved by William Faden (1750–1836). London: William Faden, 1796. Map: hand-coloured, engraved. 52.5 × 63.5 cm.

National Archives of Canada: Cartographic and Architectural Archives Division. (NMC 24667).

IV

Settlement and Population

The resource that early British North America most obviously lacked between 1760 and 1815 was people. Although the years after 1815 would see more spectacular waves of immigration, central and eastern Canada did achieve a respectable population growth in this period that helped greatly in assuring the colonies' survival and prosperity. The growth of population, the process of settlement, the expansion of urban centres and the related development of communications in this period are all stories that most Canadians know little about; yet they can be told from the documents of the period.

IV

A Record Birth Rate

By far the largest concentration of population was in Quebec. The population of that colony in 1765 was 70,000; in 1790, 161,000 and in 1814, 300,000 or about sixty per cent of the total population of British North America. Remarkably, most of Quebec's population growth came not through immigration but through natural increase. Quebec at this period had the highest birth rate ever recorded for any people of European origin — its population was doubling every twenty-five to twenty-seven years!

This 1765 census of the seignieury of Bécancour is typical of many similar documents in the National Archives. When used in conjunction with other censuses, it is extremely valuable not only for calculating population, but for tracing family history, as well as for studying occupation, family size and structure, religious composition of the population and agricultural production.

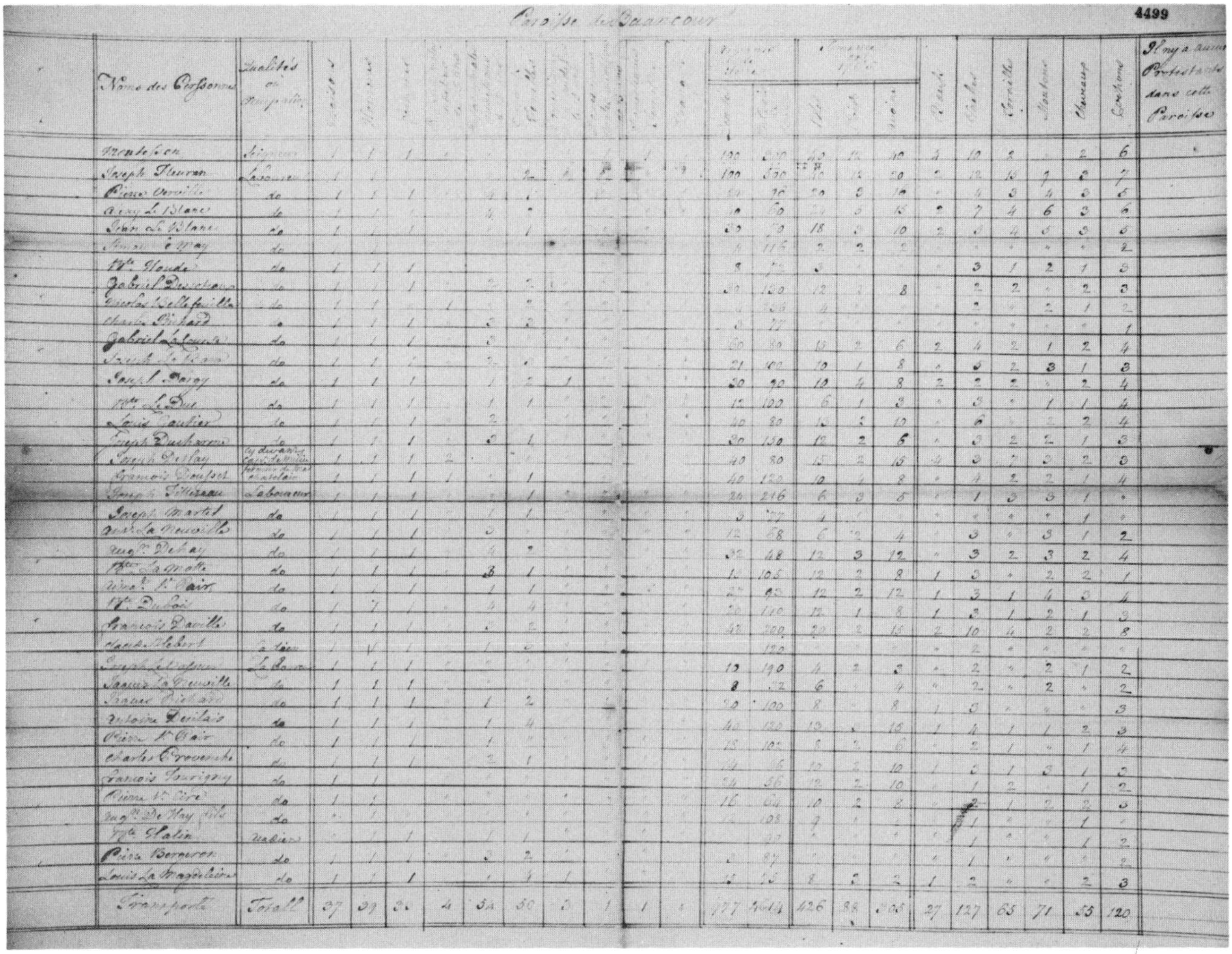

4499

Noms des Personnes

Il n'y a aucun Protestants dans cette Paroisse

Census of Bécancour, 1765.

National Archives of Canada: Manuscript Division, Quebec and Lower Canada: "S" Series, Provincial and Civil Secretaries' Offices, RG 4, A 1, vol. 11, p. 4499.

The Loyalists Transform the Face of English-Speaking British North America, 1783–1784

Although there was an existing population of 20,000 in the Maritimes and 8,000 permanent settlers in Newfoundland in 1783, the wave of Loyalist migration beginning in that year provided the British North American colonies with their first substantial English-speaking population. A total of 40,000 to 50,000 Loyalists came to British North America, approximately 35,000 to the Canadian Maritimes, 2,000 to Quebec and 7,500 to Ontario. To deal with the influx, the new provinces of New Brunswick and Cape Breton were created in 1784, and Upper Canada (Ontario) in 1791.

This view is the only surviving one by an eye-witness of the beginnings of Loyalist settlement. James Peachey was working as a surveyor in the future Upper Canada, laying out lots for the new settlers, when the Loyalists arrived. The little tent city, depicted only a few days after its establishment, was at Cornwall and was one of three base camps established for the St. Lawrence River and Bay of Quinte Loyalists. The large tent with several smaller tents beside it on the far side of the cove is probably the headquarters of the surveyors.

This watercolour is one of a series of seventeen scenes by James Peachey alphabetically keyed and depicting Quebec and the future Upper Canada in 1784 and earlier. All are now held by the National Archives. They are thought to originally have been insets on a large-scale map of the St. Lawrence River region.

Encampment of the Loyalists at Johnstow, a New Settlement, on the Banks of the River St. Laurence in Canada,
taken from [triangle symbol] marked in the Plan

Encampment of the Loyalists at Cornwall, 1784. James Peachey (fl. 1773–1797). Watercolour, pen and ink, after 1784. 16.6 × 36.5 cm.

National Archives of Canada: Documentary Art and Photography Division (Negative no. C-2001).

IV

Some Americans Petition for Land, 1792

Many Americans were attracted to the British colonies after the Loyalist immigrations of the early 1780s. Upper Canada was the greatest beneficiary of this interest: it grew from a population of 7,500 in 1784 to 71,000 in 1814, largely on the basis of American emigration. The Maritimes and Quebec also received substantial numbers.

Some Americans came as "late Loyalists," drawn by their continuing allegiance to the Crown. Many more were attracted by economic considerations such as free and plentiful land in Upper Canada. Minority religious and ethnic groups such as the Quakers, Tunkers and Moravians established settlements to escape the intolerance that was frequently evident in the new republic to the south. Heavy American settlement created increasing concerns as the possibility of another war with the United States loomed large.

This petition of 1792 is from Stephen Aldrich, William Lawing and their associates in the State of Vermont, a group of Germans seeking a township on the shores of Lake Memphramagog, Quebec, in which to settle. Since no accurate statistics on American immigration into British North America exist for this period, such documents as this one are very helpful for studying the movement.

The petition comes from a series of land petitions and related documents such as reports of surveys and copies of official decisions submitted to the Land Committee of the Executive Council in Quebec, 1764–1841. The series consists of 210 volumes or 21 metres of material.

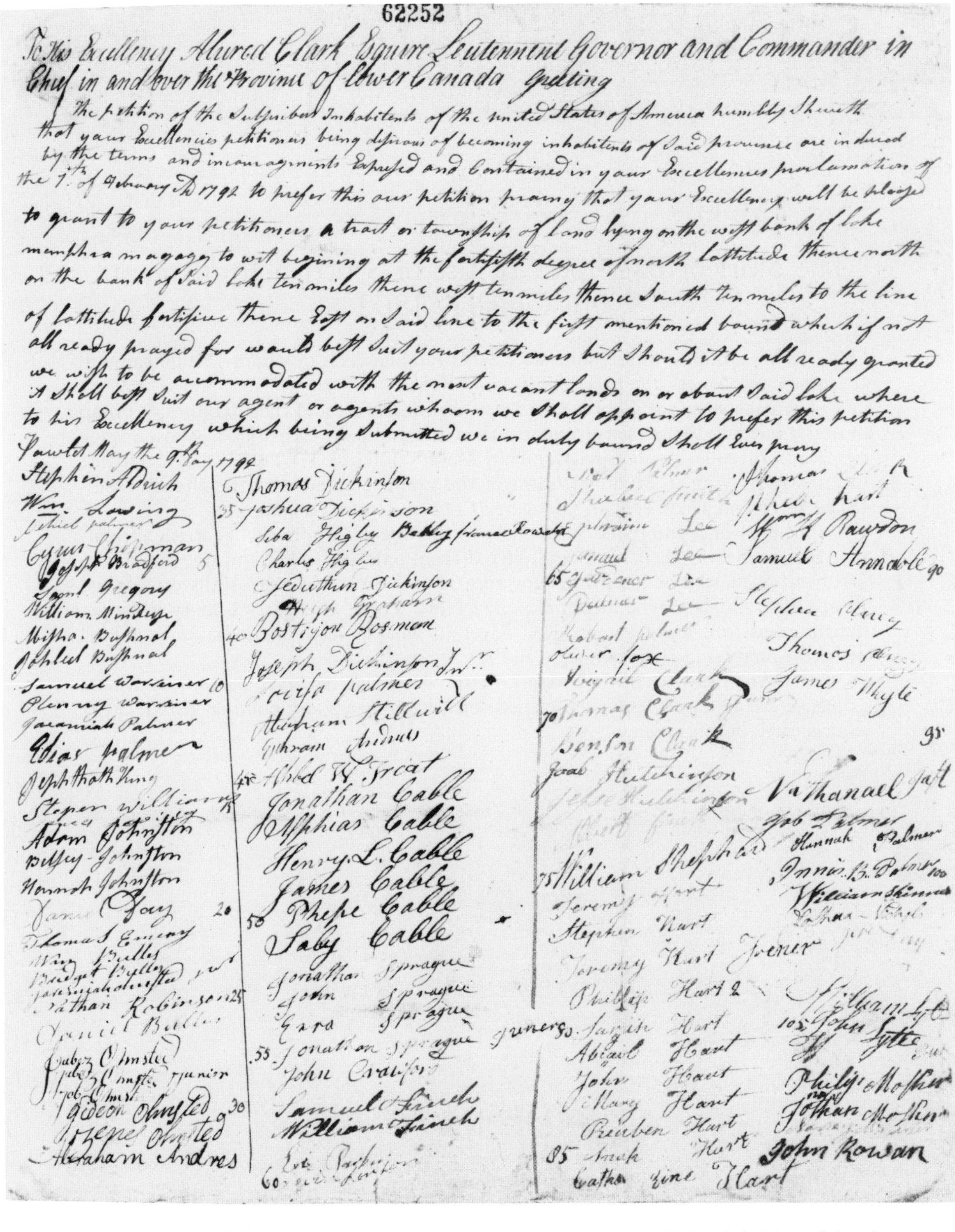
62252

To His Excellency Alured Clark Esquire Lieutenant Governor and Commander in Chief in and over the Province of Lower Canada Greeting

The petition of the Subscriber Inhabitants of the united States of America humbly Sheweth that your Excellencies petitioners being desirous of becoming inhabitants of said province are induced by the terms and incouragements Expressed and Contained in your Excellencies proclamation of the 7th of February AD 1792 to prefer this our petition praying that your Excellency will be pleased to grant to your petitioners a tract or township of land lying on the west bank of lake memphramagog to wit begining at the fortyfifth degree of north lattitude thence north on the bank of said lake ten miles thence west ten miles thence South ten miles to the line of lattitude fortyfive thence East on said line to the first mentioned bound which if not all ready prayed for would best suit your petitioners but should it be all ready granted we wish to be accommodated with the most vacant lands on or about said lake where it shall best suit our agent or agents whoom we shall appoint to prefer this petition to his Excellency which being submitted we in duty bound shall ever pray

Pawlet May the 9th Day 1792

Stephen Aldrich
Wm. Lawing
Cyrus Chipman
Joseph Bradford
Saml. Gregory
William Mindege
Elisha Bushnal
Jehiel Bushnal
Samuel Warsiner
Plenny Warsiner
Jeremiah Palmer
Elias Palmer
Stephen Williams
Adam Johnston
Hannah Johnston
Thomas Emery
Nathan Robinson
Daniel Baller
Jabez Olmstead
Gideon Olmsted
Abraham Andres

Thomas Dickinson
Joshua Dickinson
Seba Higby
Charles Higbee
Jedediah Dickinson
Hugh Graham
Bostiyon Bosman
Joseph Dickinson Jr.
Abraham Stillwill
Ephraim Andrus
Abel W. Treat
Jonathan Cable
Apphias Cable
Henry L. Cable
James Cable
Phebe Cable
Saby Cable
Jonathan Sprague
John Sprague
Ezra Sprague
Jonathan Sprague Juner
John Crawford
Samuel Finch
William Finch

Oliver Fox
Abigail Clark
Thomas Clark
Benson Clark
Joel Hutchinson
William Shepherd
Jeremy Hart
Stephen Hart
Jeremy Hart Juner
Phillip Hart
Sarah Hart
Abigail Hart
John Hart
Mary Hart
Reuben Hart
Catharine Hart

Thomas Clark
Phebe Hart
Wm. K. Rawdon
Samuel Annable
Thomas
James Whyte
Nathanael Hart
Job Palmer
Hannah Palmer
John Lytle
Philip Mosher
Jotham Mosher
John Rowan

Petition of Stephen Aldrich *et al.* for a township, 1792.

National Archives of Canada: Manuscript Division, Executive Council: Lower Canada. Land Petitions, RG 1, L 3 L, vol. 126, p. 62252.

The Skirl of Bagpipes: A List of Scottish Immigrants to Canada, 1802

One notable group of immigrants were Scots Highlanders, of whom 15,000 came to British North America between 1770 and 1815.

The page shown is a portion of a list of immigrants and their families, a group of nearly five hundred settlers from Lochaber, Inverness-shire, Scotland, whose voyage to Canada in 1802 was led by Archibald McMillan (circa 1761–1832), a merchant. Originally arriving in Montreal, most of the group gravitated to the already established Highland settlement in Glengarry County, Upper Canada.

The clansmen emigrated voluntarily in the face of "improved" Scottish agriculture that took away their farms and offered them only small crofts to live on. Before 1815 and unassisted by the British government, the Scots had successfully established Prince Edward Island, the Pictou region of Nova Scotia, Glengarry County in Upper Canada, and to a lesser extent, Red River in what is now Manitoba as Highland districts, preserving their language and traditions.

The Archibald McMillan papers in the National Archives contain unusually extensive accounts, correspondence, petitions, agreements and nominal lists relating to this early immigration.

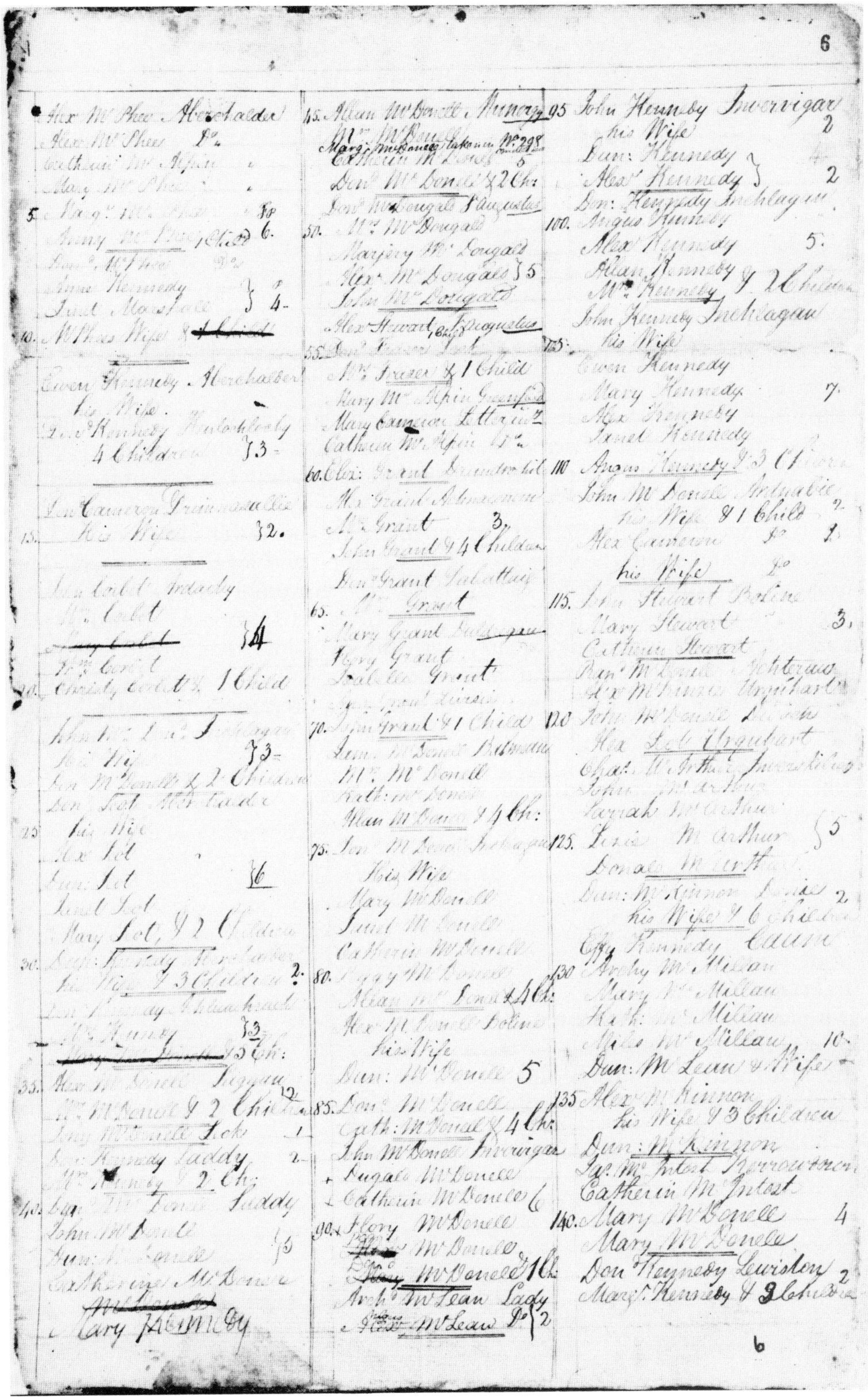

List of Scottish immigrants, 1802.

National Archives of Canada: Manuscript Division, Archibald McMillan and Family papers, MG 24, I 183, p. 6.

The Theory: A Model Township, 1790

Rapid expansion of population caused government officials to give increasing thought to the proper organization of settlements. Although French Canadians would continue to use the seigneury as the unit of settlement, the township was the unit used by English-speaking Canadians.

Government officials, concerned about American and lower class immigrants, wished to attract and strengthen the growth of a "strong and loyal Aristocracy." This plan, proposed by Lord Dorchester (1724–1808), the Governor in Chief of Quebec, was designed to encourage the formation of local elites. His proposed township plan was to include a town one mile square, with one-acre lots that would appeal to prosperous residents. The town was to have a buffer of a half-mile around it, followed by park lots of twenty-four acres reserved for the most prominent residents. Ample provision was made for schools, churches, courts and jails to develop proper attitudes and to punish wrong ones.

Other features are explained by an alphabetic code:

A – Reserves to the Crown
B and C – Church, parsonage and schoolhouse
D – Gaol and courthouse
E – Workhouse
F – Church yards, hospitals, etc.
G – Public squares
H – Market-places
I – Town park for the schoolmaster
K – Town park for a minister

The plan bears the initials and arrowhead stamp of the Board of Ordnance, which was responsible for the supply of maps as well as other equipment to the British military forces.

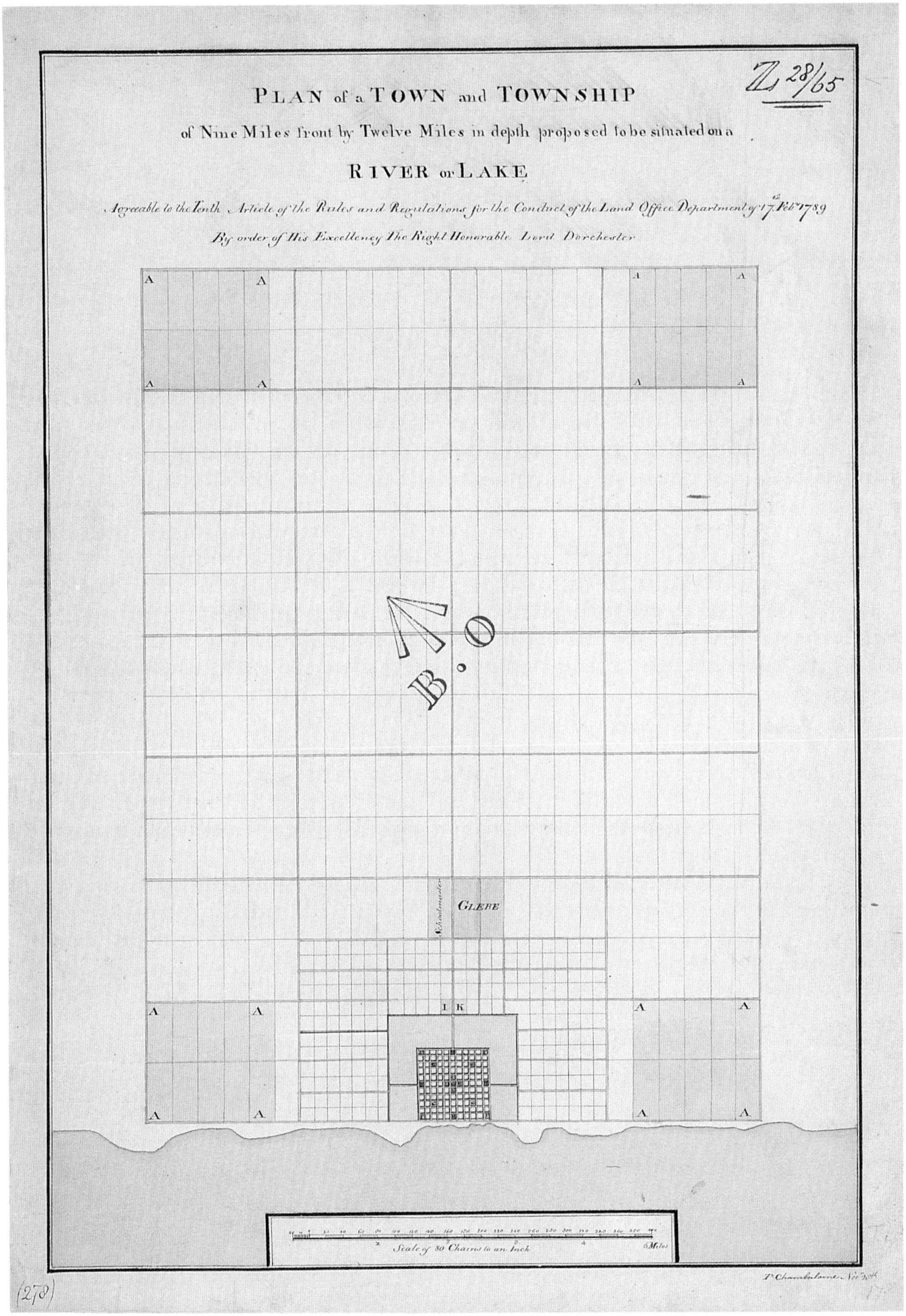

"Plan of a Town and Township of Nine Miles front by Twelve Miles in depth proposed to be situated on a River or Lake." Ts. Chamberlaine. Plan: manuscript, hand-coloured, 1789, 43.0 × 29.7 cm.

National Archives of Canada: Cartographic and Architectural Archives Division (NMC 273).

The Reality: Diagram of Dunham Township, Quebec, 1796

The township pattern that actually emerged in central British North America was different from the rather abstract theories of British officials. A minority of townships had towns within them. Dunham Township, displayed here, did not. The location and shape of real towns were determined more by local economic and geographical factors than by official theory. Still the townships did display some of the essential characteristics evident in official plans. They were rectangular or square, with their lots laid out in a grid pattern. The typical township was 16 kilometers square, or if on navigable water, 19 kilometres in depth with a 14-kilometre water frontage. Modifications due to local circumstances were frequent. Although they did not generally have reserves of land laid out in blocks as in the official theory, the townships did have a seventh part of their land set aside "for use of the Protestant clergy" — called the Clergy Reserves — and a further seventh set aside for the government — called the Crown Reserves. Money from the sale of these lots was supposed to be used to aid the officially recognized churches and government projects. The Clergy and Crown Reserves were scattered in a "chequer board" pattern intended to place them evenly through a township. They are marked in grey and red respectively in this plan. Being held for later and more profitable sale, the reserves began to impede settlement by about 1820.

This survey is a certified copy prepared in 1796 for reference from the original, then kept in the Surveyor General's Office in Québec, which was responsible for the conduct of land surveys and is the major source of detailed maps chronicling the settlement of the land.

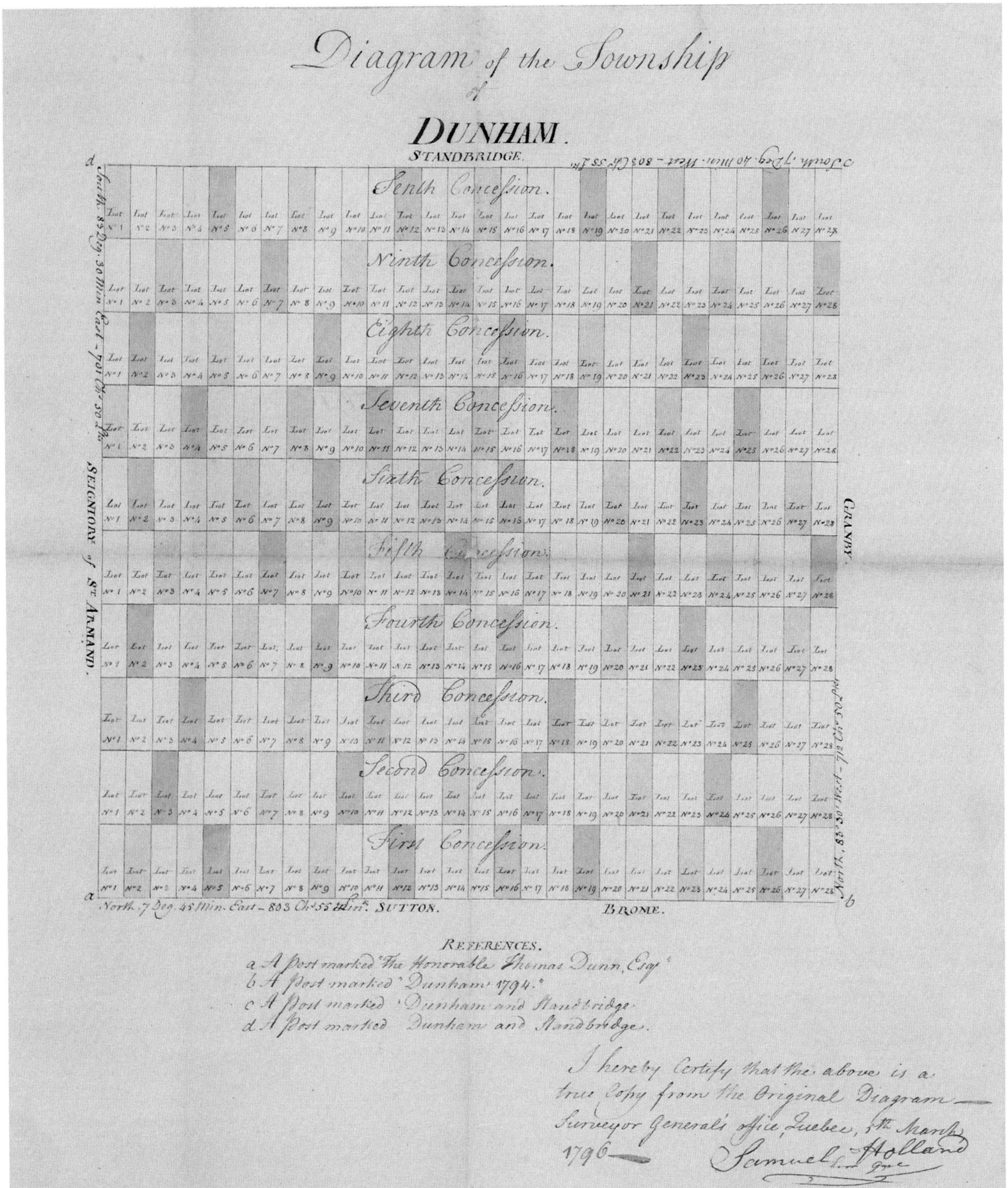

"Diagram of the Township of Dunham." Certified by Samuel Holland (1728–1801). Plan: manuscript, hand-coloured, 1796, 39.3 × 33.8 cm.

National Archives of Canada: Cartographic and Architectural Archives Division (NMC 1330).

Conditions of Land Granting: Yonge Street, 1798

Beyond the establishment of settlement patterns and the granting of land, colonial governments found it necessary to take measures to ensure that the land granted was actually settled. Conditions on very attractive sites, like Yonge Street, the main artery running out of York (Toronto), sounded stringent.

The insistence that owners build a house and fence in five acres within a year was to prevent land from being monopolized by speculators who would do nothing but wait until the improvements of others in the neighbourhood pushed land values up. There was little government money for expensive projects such as road-building and maintenance, and the official regulation that landowners labour on local roads was virtually universal. Regulations were easier to make than put into effect, however; they were frequently ignored, and summonses and fines were difficult to enforce.

A manuscript note on the side of this handbill states that Loyalists were not eligible for grants on Yonge Street — a somewhat ironic application of the special privileges the government awarded them.

Handbills like this one would have been posted locally. Often copies survive only because examples were placed in official government records, now deposited in archives.

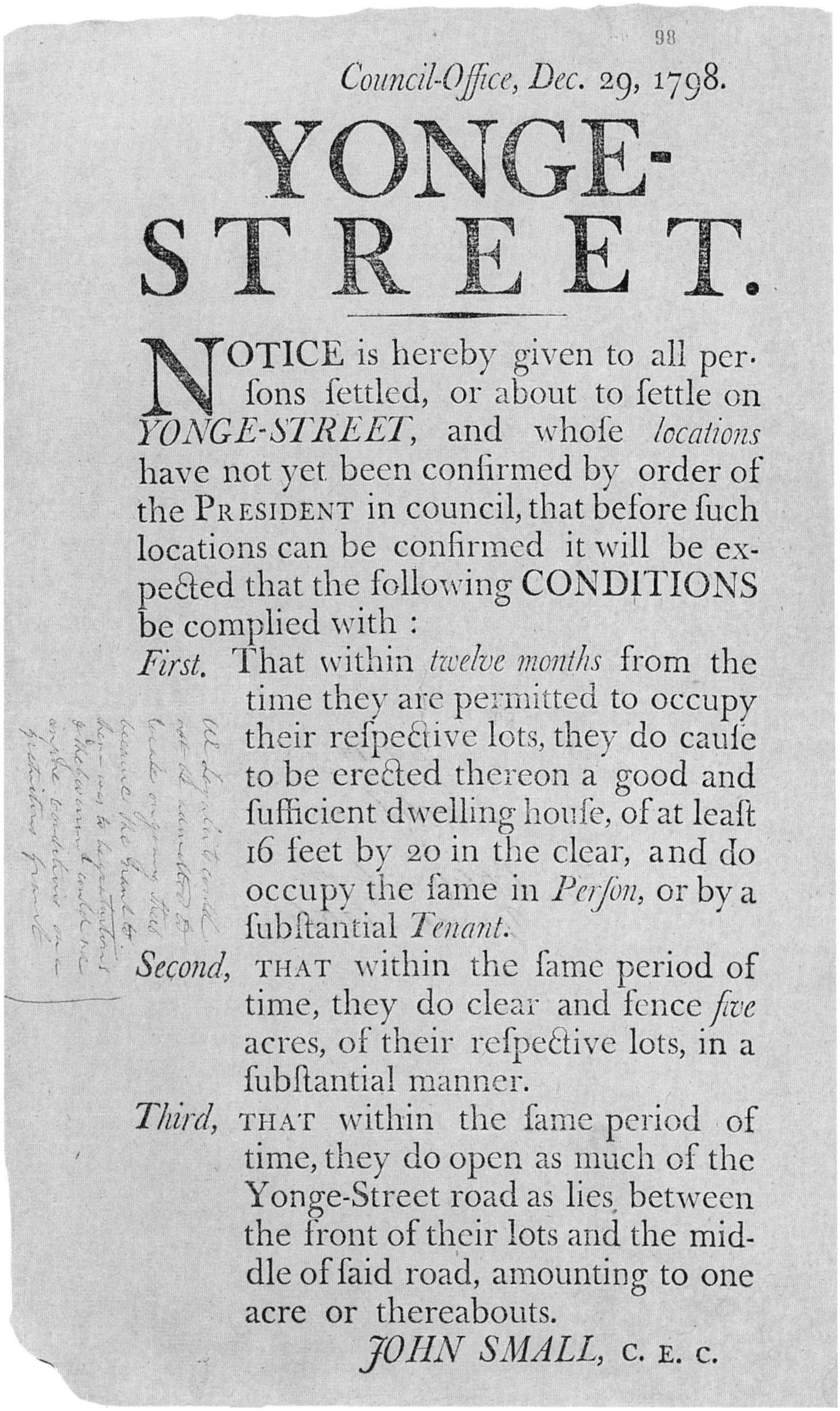

98

Council-Office, Dec. 29, 1798.

YONGE-STREET.

NOTICE is hereby given to all perſons ſettled, or about to ſettle on *YONGE-STREET*, and whoſe *locations* have not yet been confirmed by order of the PRESIDENT in council, that before ſuch locations can be confirmed it will be expected that the following CONDITIONS be complied with :

First. That within *twelve months* from the time they are permitted to occupy their reſpective lots, they do cauſe to be erected thereon a good and ſufficient dwelling houſe, of at leaſt 16 feet by 20 in the clear, and do occupy the ſame in *Perſon*, or by a ſubſtantial *Tenant*.

Second, THAT within the ſame period of time, they do clear and fence *five* acres, of their reſpective lots, in a ſubſtantial manner.

Third, THAT within the ſame period of time, they do open as much of the Yonge-Street road as lies between the front of their lots and the middle of ſaid road, amounting to one acre or thereabouts.

JOHN SMALL, C. E. C.

Yonge Street Settlement Regulations.
Broadside, 1798.

National Archives of Canada:
Manuscript Division, Upper Canada:
Submissions to the Executive Council on
State Matters, 1791–1841, RG 1, E 3,
vol. 100, p. 98.

A Royal Town: Halifax, 1800

While settlement grew in the rural areas of British North America, its cities were also developing. Founded in 1749, Halifax by 1790 was still a struggling town of shabby wooden structures, defended by the tumble-down remains of forts dating from the American Revolution. Its exports were small and its mercantile activity risky.

The Napoleonic Wars were buoying up the city's economy by the time Edward, Duke of Kent, son of King George III, arrived in Halifax in 1794 to be military Commander-in-Chief of Nova Scotia. When he left in 1800, Halifax was studded with excellent public and military buildings, and surrounded by powerful batteries that made it the strongest fortress in the world outside Europe.

The fort on George's Island, from which this view was taken, was a symbol of Halifax's military importance. It was entirely rebuilt and modernized by Edward, as was the Citadel, seen atop the hill in the centre of the view. On the left slope of Citadel Hill, the large mansion on the horizon is Belle Vue, Edward's handsome wooden residence, with its wide Corinthian portico. Government House, whose corner stone was laid the year this view was sketched by George Parkyns, is to the left, nearer to the Citadel and below it. In 1800 the Duke also laid the corner stone of St. George's Church, the round building to the right of the town. Merchants were growing wealthy and, influenced by the Duke's example, were also building finer homes and bigger stores. Even the common folk were improving their tenements. Edward left a town with a new and lofty tone and a vigorous outlook on the world.

George Isham Parkyns (1750–1820) was an English watercolourist and engraver. He lived in Brooklyn in the United States from 1793, publishing a series of aquatint engravings of American cities. He visited Halifax in 1800 before returning to England where he published a series of four aquatints of Halifax. The National Archives holds all four aquatints as well as a view of Halifax by Parkyns published in the *Colonial Journal*, Vol. 6 (London, 1817).

View of Halifax from Georges Island.
George Isham Parkyns (1750–1820).
Etching and aquatint in brown ink with watercolour, circa 1801.
33.0 × 54.6 cm.

National Archives of Canada: Documentary Art and Photography Division (Negative no. C-40306).

Québec City: Comfort and Squalor, 1804

Québec City, then as now, was considered one of the most spectacularly beautiful cities of North America. Its extensive line of commercial wharfs, carefully delineated on this military map, spoke of its prosperity, while the new suburbs pushing out to the west of the city beyond its walls proclaimed its growth. Its citadel and fortifications indicated heavy investment of public money and gave the city its military colour. Québec was lively, bustling and, by colonial standards, urbane and sophisticated.

Québec City, however, also exhibited the filth, poverty and danger common to cities of the period. A prominent citizen, William Smith, spoke of approaching the city by avenues full of "noxious vapours" and "encumbered by heaps of old shoes, cast mocassins . . . bones, dead cats and dogs . . . the emptying of slaughterhouses and cleaning of stables." Poverty was in clear evidence. Every day in winter crowds of beggars walked the streets with large bags to gather food from passers-by.

Fire was an ever-present danger, and protection against it consisted of ordinances such as one that required all carters in the city to report to the scene of a fire with a horse, cart, and cask, if they had one, to cart water and remove goods. There were two major fires between 1790 and 1815, each of which left many families homeless. Thus citizens of Québec lived surrounded by beauty and comfort, but also by appalling squalor and the risk of disaster.

This plan accompanied a report on Quebec's fortifications by Gother Mann, Major General Commanding, Royal Engineers. It was prepared in the Engineers' Drawing Room, Québec City. The military's concern with the city as a prime fortification meant that plans of it were frequently prepared.

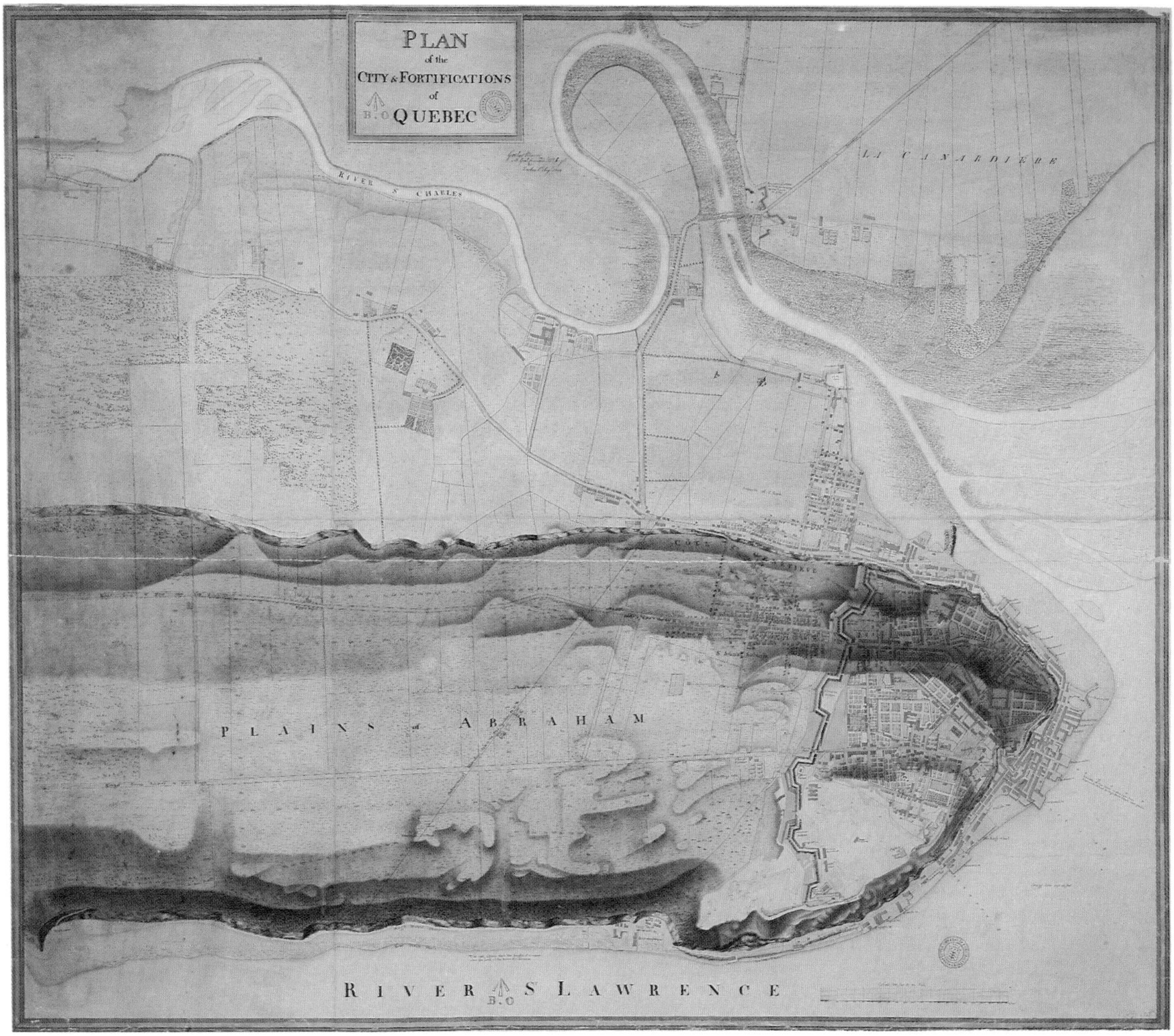

Plan of the City and Fortifications of Québec City, 1 August 1804.
Gother Mann (1747–1830), Major General Commanding, Royal Engineers.
Map: manuscript, hand-coloured.
142.5 × 167.3 cm.

National Archives of Canada: Cartographic and Architectural Archives Division (NMC 95875).

A Capital Among the Tree Stumps: York (Toronto), circa 1803

Unlike Québec City and Halifax, which had developed strategic and economic functions, York, Upper Canada, was a hothouse community forced ahead of its natural growth by its social position as capital. Many towns and villages in British North America still sat, like York, amidst stumps, with the forest looming behind them. Few, however, would have had such elaborate shops and houses.

The east end of the town along Front Street is seen in this painting, stretching from Cooper's Tavern on King Street around to the town blockhouse, a place for citizens to take shelter in case of attack. The town was only ten blocks long in total.

Cooper's Tavern, to the left of this view, was advertised in 1801 as being "as nearly on the footing of an English Inn as local circumstances will permit. . . ." Its owner, William Cooper, was an example of the flexibility necessary for success in a pioneer town: he was at various times, and often concurrently, a tavern keeper, school teacher, preacher, butcher, wharfinger, miller and auctioneer. The house behind the tavern belonged to Duncan Cameron, a Scots merchant, involved for a few years in a local trade in furs, while the next was that of William Warren Baldwin, an Irishman who, although a qualified doctor, maintained a comfortable and distinguished law practice. Baldwin was destined to become a major figure in reform politics. His neighbour to the right, William Allan, was a merchant and, like most of the major merchants of Upper Canada, a Scot. The last home belonged to Peter Russell, a government official who had been administrator of the province. Russell maintained the hundred acre lot he had been granted as a moderately successful farm and attempted, with difficulty, to live the leisurely life of a British gentleman. The two red brick single-storey structures beside the blockhouse were designed as the wings of a lieutenant-governor's residence that was never built. They served for meetings of the legislature, sessions of the courts, and church services and stood at the foot of what is now Parliament Street.

Three variant versions of this watercolour are known. Elizabeth Frances Hale (1774–1826) is likely to have copied this version from ones done in the autumn of 1803 by Edward Walsh.

York, Upper Canada. Elizabeth Frances Hale (1774–1826). Watercolour, pen and ink over pencil, 1804. 28.3 × 44.5 cm.

National Archives of Canada: Documentary Art and Photography Division (Negative no. C-40137).

IV

The Mail Gets Through – Maybe, 1811–1812

The provision of adequate transportation and communications was a very major undertaking in early British North America. The remarks on this way-bill, carried by couriers attempting to get the mail from Halifax to Québec City in the dead of winter, dramatize the problems. Indeed, it is not even clear that the mail, after more than a month, actually did get through. The last notations are at Madawaska, still almost two hundred miles from Québec City.

A way-bill is a list of goods on conveyance. In this particular case, couriers were under instructions to have the postmasters at various points along their route note the day and time of the arrival and departure of the mail. Any delays were to be noted and certified by a responsible person. "In this," the instructions sternly warned, "you [the courier] are not to fail."

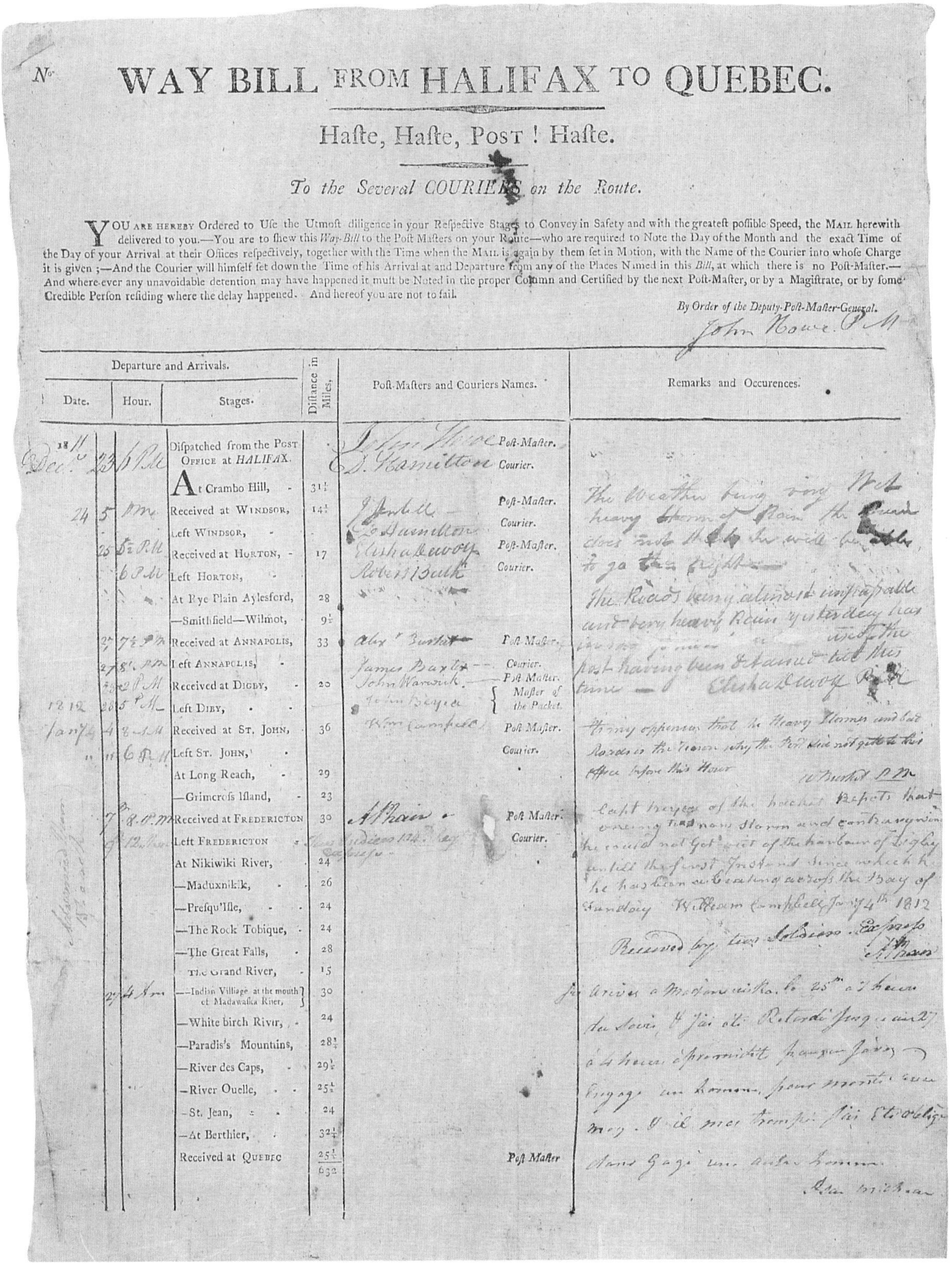

No.

WAY BILL FROM HALIFAX TO QUEBEC.

Hafte, Hafte, Post ! Hafte.

To the Several COURIERS on the Route.

YOU ARE HEREBY Ordered to Ufe the Utmoft diligence in your Refpective Stages to Convey in Safety and with the greateft poffible Speed, the MAIL herewith delivered to you.—You are to fhew this *Way-Bill* to the Poft Mafters on your Route—who are required to Note the Day of the Month and the exact Time of the Day of your Arrival at their Offices refpectively, together with the Time when the MAIL is again by them fet in Motion, with the Name of the Courier into whofe Charge it is given ;—And the Courier will himfelf fet down the Time of his Arrival at and Departure from any of the Places Named in this *Bill*, at which there is no Poft-Mafter.—And where-ever any unavoidable detention may have happened it muft be Noted in the proper Column and Certified by the next Poft-Mafter, or by a Magiftrate, or by fome Credible Perfon refiding where the delay happened. And hereof you are not to fail.

By Order of the Deputy-Poft-Mafter-General.

John Howe P.M.

Departure and Arrivals.			Diftance in Miles.	Poft-Mafters and Couriers Names.	Remarks and Occurences.
Date.	Hour.	Stages.			
		Difpatched from the POST OFFICE at *HALIFAX*.		Poft-Mafter. Courier.	
		At Crambo Hill,	31½		
		Received at WINDSOR,	14½	Poft-Mafter.	
		Left WINDSOR,		Courier.	
		Received at HORTON,	17	Poft-Mafter.	
		Left HORTON,		Courier.	
		At Rye Plain Aylesford,	28		
		—Smithfield—Wilmot,	9½		
		Received at ANNAPOLIS,	33	Poft-Mafter.	
		Left ANNAPOLIS,		Courier.	
		Received at DIGBY,	20	Poft-Mafter. Mafter of the Packet.	
		Left DIBY,			
		Received at ST. JOHN,	36	Poft-Mafter.	
		Left ST. JOHN,		Courier.	
		At Long Reach,	29		
		—Grimcrofs Ifland,	23		
		Received at FREDERICTON	30	Poft-Mafter.	
		Left FREDERICTON		Courier.	
		At Nikiwiki River,	24		
		—Maduxnikik,	26		
		—Prefqu'Ifle,	24		
		—The Rock Tobique,	24		
		—The Great Falls,	28		
		The Grand River,	15		
		—Indian Villiage at the mouth of Madawafka River,	30		
		—White birch Rivir,	24		
		—Paradis's Mountains,	28¼		
		—River des Caps,	29½		
		—River Ouelle,	25½		
		—St. Jean,	24		
		—At Berthier,	32¼		
		Received at QUEBEC	25½	Poft-Mafter	
			632		

Way Bill from Halifax to Quebec. Printed notice with manuscript additions, 1811–1812.

National Archives of Canada: Manuscript Division, Miscellaneous Documents, MG 55/24, no. 59.

V

Political and General Social Development, 1784–1812

The political and social development of the British North American colonies was diversified, with no colony repeating the pattern of another. Politics in Quebec, for example, were fairly complex and gave rise to established party groupings and sophisticated political theory, while in Prince Edward Island and Newfoundland, they focused on single issues. Each colony faced its own particular problems; regional diversity is not a new phenomenon. Yet politics of the colonies did follow a basic pattern of contention between local residents and imperial authorities as many colonists struggled to gain the powers and alterations necessary to work out their own solutions to their own problems. In general, it was a period of political frustration when many more problems were articulated than solutions found. Political agitations often tended to end in quiescence rather than resolution. Still, shared experiences would be carried forward into later periods to produce more viable solutions.

V

Upper Canada

Following an initial influx of population into what had been the upper reaches of Quebec, the Constitutional Act of 1791 divided the old Province of Quebec to create the new colony of Upper Canada (Ontario). Its first Lieutenant-Governor, John Graves Simcoe (1752–1806), a veteran of the Revolutionary War, attempted to make the new colony a bastion of British influence in the heart of the continent. Simcoe advocated the encouragement of a local artistocracy, and the foundation of churches, schools and universities based on British models. He encouraged rapid settlement — and thus the rapid surveying of townships, as the map shows — the firm establishment of new towns such as York (Toronto) and London, and the quick development of a road network, as exemplified here by Dundas and Yonge Streets. Simcoe was only partially successful in his aims. His successors lacked his vision and energy, and Upper Canada remained very North American in its outlook.

David William Smith (1764–1837) was the first Surveyor General of Upper Canada, a position that gave him an excellent opportunity to prepare this, the first accurate, detailed map of what is now southern Ontario. A careful examination of it yields information on the location and early names of towns, road networks, the position of former settlements of the French period, Indians settled after the American Revolution, and even the settlement of French aristocrats fleeing the French Revolution. Other editions of the map followed in 1813, 1818 and 1838, all of which are held by the National Archives.

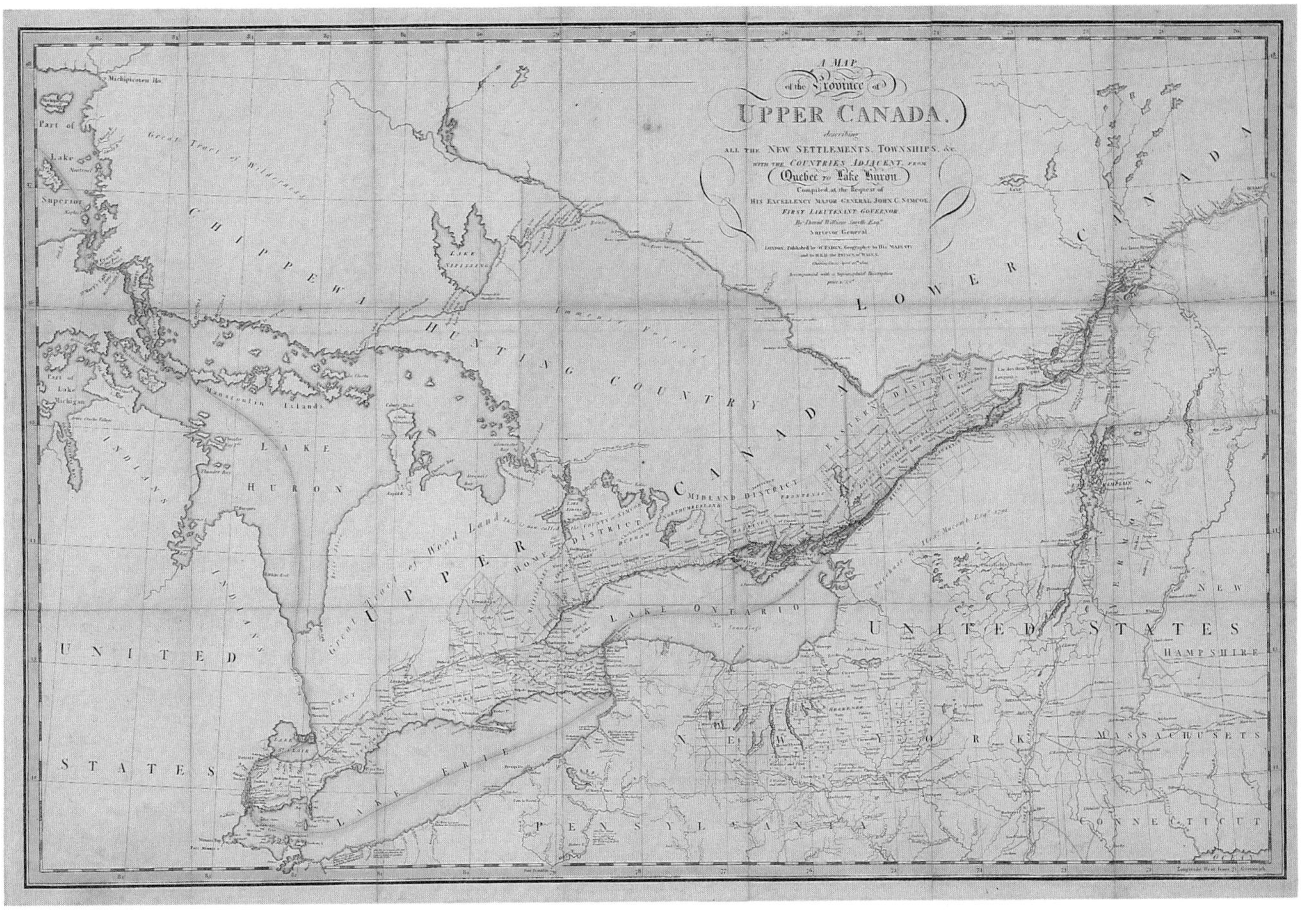

A Map of the Province of Upper Canada describing All the New Settlements, Townships, & c. . . . . David William Smith (1764–1837). London: William Faden, 1800. Map: hand-coloured, engraved. 55.0 × 83.6 cm.

National Archives of Canada: Cartographic and Architectural Archives Division (NMC 98186).

Quebec

Quebec was the largest, most densely populated and most developed of the British North American colonies. Settlement, as this map indicates, continued to be focused along the St. Lawrence River, which facilitated communication and trade. The upper reaches of the St. Lawrence and the Great Lakes were cut off from the colony when the "Pays d'En Haut" was separated off by the Constitutional Act of 1791 to form Upper Canada. The coming of the Loyalists had increased the non-French-speaking population from 4 to 9 per cent, while further American immigration increased it to 12.5 per cent by 1791. Their increasing numbers in turn raised the expectations of the English group that the colony would become more fully Anglo-Saxon in its culture and institutions. Quebec, however, remained the only major region in North America where the majority spoke French. French and English often lived side by side, but did not integrate. Tensions became increasingly frequent.

A new economy was emerging in Quebec between 1790 and 1815, which encouraged the growth of new classes of businessmen and professionals. Their clashes with each other and with British officials, sharpened by ethnic tensions, led to more complex political development here than anywhere else in British North America.

This map, on the large scale of eight miles to the inch, is laid out into districts and townships. Only a portion of it is shown here. At its full extent, it embraces the country on both sides of the St. Lawrence from the Island of Anticosti to the boundary of Upper Canada. There are several descriptive notes on the map. Churches, windmills and watermills as well as county lines, roads, settlements and "old French grants" are shown by means of symbols and lines according to the "references" engraved in the bottom left of the map.

The map was accompanied by a pamphlet by William Vondenvelden and Louis Charland entitled *Extraits des titres des anciennes concessions de terre en fief et seigneurie . . .* (Quebec, 1803) which gives a description of the location of the seigneuries as well as the date when they were granted. The National Archives holds a copy.

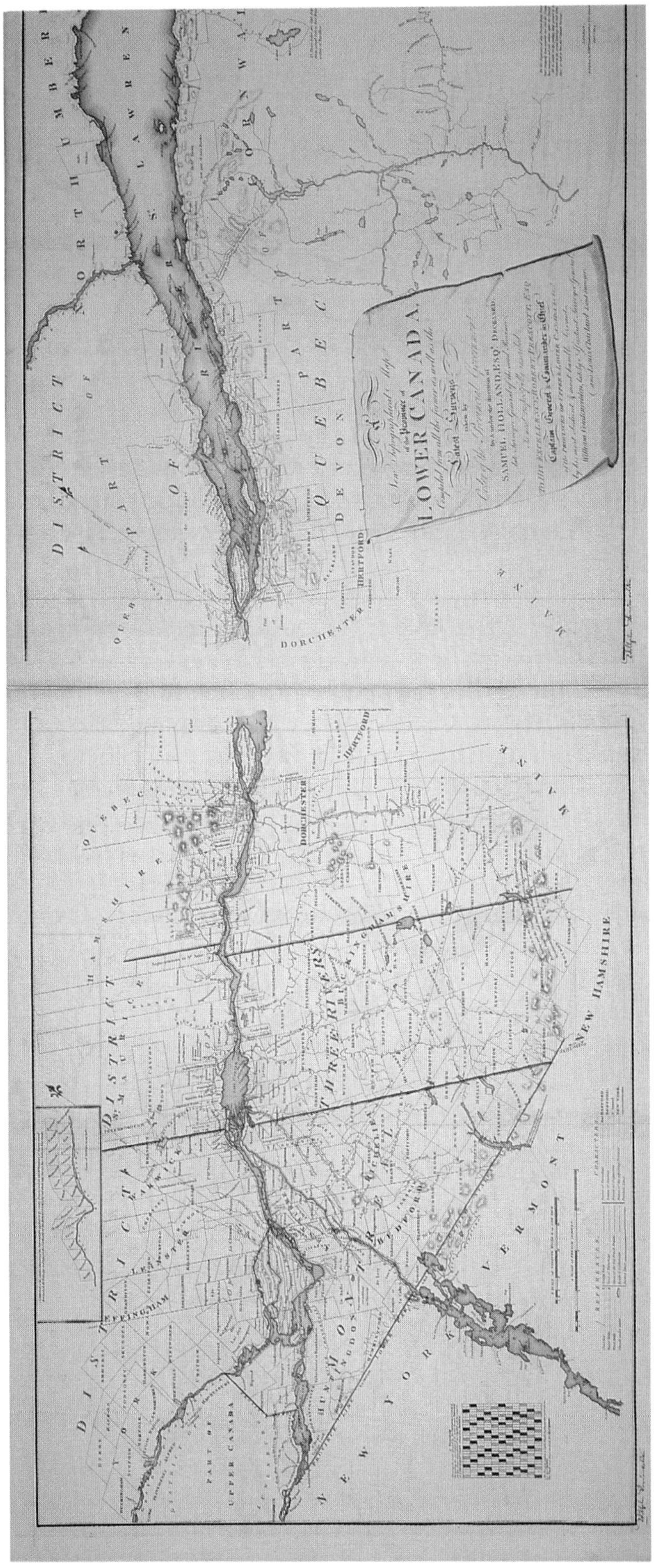

A New Topographical Map of the Province of Lower Canada . . . . William Vondenvelden and Louis Charland. London: Wm. Vondenvelden, 1803. Map: hand-coloured, engraved. Left sheet 59.0 × 77.6 cm. Centre sheet 59.0 × 78.2 cm. Right sheet 59.0 × 78.2 cm (detail).

National Archives of Canada: Cartographic and Architectural Archives Division (NMC 98187).

A Massive Counter-Petition Attempts to Avoid Reform in Quebec, 1784

Authoritarian and often arbitrary military government during the American Revolution led certain elements in Quebec society to press for representative government in the form of an assembly. Leaders in the movement were French- and English-Canadian merchants, French-Canadian professionals, Loyalists, and an elite of French-Canadian tradesmen and farmers. In 1784, they gathered 2,300 signatures in a petition for representative government. Opposition to this reform movement was led by French-Canadian seigneurs who felt their interests were well served by present conditions and feared the results of popular government. The sought-after reform was granted in the Constitutional Act of 1791, which created an assembly. The winning of an assembly would not have been possible without the participation of an important segment of French-Canadian society in the reform movement. French Canada was rapidly acquiring skill in using British parliamentary institutions and practices to express its needs and desires.

The counter-petition organized by seigneurs to oppose reform is illustrated here. Although it has 2,400 signatures, only a small number of which appear in the illustration, many names are inscribed in only a few hands. Most of the names, in fact, were recorded en masse at general meetings of habitants by seigneurs who more assumed than solicited support.

Au Roi

Sire

de votre Majesté

Petition for civil and religious liberties from the Roman Catholic citizens and inhabitants of Montreal, 1784 (detail).

National Archives of Canada: Manuscript Division: MG 23, G I 6.

Posters from the First Quebec Election, 1792

The first elections for an assembly in Quebec were held in 1792. It sat in 1793. Because the property qualifications used to established the right to vote were based on British models, they gave the franchise to virtually every male head of a household in land-rich British North America, and politics from the beginning had a strong democratic tinge.

Before 1791, English and French elites had cooperated temporarily on political reform. From the first sitting of the Assembly, conflicts between the two groups rapidly emerged. Printed in both French and English, this campaign poster from Quebec's first election is meant to argue the harmony of interests between English merchants and French Canadians. It also lays out, however, the elements of constitutional, social, ethnic and economic conflict that would continue to be battlegrounds between these two groups to 1815 and well beyond.

This campaign literature was printed by Samuel Neilson (1771–1793) of Québec City. His order books in the Neilson papers at the National Archives indicate that seven hundred copies were initially printed. Only four, including the two illustrated, now survive.

To the Electors of Lower Canada,

And thoſe of the County and Towns of Quebec in particular.

SINCE the cautionary addreſs which we made you in the Gazette of the 17th. inſtant there have been diſtributed among the people a variety of Hand-bills, ſome recomendatory of Candidates and ſome juſtificatory of themſelves, and among the number is one *deſamatory*; all of them are innocent and decent except the laſt mentioned, which abounds with illiberality and falſehood; we ſhall therefore diſſect it and endeavour to confute the arguments and deſtroy the inſinuations contained in it.

The author of the " AVIS AUX CANADIENS " ſtates, 1ſt. That it appears to be agreed upon between the Britiſh Merchants that they ought to be the only Repreſentatives in the Houſe of Aſſembly.

2d. That by their canvaſſing jointly---they have concerted a Coalition, which diſcovers their great illiberality (which he ironically calls *liberality*) for the Canadians.

3d. That if the Engliſh Merchants are elected, the fundamental Laws of the Canadians will derive no advantage or be perhaps altered and injured.

4th. That the ſmalleſt " *Reverſe* " may take them out of the Province, and therefore they ought to have no pretenſions to concern themſelves about it.

5th. That there ſhould be ſuch a union of intereſts between the Electors and Repreſentatives, that whatever Laws may be made by the Legiſlature ſhall equally affect all the members of the Houſe of Aſſembly as well as the body of the people, by which he would inſinuate that there is no connexion or communication of intereſts between the Britiſh Merchants and the Body of the people.

The firſt and ſecond aſſertions are proved to be palpable falſehoods, by the diviſion that every man ſees exiſts in the Lower Town; where the Engliſh Intereſt is divided by four or five Candidates ſtanding on their own ſtrength unconnected with each other and ſupported by different friends. It is likewiſe too notorious that the Merchants never affected to think that they had an excluſive right to be returned Repreſentatives; they poſſeſs too much good ſenſe and equity to look for a monoply, it is their common converſation that the Election ſhould be free and open to every man, that the people ſhould chooſe without Bias ſuch characters (whether Merchants or Seigneurs or No-ſeignieurs) as they think will make the beſt Laws for the Agriculture, as well as for the Commerce of the Country. And, it is we believe the firſt time that the Mercantile body have ever been ſuſpected of want of *Liberality* towards the Canadians, either in the line of trade or in perſonal reſpect;

They have been exceedingly liberal in their dealings with the Canadians, and inſtead of treating them with hauteur, ſcorn, and inſult, they have conſidered them as men, friends, neighbours and Fellow citizens, equal in the Eye of the Law with themſelves.

In anſwer to the third inſinuation, we do inſiſt no proof appears that the Britiſh Merchants have ever attempted to get the fundamental Laws of the Country altered. They wiſhed for good and ſalutary Laws for all ranks of people, that every man might be ſecure in the free Enjoyment of his Liberty and property; and where they felt a grievance, they complained and applied for Redreſs; when they aſked for laws to ſecure circulating commercial property, they did at the ſame time in a very pointed manner recommend that the rights and intereſts of the Seigneur, the Miller, the Curé, and the Habitants ſhould be ſecured.

The Author of " AVIS AUX CANADIENS " by the fourth inſinuation betrays either great Diſloyalty or groſs ignorance; for if by the word " *Reverſe* " he means the *the change of Sovereigns*, he may be pronounced a Traitor to the King and People of Great Britain from whom he enjoys a very honorable and lucrative place, and we are bold to ſay that he is the only Traitor in the Country; if by " Reverſe " he means only the viciſſitudes of fortune among individual Merchants, and that if they do not ſucceed in their commercial enterpriſe, they muſt return from whence they came, we may laugh at his ſtupidity, and while we deſpiſe the impotence of his malice, we will inform him that, under the Britiſh Government, the generation of Merchants is like the generation of men; and that if by any wiſe Reſolution of the Author of the handbill and his Coadjutors all the Britiſh Merchants were expelled the Country, double the number would reſort to the Province from Great Britain: ſo truly may the ancient Proverb " Non deficit alter " be applied upon this ſubject. We ſee (almoſt daily) that " *Reverſes* " in the courſe of Nature take away the Merchants as they do *Seigneurs*, and yet we find no vacuum in the Mercantile ſyſtem; others riſe and ſpring up to fill the place of thoſe that death has called away; and though the ſythe of time mows ~~them~~ men down without diſtinction (Merchants Seigneurs and others,) it deſtroys not Commerce, for that will live as long as time itſelf; nothing can deſtroy Commerce but oppreſſive and arbitrary principles, ſuch as the author of the handbill poſſeſſes, and it is to be hoped that among the few Corners of the earth where it may find refuge it may be countenanced in Canada hereafter. The Britiſh Merchants have a million and a half of money circulating in the two provinces of Canada; There are ſome hundreds of thouſands of Buſhels of wheat annually exported from Lower Canada by the Britiſh Merchants, beſides many other exports to a great amount; ſurely theſe are great and important enterpriſes and riſques; they have cauſed the value of lands and Houſes from one end of the province to the other to be doubled at leaſt, and under our preſent Government there is every reaſon to expect they will ſtill increaſe. The Britiſh Merchant may be conſidered the beſt friend to the Farmer and to the Cultivator of the land, whoſe induſtry he rewards, and towards whom he always caries himſelf with reſpect and civility. It may therefore be preſumed that he has a very ſtrong title and great pretenſion to concern himſelf in the welfare and Legiſlation of the Country.

Ce que nous avons dit dans l'article quatriéme peut être appliqué et conſidéré comme une réponſe complete à la cinquiéme inſinuation, " qu'il n'y a aucune communion ni lien d'intêret réciproque " entre le peuple du Canada et les Marchands Britaniques." Rien ne peut prouver plus clairement un interet et une union commune que le grand avancement que le commerce a procuré dans les propriétés agriculturales et foncieres, ſous la direction des Marchands Britaniques; l'un et l'autre s'avancent réciproquement. Rien ne peut manifeſter plus invinciblement une ſympathie pour les Canadiens comme hommes et Citoyens, que le reſpect amical et la civilité ſociale que les Marchands Britaniques leur témoignent à tous. Enfin il ne peut y avoir dans la nature un lien d'union entre des hommes de rangs différens plus intime que celui provenant de ce que le Marchand ſait et prévoit qu'il ne peut donner ſa ſanction à aucune loi qui dans un tems ou dans l'autre ne l'affecte lui-même ainſi que ſes amis, ſes parens et ſes deſcendans, auſſi amplement et auſſi effectivement qu'aucun cultivateur On peut dire avec confiance que peu de ſeigneurs ont de pareils ſentimens et ſont de pareilles reflexions, parcequ'ils eſperent que leurs deſcendans, quelques indignes qu'ils en ſoient, continueront d'être Seigneurs juſqu'aux ſiécles les plus reculés. Nous concluons de là qu'il y a une plus grande union d'interêt, plus de ſentimens de ſympathie et une opération des lois plus égale entre la maſſe du peuple et le Marchand qu'entre le peuple et les Seigneurs. Conſéquemment les Marchands ont le droit inconteſtable de s'offrir avec les autres Citoyens comme Candidats pour repréſenter le peuple, qui les trouvera dignes de ſa confiance.

Les Négocians renoncent à toutes diſtinctions Nationales; ils ne regardent tout le peuple de la province que comme Citoyens Canadiens zélément attachés au Roi et au peuple de la Grande Bretagne. Les Négocians continueront de former une grande et reſpectable partie de la Société, quand le nom de Seigneur ne ſe trouvera plus que dans l'hiſtoire. Afin de manifeſter l'ignorance de l'Auteur de l'*Avis aux Canadiens*, nous lui ferons quelques queſtions qui s'appliquent avec beaucoup d'aptitude à la préſente occaſion.

Qui eſt-ce qui donne du pain à l'ouvrier? Le Marchand. Qui eſt-ce qui donne de l'emploi aux nombreux Mécaniques, Artiſans et Navigateurs, dont la ville de Québec abonde? le Marchand. Qui eſt-ce qui fait circuler les propriétés et répand les richeſſes dans tout le païs, qui donne la vie et la vigueur à l'agriculture? Le Marchand.

Qui eſt-ce qui a contribué à augmenter les revenus des Seigneurs, ainſi que la valeur des produits des terres pour les cultivateurs? Le Marchand.

Citoyens Canadiens, vous ſavez que tout cela eſt vrai. Peut on vous faire croire que vous ne devez pas donner vos voix aux Marchands, dont les intérêts ſont les mêmes que les vôtres? D'autres profeſſions peuvent s'élever ſur votre ruines; celle des Marchands ne peut fleurir qu'autant que vous proſpérez; ſi vous êtes ruinés, le Marchand l'eſt auſſi, ſon intérêt et le vôtre ſont inſéparables. Les Seigneurs ont tenu à votre égard une conduite deſpotique; ils ſe ſont efforcés de la continuer; les Marchands au contraire ont uni leurs efforts aux vôtres pour vous procurer un gouvernement libre et des loix équitables, qui vous aſſurent le libre exercice de votre Religion.

Pour vous convaincre combien nous avons vos intérêts à cœur, pour vous montrer. notre zèle honête pour le bienêtre et la proſpérité des citoyens Canadiens, au lieu d'imiter l'indigne exemple de l'auteur en queſtion, nous nous propoſons de vous indiquer la nature et les conſéquences d'une élection, et quelles ſont les qualifications que doivent avoir les repréſentans que vous élirez, ſoit Marchands, ou Seigneurs.

Probus.

QUEBEC, 12 MAI, 1792.

Aux Electeurs du Bas Canada, et à ceux du Comté et des Villes de Québec en particulier / To the Electors of Lower Canada and those of the County and Towns of Quebec in particular. Probus [John Young?]. Québec City: Samuel Neilson, 1792. Pamphlet.

National Archives of Canada: Library (Negative nos. C-54628 and C-54631).

A French-English Clash in the Quebec Assembly, 1805

From the very first meeting of the Legislative Assembly, its members quickly divided themselves into two parties. The British party consisted of British officials and merchants who were interested in the commercial and demographic development of the English part of the population. They wished to control the Assembly in order to vote laws in their interest. They wished ultimately to see Quebec an English colony and French-Canadians assimilated. The British party generally received strong support from the Governor and his officials.

The French-Canadians grouped together in the *Parti canadien* comprised notaries, lawyers, doctors, surveyors, some artisans and shop-keepers, and well-to-do farmers. They extolled the British constitution and wished to use their rights under it to protect and promote the *nation canadienne*.

The struggle between the two parties very often revolved around control of finances. The British party exploded into bitter denunciations of the *Parti canadien*, for instance, in 1805 when the French Canadian majority in the Assembly passed a bill allowing taxes on commerce — not land, as the merchants had requested — for the building of new jails in Québec and Montreal. The proposed taxes are outlined in the resolutions reproduced here from the *Journals of the Assembly of Lower Canada*.

A vote in the Lower Canadian (Quebec) House of Assembly in April 1794, a few months after its first session opened, authorized the printing of its proceedings in both French and English. The publication of its *Journal* was awarded to John Neilson, Samuel's successor. His firm continued to print the *Journals* until the Rebellion of 1837. The National Archives has a complete original set of these publications.

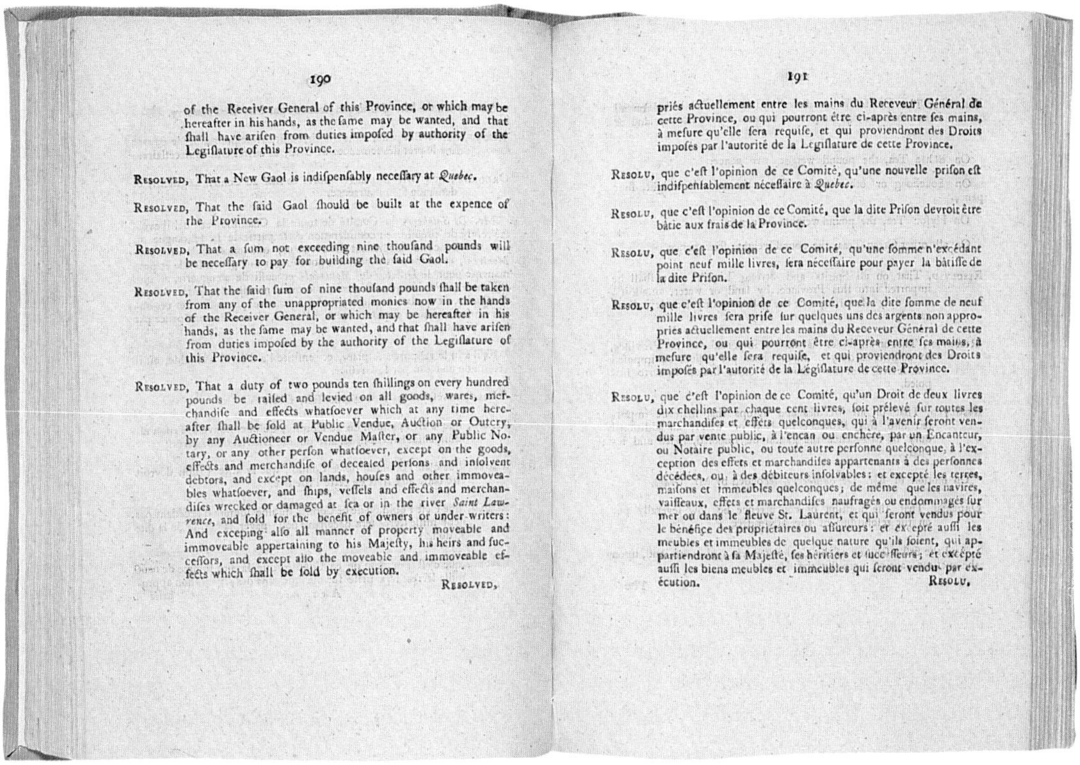

190

of the Receiver General of this Province, or which may be hereafter in his hands, as the ſame may be wanted, and that ſhall have ariſen from duties impoſed by authority of the Legiſlature of this Province.

RESOLVED, That a New Gaol is indiſpenſably neceſſary at *Quebec*.

RESOLVED, That the ſaid Gaol ſhould be built at the expence of the Province.

RESOLVED, That a ſum not exceeding nine thouſand pounds will be neceſſary to pay for building the ſaid Gaol.

RESOLVED, That the ſaid ſum of nine thouſand pounds ſhall be taken from any of the unappropriated monies now in the hands of the Receiver General, or which may be hereafter in his hands, as the ſame may be wanted, and that ſhall have ariſen from duties impoſed by the authority of the Legiſlature of this Province.

RESOLVED, That a duty of two pounds ten ſhillings on every hundred pounds be raiſed and levied on all goods, wares, merchandiſe and effects whatſoever which at any time hereafter ſhall be ſold at Public Vendue, Auction or Outcry, by any Auctioneer or Vendue Maſter, or any Public Notary, or any other perſon whatſoever, except on the goods, effects and merchandiſe of deceaſed perſons and inſolvent debtors, and except on lands, houſes and other immoveables whatſoever, and ſhips, veſſels and effects and merchandiſes wrecked or damaged at ſea or in the river *Saint Lawrence*, and ſold for the benefit of owners or under-writers: And exceping alſo all manner of property moveable and immoveable appertaining to his Majeſty, his heirs and ſucceſſors, and except alſo the moveable and immoveable effects which ſhall be ſold by execution.

RESOLVED,

191

priés actuellement entre les mains du Receveur Général de cette Province, ou qui pourront être ci-après entre ſes mains, à meſure qu'elle ſera requiſe, et qui proviendront des Droits impoſés par l'autorité de la Legiſlature de cette Province.

RESOLU, que c'eſt l'opinion de ce Comité, qu'une nouvelle priſon eſt indiſpenſablement néceſſaire à *Quebec*.

RESOLU, que c'eſt l'opinion de ce Comité, que la dite Priſon devroit être bâtie aux frais de la Province.

RESOLU, que c'eſt l'opinion de ce Comité, qu'une ſomme n'excédant point neuf mille livres, ſera néceſſaire pour payer la bâtiſſe de la dite Priſon.

RESOLU, que c'eſt l'opinion de ce Comité, que la dite ſomme de neuf mille livres ſera priſe ſur quelques uns des argents non appropries actuellement entre les mains du Receveur Général de cette Province, ou qui pourront être ci-après entre ſes mains, à meſure qu'elle ſera requiſe, et qui proviendront des Droits impoſés par l'autorité de la Légiſlature de cette Province.

RESOLU, que c'eſt l'opinion de ce Comité, qu'un Droit de deux livres dix chellins par chaque cent livres, ſoit prélevé ſur toutes les marchandiſes et effets quelconques, qui à l'avenir ſeront vendus par vente public, à l'encan ou enchère, par un Encanteur, ou Notaire public, ou toute autre perſonne quelconque, à l'exception des effets et marchandiſes appartenants à des perſonnes décédées, ou à des débiteurs inſolvables: et excepté les terres, maiſons et immeubles quelconques; de même que les navires, vaiſſeaux, effets et marchandiſes naufragés ou endommagés ſur mer ou dans le fleuve St. Laurent, et qui ſeront vendus pour le bénéfice des propriétaires ou aſſureurs: et excepté auſſi les meubles et immeubles de quelque nature qu'ils ſoient, qui appartiendront à ſa Majeſté, ſes héritiers et ſucceſſeurs; et excépté auſſi les biens meubles et immeubles qui ſeront vendus par exécution.

RESOLU,

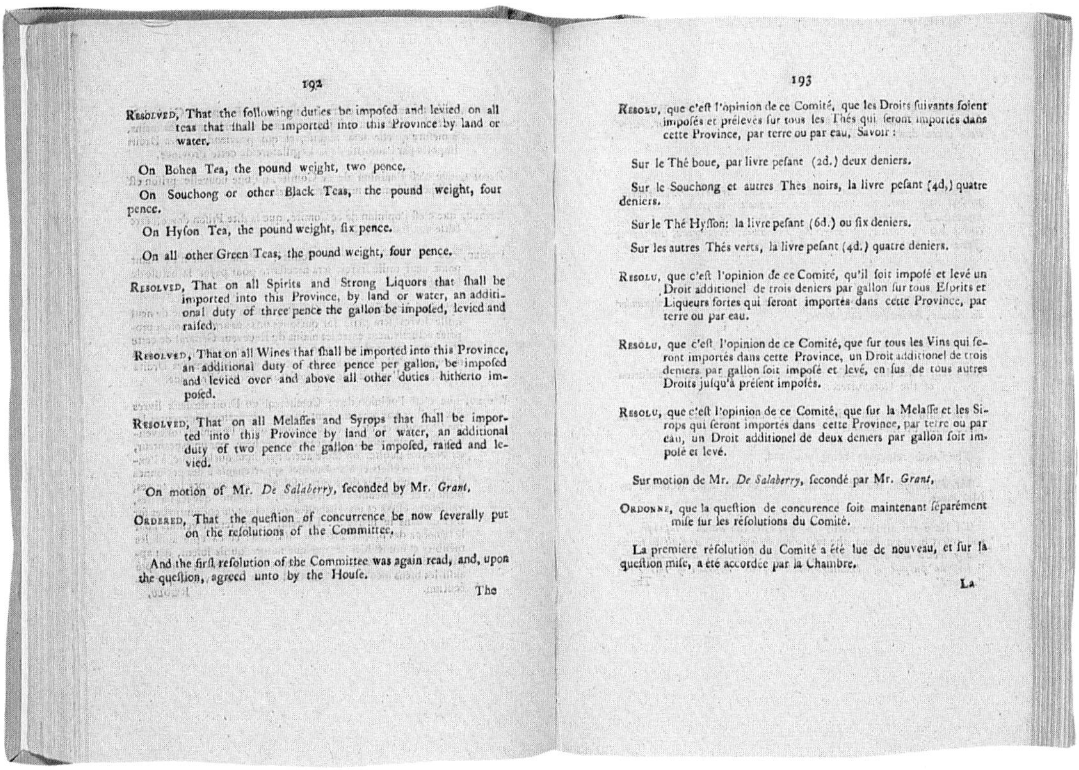

192

RESOLVED, That the following duties be impoſed and levied on all teas that ſhall be imported into this Province by land or water.

On Bohea Tea, the pound weight, two pence.

On Souchong or other Black Teas, the pound weight, four pence.

On Hyſon Tea, the pound weight, ſix pence.

On all other Green Teas, the pound weight, four pence.

RESOLVED, That on all Spirits and Strong Liquors that ſhall be imported into this Province, by land or water, an additional duty of three pence the gallon be impoſed, levied and raiſed.

RESOLVED, That on all Wines that ſhall be imported into this Province, an additional duty of three pence per gallon, be impoſed and levied over and above all other duties hitherto impoſed.

RESOLVED, That on all Melaſſes and Syrops that ſhall be imported into this Province by land or water, an additional duty of two pence the gallon be impoſed, raiſed and levied.

On motion of Mr. *De Salaberry*, ſeconded by Mr. *Grant*,

ORDERED, That the queſtion of concurrence be now ſeverally put on the reſolutions of the Committee.

And the firſt reſolution of the Committee was again read, and, upon the queſtion, agreed unto by the Houſe.

The

193

RESOLU, que c'eſt l'opinion de ce Comité, que les Droits ſuivants ſoient impoſés et prélevés ſur tous les Thés qui ſeront importés dans cette Province, par terre ou par eau, Savoir:

Sur le Thé boue, par livre peſant (2d.) deux deniers.

Sur le Souchong et autres Thes noirs, la livre peſant (4d.) quatre deniers.

Sur le Thé Hyſſon: la livre peſant (6d.) ou ſix deniers.

Sur les autres Thés verts, la livre peſant (4d.) quatre deniers.

RESOLU, que c'eſt l'opinion de ce Comité, qu'il ſoit impoſé et levé un Droit additionel de trois deniers par gallon ſur tous Eſprits et Liqueurs fortes qui ſeront importés dans cette Province, par terre ou par eau.

RESOLU, que c'eſt l'opinion de ce Comité, que ſur tous les Vins qui ſeront importés dans cette Province, un Droit additionel de trois deniers par gallon ſoit impoſé et levé, en ſus de tous autres Droits juſqu'à préſent impoſés.

RESOLU, que c'eſt l'opinion de ce Comité, que ſur la Melaſſe et les Sirops qui ſeront importés dans cette Province, par terre ou par eau, un Droit additionel de deux deniers par gallon ſoit impoſé et levé.

Sur motion de Mr. *De Salaberry*, ſecondé par Mr. *Grant*,

ORDONNE, que la queſtion de concurence ſoit maintenant ſéparément miſe ſur les réſolutions du Comité.

La premiere réſolution du Comité a été lue de nouveau, et ſur la queſtion miſe, a été accordée par la Chambre.

La

Journals of the House of Assembly of Lower Canada./Journaux de la Chambre d'Assemblée du Bas-Canada. Quebec: John Neilson, 1805, pp. 190–193.

National Archives of Canada: Library (Negative nos. C-130542 and C-130543).

Governor Craig and the Suppression of the *Parti canadien*, 1810

As the *Parti canadien* continued to vigorously push its programs, an atmosphere of crisis developed. A stern pro-British Governor, Sir James Craig (1748–1812) — pictured here — dissolved the legislature twice, in 1809 and 1810. Finally, in the middle of the 1810 electoral campaign, the Governor took advantage of some daring articles that had appeared in the French Canadian party's paper, *Le Canadien*, to seize its press and imprison its editors and some of its distributors — more than twenty persons in all. With its chief members in jail, the *Parti canadien* experienced a leadership crisis that it did not resolve until the late 1820s. The *Parti* was relatively quiescent, and for a period Quebec politics exhibited at least a surface calm.

His Excellency Sir James Henry Craig . . . . Anonymous. Hand-coloured mezzotint. 32.7 × 25.5 cm.

National Archives of Canada: Documentary Art and Photography Division (Negative no. C-24888).

Nova Scotia

The Loyalists and disbanded soldiers who came to Nova Scotia during and after the American Revolution created a tremendous surge in its population — they increased it by two-thirds — and their coming can be said to mark the effective beginning of British Nova Scotia. One result was the separation of New Brunswick and Cape Breton from Nova Scotia as separate colonies. Cape Breton was reattached in 1820. The Loyalist John Wentworth (1737–1820) used his long term as Governor of Nova Scotia (1792–1808) to establish Loyalist control of the higher levels of government. As a result, Loyalists did not find it necessary to push their claims vigorously, and distinct Loyalist influence disappeared rapidly.

Wentworth clashed constantly with a "country party" led by William Cottnam Tonge (1764–circa 1825). Despite Wentworth's efforts, the Assembly gained control over the disposition of road moneys, the chief source of local patronage. Since the military governors who followed did not challenge this arrangement, relative political calm marked Nova Scotian politics until well into the 1830s.

This map is an inset taken from Purdy's *Map of Cabotia*, which covers large portions of Canada east of Lake Superior. The *Cabotia* map is unique in that it is the only large-scale map of British North America of the time that has such a broad scope of area coverage and information. The Nova Scotia section gives detailed information on settlements and especially on roads. A note explains why St. John's Island was renamed Prince Edward Island.

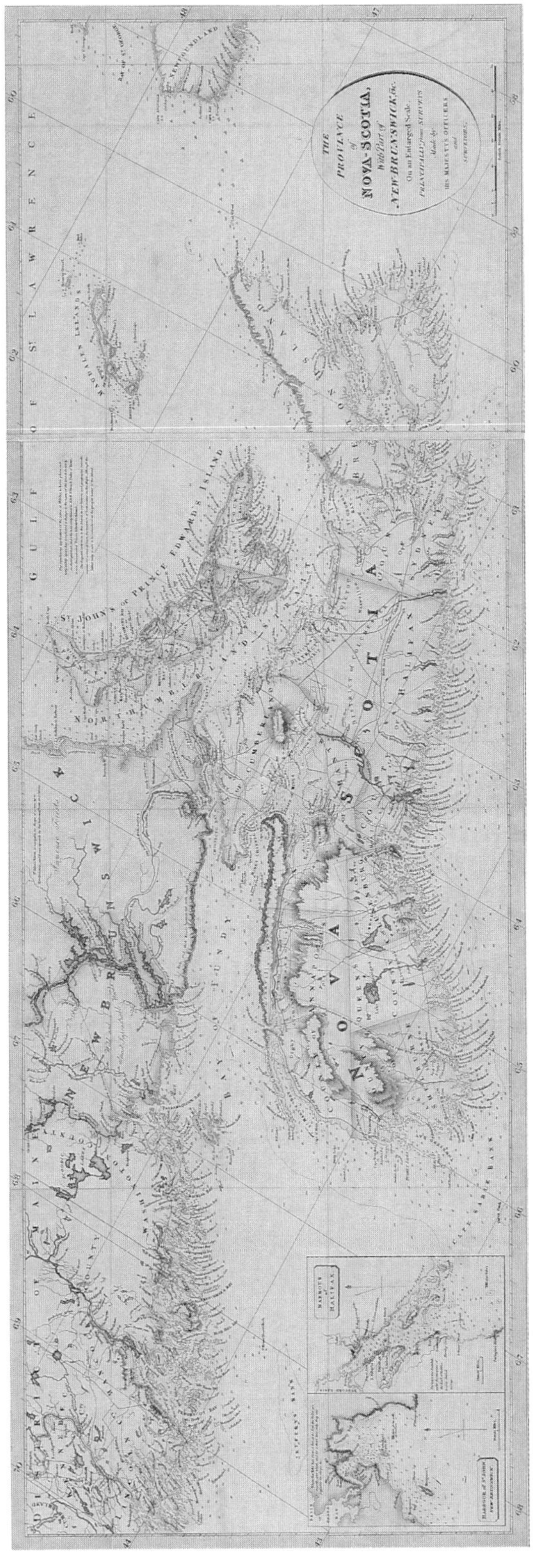

The Province of Nova Scotia with Part of New Brunswick & c. . . . John Purdy.
Map: hand-coloured, engraved,
35.5 × 105.0 cm.
Inset in *A Map of Cabotia Comprehending the Provinces of Upper and Lower Canada, New-Brunswick, and Nova Scotia, with Breton Island, Newfoundland & c. . . .*
Engraved by Thompson and Hall.
London: Whittle and Laurie, 1814.

National Archives of Canada:
Cartographic and Architectural Archives
Division (NMC 98208).

New Brunswick

New Brunswick was pre-eminently "the Loyalist province." Its population, less than 4,000 before 1784 (including Acadians who had returned after the expulsion), was suddenly augmented by approximately 14,000 Loyalist refugees who came to the north shore of the Bay of Fundy as well as the St. Croix River Valley and established their major settlements along the Saint John River Valley.

The "Negro settlement" mentioned on this map of settlement along the Saint John River is a reminder that 3,000 of the Loyalists coming to the Maritimes were blacks. The map shows fairly compact settlement along the river between Saint John, the commercial centre at the mouth, and Fredericton, the government capital. Virgin, almost impenetrable forest that covered most of the province encouraged this settlement pattern. Roads, as can be seen, were extremely limited. The mills dotted along the river were a witness to an early optimism concerning agriculture and lumbering, but the quality of the land was poor and settlers could not compete effectively with cheaper American timber production. Settlers began to leave and the economy became depressed. Economic difficulties led to intense controversies over regional, social and religious issues in politics, with a very vocal opposition led by the brilliant and erratic Scot, James Glenie (1750–1817).

As lumbering became more prosperous in the early nineteenth century, however, tensions subsided. Those years saw Scottish and Irish immigration into the colony that would eventually submerge the Loyalist element. Encouraged by lumbering, population began to spread out from the shore and the river valleys in a much less compact fashion.

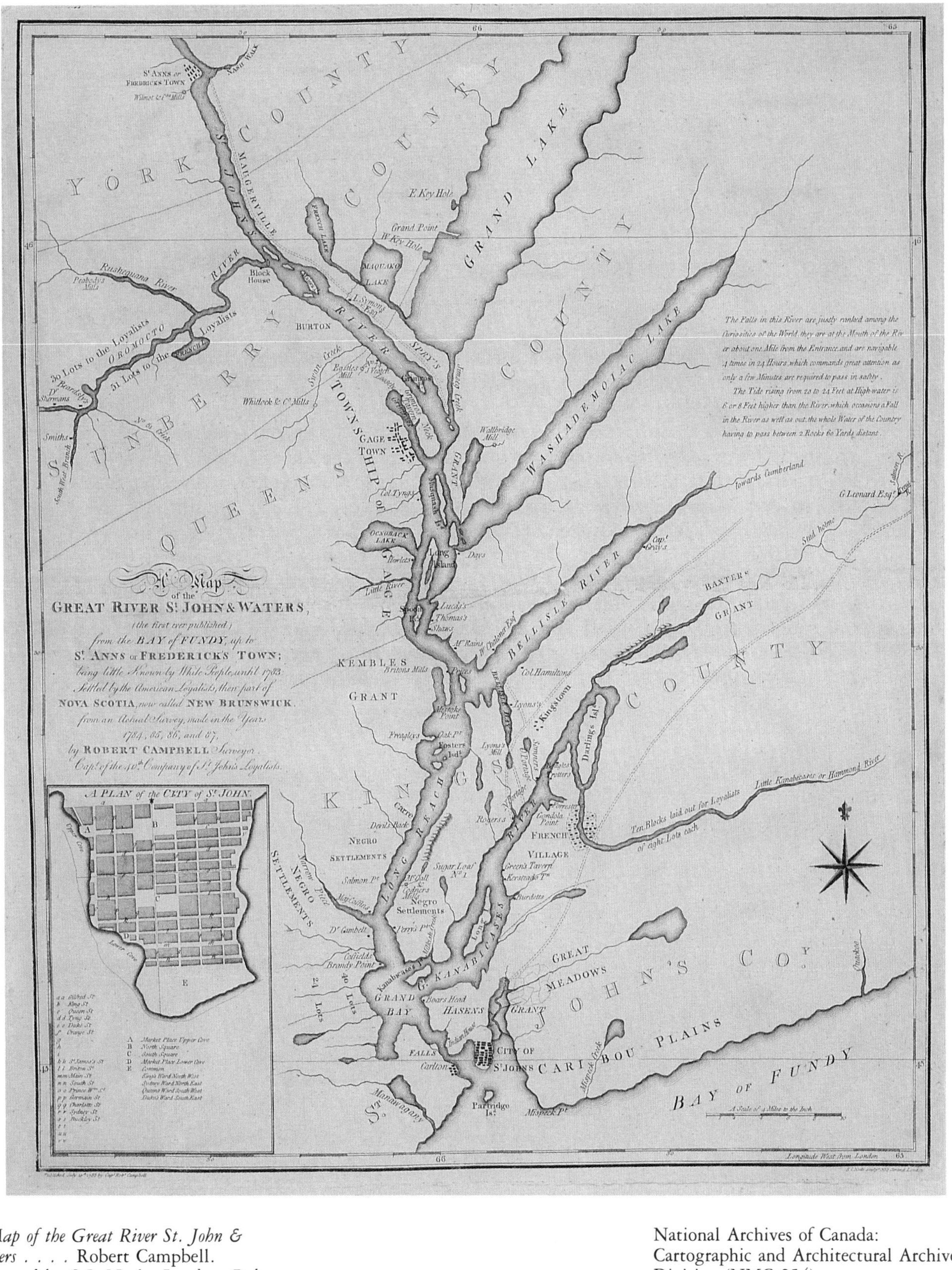

A Map of the Great River St. John & Waters . . . . Robert Campbell. Engraved by S.I. Neele. London: Robert Campbell, 1788. Map: engraved, 59.9×40.2 cm.

National Archives of Canada: Cartographic and Architectural Archives Division (NMC 254).

V

Prince Edward Island Through Rose-Coloured Glasses, 1779

The Island of St. John (Prince Edward Island after 1799) experienced major problems that induced some of its large landowners to advertise for settlers.

In 1767, sixty-seven townships of 20,000 acres each had been granted by lottery to military officers and others to whom the British government owed favours. The proprietors were required to settle their lands to fulfil the terms of their grants, but few made an effort to do so. The island had vast areas of undeveloped land, yet those who wished to settle had to pay steep rents or purchase fees. As a result, PEI was largely neglected. The population of Newfoundland, in fact, increased more quickly.

In this example of slick salesmanship, one of the proprietors, Robert Clark, attempts to attract "Industrious Farmers and Tradesmen with some Property" who in PEI "may live in a comfortable manner, unknown to people of their station in this country [England]." Clark, perhaps not surprisingly, ignores the problems of the Island and promotes its natural advantages. He describes it, on the page shown here, as being like England only much better — a veritable Garden of Eden.

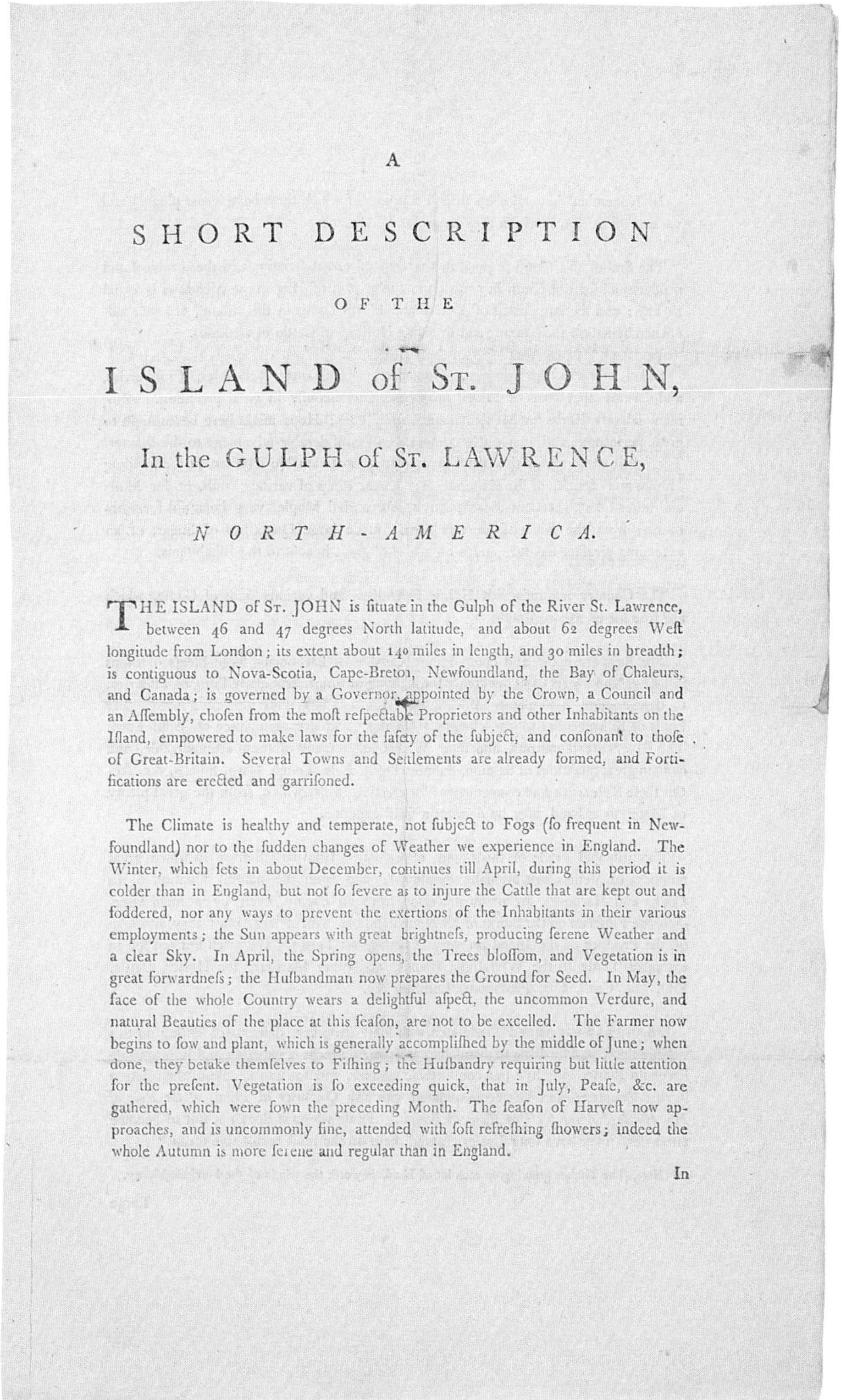

A

SHORT DESCRIPTION

OF THE

ISLAND of St. JOHN,

In the GULPH of St. LAWRENCE,

NORTH-AMERICA.

THE ISLAND of St. JOHN is ſituate in the Gulph of the River St. Lawrence, between 46 and 47 degrees North latitude, and about 62 degrees Weſt longitude from London; its extent about 140 miles in length, and 30 miles in breadth; is contiguous to Nova-Scotia, Cape-Breton, Newfoundland, the Bay of Chaleurs, and Canada; is governed by a Governor, appointed by the Crown, a Council and an Aſſembly, choſen from the moſt reſpectable Proprietors and other Inhabitants on the Iſland, empowered to make laws for the ſafety of the ſubject, and conſonant to thoſe of Great-Britain. Several Towns and Settlements are already formed, and Fortifications are erected and garriſoned.

The Climate is healthy and temperate, not ſubject to Fogs (ſo frequent in Newfoundland) nor to the ſudden changes of Weather we experience in England. The Winter, which ſets in about December, continues till April, during this period it is colder than in England, but not ſo ſevere as to injure the Cattle that are kept out and foddered, nor any ways to prevent the exertions of the Inhabitants in their various employments; the Sun appears with great brightneſs, producing ſerene Weather and a clear Sky. In April, the Spring opens, the Trees bloſſom, and Vegetation is in great forwardneſs; the Huſbandman now prepares the Ground for Seed. In May, the face of the whole Country wears a delightful aſpect, the uncommon Verdure, and natural Beauties of the place at this ſeaſon, are not to be excelled. The Farmer now begins to ſow and plant, which is generally accompliſhed by the middle of June; when done, they betake themſelves to Fiſhing; the Huſbandry requiring but little attention for the preſent. Vegetation is ſo exceeding quick, that in July, Peaſe, &c. are gathered, which were ſown the preceding Month. The ſeaſon of Harveſt now approaches, and is uncommonly fine, attended with ſoft refreſhing ſhowers; indeed the whole Autumn is more ſerene and regular than in England.

In

A Short Description of the Island of St. John, in the Gulph of St. Lawrence, North America. Robert Clark. [London?], 1779, p. 1.

National Archives of Canada: Library (Negative no. C-130540).

A Prince Edward Island Exposé, 1808

In this pamphlet, an anonymous resident of Prince Edward Island sets out with humour and determination to right the false impression given by the last item and other similar productions. He has lived, the author says, for twenty years on the Island and has seen "establishments landed for the most improved and refined agriculture, when there was not a good farmer on the Island; splendid curricles and wheeled carriages, when there was but one road, and that a short one, sufficient for a small cart; illumination lamps, when there was scarcely a window sufficiently large to hold a dozen; and opera hats, when the hall doors would hardly admit them on the wearer's head. Poor people have been told of spontaneous crops in the wilderness; and cleared lands in places where they hardly find their way twenty yards straight forward."

The land question dominated politics on the Island from 1763 until it entered Confederation in 1873.

49

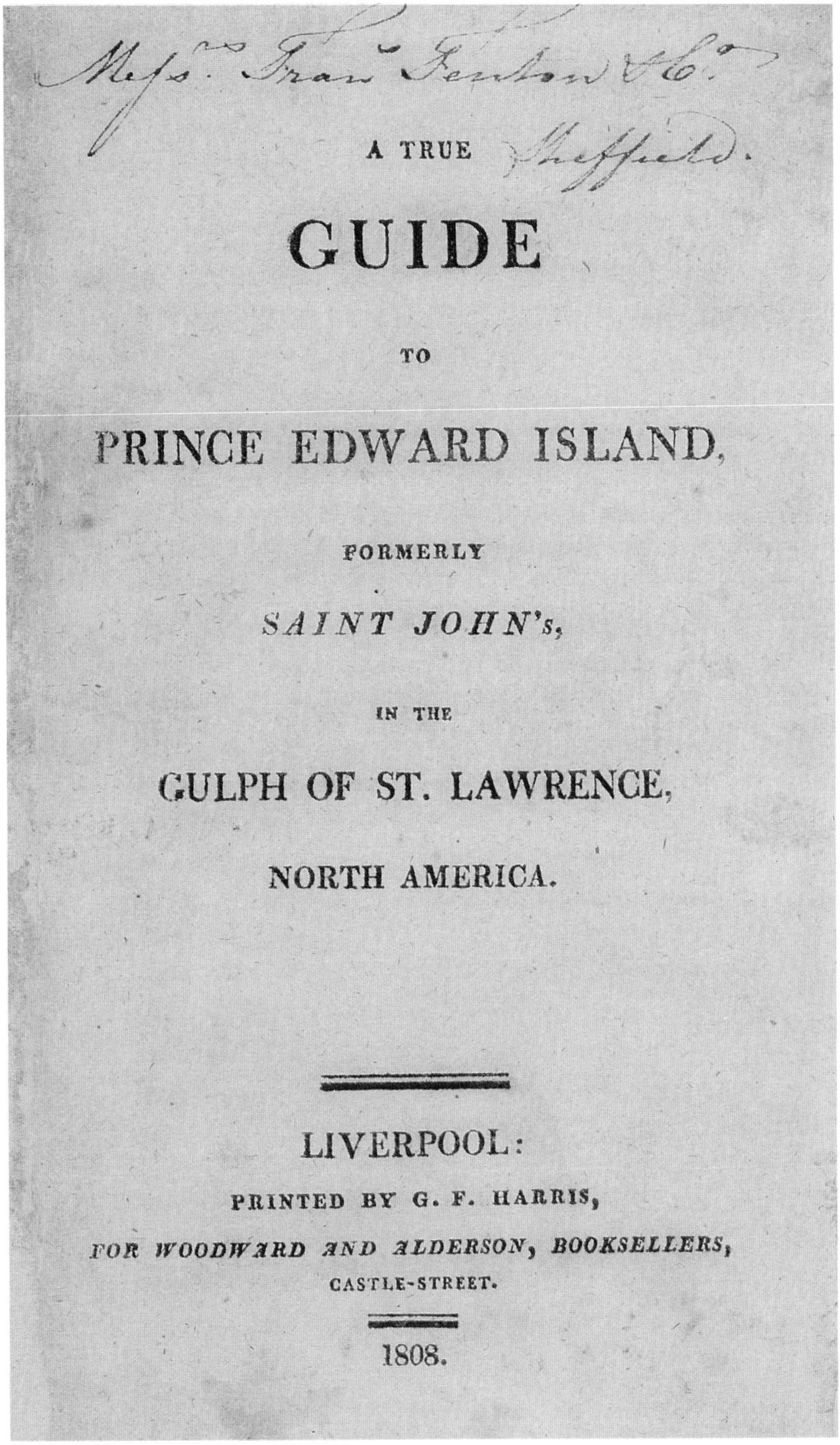

Messrs. Fran. Fenton & Co.

Sheffield.

A TRUE

GUIDE

TO

PRINCE EDWARD ISLAND,

FORMERLY

SAINT JOHN's,

IN THE

GULPH OF ST. LAWRENCE,

NORTH AMERICA.

LIVERPOOL:

PRINTED BY G. F. HARRIS,

FOR WOODWARD AND ALDERSON, BOOKSELLERS,

CASTLE-STREET.

1808.

A True Guide to Prince Edward Island, formerly Saint John's, in the Gulph of St. Lawrence, North America. Anonymous. Liverpool: G.F. Harris for Woodward and Alderson, 1808. Pamphlet. Title page.

National Archives of Canada: Library (Negative no. C-130530).

V

Newfoundland: The Colony that Wasn't Supposed to Be, 1813

In order to make the Grand Banks off Newfoundland a "nursery for British seamen," Newfoundland was officially not supposed to have any permanent settlement. Fishermen would then, in theory, be forced to sail the Atlantic twice a year and would become competent seamen who could be conscripted in time of war. The island was not allowed to have civil government or even any agriculture; yet by 1812, it had a population approaching 40,000. Prosperity and heavy increases in population made British policy increasingly untenable. In a forceful pamphlet, *Letter to Members of Parliament* (1812), William Carson (1770–1843), the District Surgeon, convinced British officials that starvation and public disorder would follow unless the ban on agriculture was lifted. In 1813, Carson followed with the pamphlet illustrated here, *Reasons for Colonizing the Island of Newfoundland*, in which he argued for civil government and a local legislature. Other issues, however, seemed more important when the end of the War of 1812 brought depression and social unrest.

REASONS

FOR

COLONIZING

THE ISLAND OF

NEWFOUNDLAND,

IN A LETTER ADDRESSED TO

THE INHABITANTS.

BY

WILLIAM CARSON, M. D.

Author of a letter to the Members of Parliament of the United Kingdom of GREAT BRITAIN *and* IRELAND, *on the address of the Merchants and Inhabitants of SAINT JOHN'S, in the Island of NEWFOUNDLAND, to the*

PRINCE REGENT.

GREENOCK:

PRINTED BY WILLIAM SCOTT,

AND SOLD BY SIR RICHARD PHILLIPS, LONDON; ALO BY THE BOOK-SELLERS OF GREENOCK, GLASGOW AND EDINBURGH.

1813.

Reasons for Colonizing the Island of Newfoundland, in a Letter Addressed to the Inhabitants. William Carson, M.D. (1770–1843). Greenock, Scotland: W. Scott, 1813. Title page.

National Archives of Canada: Library (Negative no. C-130544).

VI

Economy

If the future Canada consisted of a series of fragmented and isolated communities in the years after 1760, its economy provided an important if tenuous source of unity. Shared occupations in the fur trade, lumbering and the fisheries gave individuals a common bond. The harvesting and shipping of fur, wood and fish linked areas of British North America to each other and to the outside world.

The single most important export of Canada in 1760 was fur. Obtained from the native peoples in the northern and western interior by two major transportation routes, one operating from Montreal via the Great Lakes and the other through Hudson and James Bays into the interior, fur linked Quebec to a vast transcontinental hinterland. Fur, however, rapidly declined in importance after 1800 as supplies were depleted, fashions changed and the Napoleonic Wars disrupted its markets.

Fortunately, the Napoleonic Wars created a market in Britain for lumber from all of central and eastern British North America — especially for masts for naval vessels. Lumber thus rapidly replaced fur as Canada's chief export. Expanded lumber exports in turn sparked more local production of ships to carry it.

Their fisheries linked the Maritimes and Newfoundland to Europe, and they prospered in the later phases of the Napoleonic Wars, because of links to the West Indies.

Tables Reveal the Extent and Value of the Montreal Fur Trade, 1767

These informative tables prepared in 1767 by the Commissary of Indian Affairs at Fort Michillimackinac on upper Lake Michigan tell much about the fur traders who operated from Montreal, their sponsors, cargoes, destinations and the value of their furs.

The Montreal fur traders travelled via the Great Lakes and westwards to the Prairies. By the late 1760s they had reached to the Saskatchewan River. A number of traders, as the tables show, operated down the Mississippi deep into what is now the United States.

The many names listed emphasize that the Montreal trade was composed in this period of a number of small, independent firms. The French dominated, but the number of English names underlines the growing Anglo-Saxon influence.

Furs were very important to the economy of Quebec. At this date, they were almost eighty per cent of its exports.

This document, like the 1775 census of Nova Scotia (see Item 19), came to the second Earl of Dartmouth for his information in his capacity as a British official concerned with the colonies. Both documents demonstrate the breadth and detail of matters in the colonies with which imperial officials were expected to concern themselves.

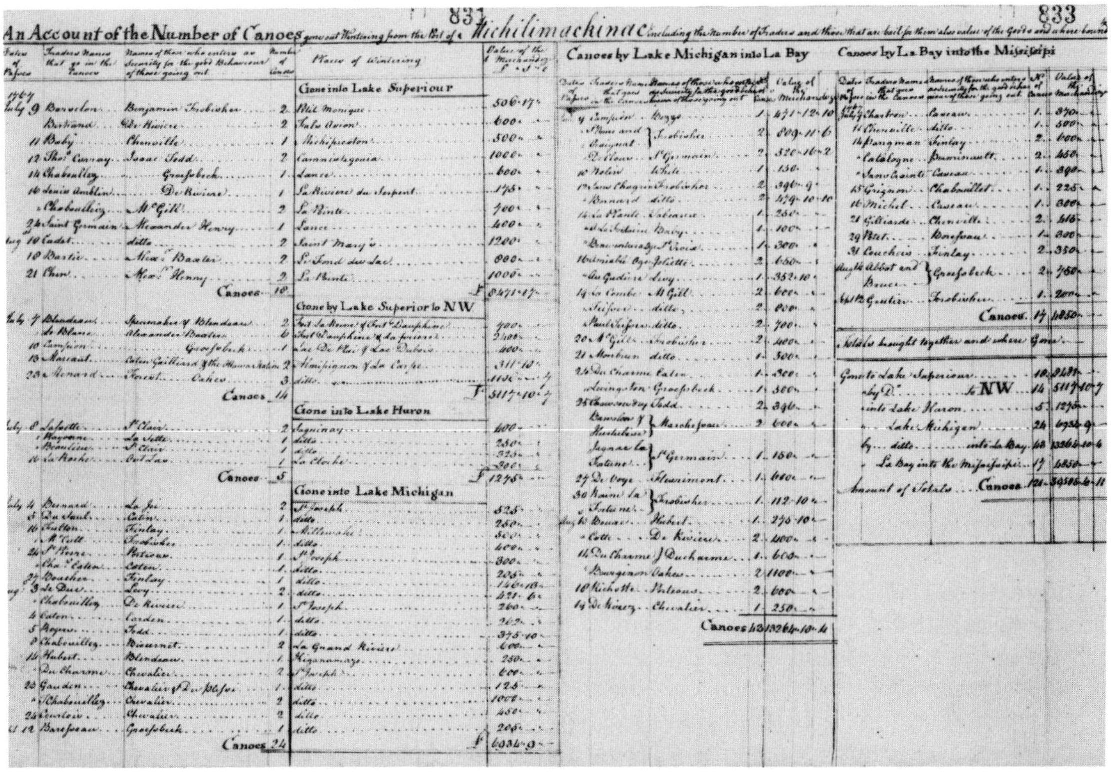

An Account of the Number of Canoes gone out Wintering from the Post of Michilimackinac

Gone into Lake Superiour

Gone by Lake Superior to NW

Gone into Lake Huron

Gone into Lake Michigan

Canoes by Lake Michigan into La Bay

Canoes by La Bay into the Missisipi

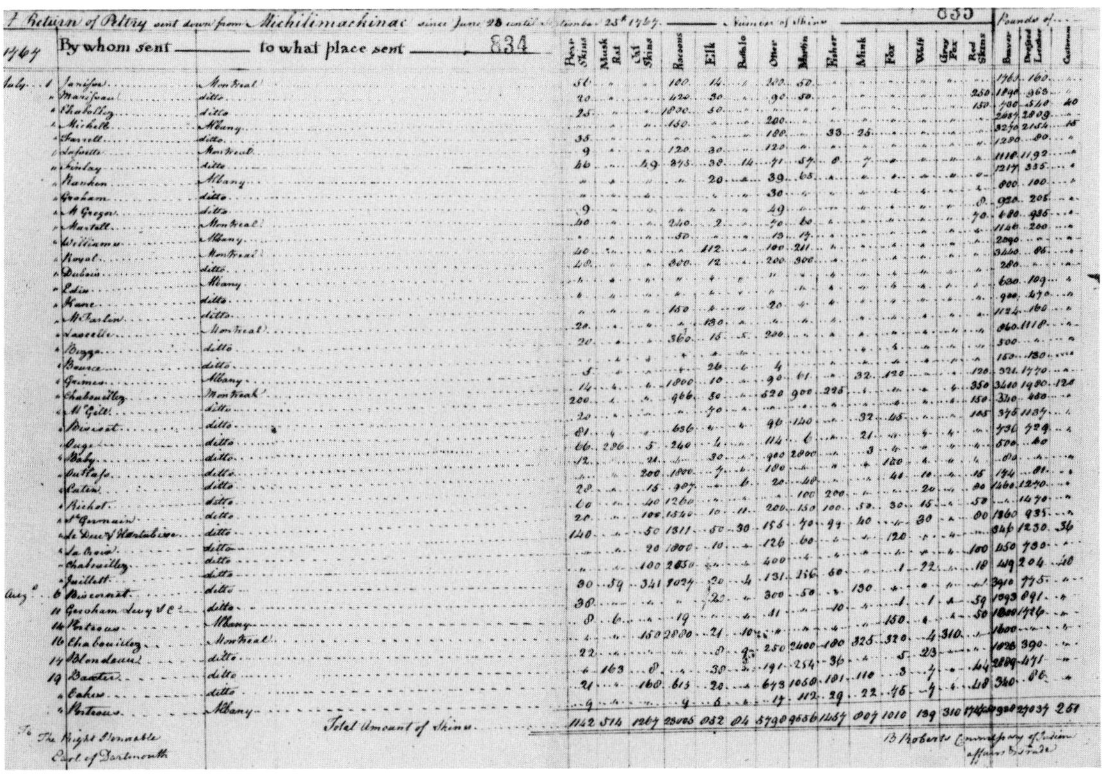

Return of Peltry sent down from Michilimackinac

By whom sent — to what place sent

Total Amount of Skins

B. Roberts

Returns relating to the fur trade, Michillimackinac, June–September, 1767. B. Roberts.

National Archives of Canada: Manuscript Division, Dartmouth papers, MG 23, A 1, vol. 1, pp. 831–835.

A Voyageur Signs Up with the North West Company, 1787

Joseph Laverdure, a Canadian voyageur, has made his "x" on this *engagement*, agreeing to the position, destination, terms and payment offered him in 1787 by the North West Company. In the twenty years since 1767, growing competition and increasing distances to unexhausted trapping grounds had forced individual Montreal traders to consolidate. A consortium of firms, the North West Company, had risen to dominate the trade. It is no accident that the other two names mentioned in the agreement, Pond and Grant, were English. English-speakers now controlled the Montreal trade, with French Canadians supplying only fifteen per cent of the trade goods. Working in the fur trade was still, however, very much part of Québécois life. In the 1780s, one third of all men of a suitable age were engaged in the fur trade at some time.

Engagements such as this one, as well as fur trade licences and export statistics, are valuable sources for studying who was involved in the fur trade, the areas of trade, the value of goods, and many other aspects of the trade. The National Archives holds many such documents in its government records as well as in its private papers.

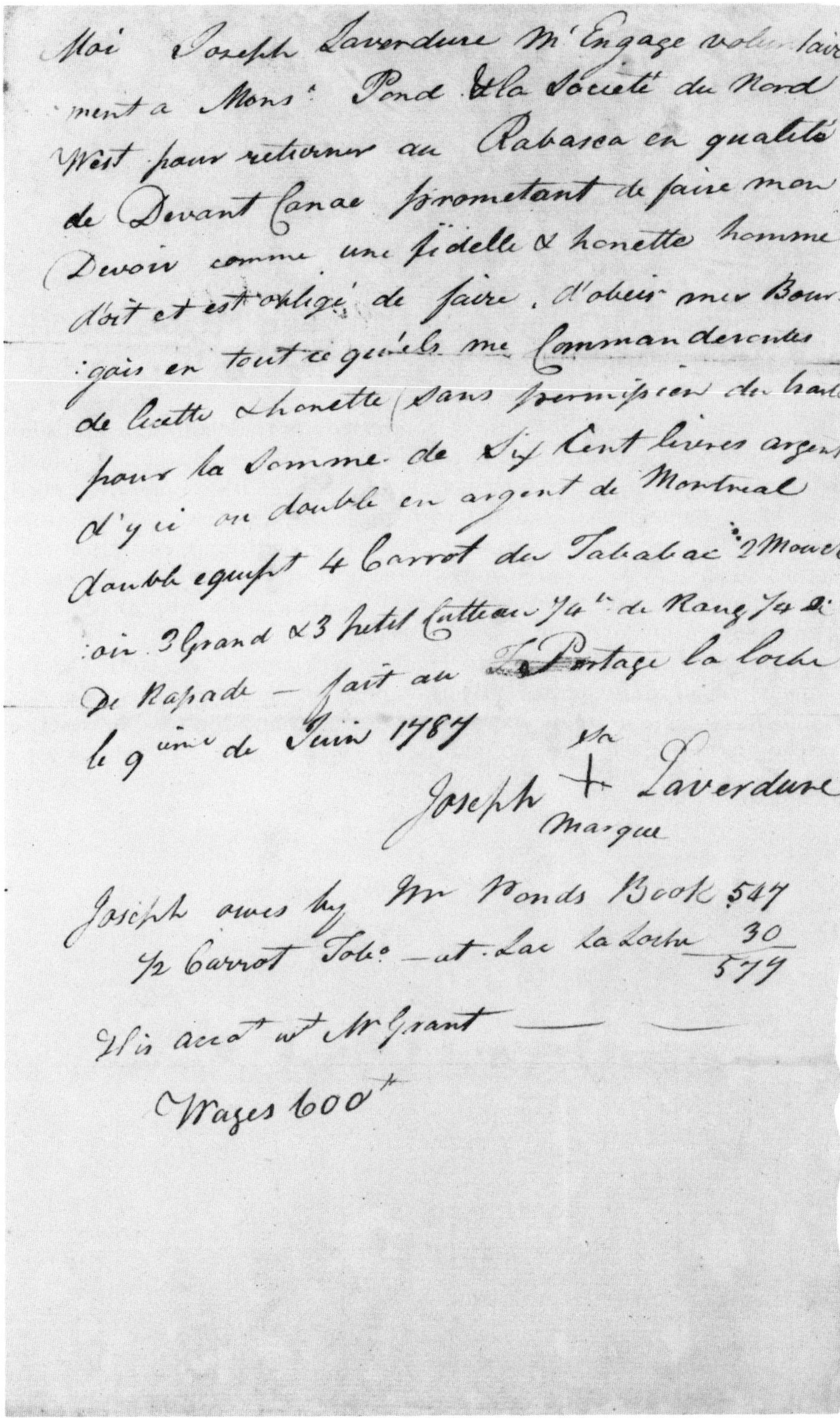

Moi Joseph Laverdure m'Engage volontaire
ment a Mons: Pond & la Societé du Nord
West pour retourner au Rabasca en qualité
de Devant Canoe promettant de faire mon
Devoir comme une fidelle & honette homme
doit et est obligé de faire, d'obeir aux Bour
:geois en tout ce qu'ils me Commanderont
de licette & honette (sans permission de traite
pour la somme de Six Cent livres argent
d'y ci ou double en argent de Montreal
double equipt 4 Carrot de Tabac 2 Mouch
:oir. 3 Grand & 3 petit Catteau 74 de Rang 74 d
de Rapade — fait au Portage la Loche
le 9ieme de Juin 1787

Joseph + Laverdure
sa marque

Joseph owes by Mr Ponds Book 547
1/2 Carrot Tobo — at Lac la Loche 30
577

His accot wt Mr Grant — —

Wages 600

Engagement of Joseph Laverdure as a voyageur with the North West Company, 9 June 1787.

National Archives of Canada: Manuscript Division, Charles Bell collection, MG 19, A 30, unpaginated.

VI

Join the Hudson's Bay Company and See the World: A Recruiting Poster, circa 1815

The Hudson's Bay Company, because it conducted its trade through Hudson and James Bays, imported its labour by ship directly from Great Britain. It sometimes recruited employees with posters such as this. Many were Orkneymen from northern Scotland. These young men found life with the Company exotic, challenging and often profitable, but their work was also demanding, with long periods at isolated posts and few if any prospects of returning home until the end of their working lives.

Unlike the looser associations of Montreal fur traders, the Hudson's Bay Company was a single company with at least a theoretical monopoly of the fur trade on all lands drained by rivers flowing into Hudson and James Bays. Until the 1770s, the Company tended to sit complacently at its posts on the shores of the bays waiting for the Indians to come to it. Increasing competition from Montreal, however, drew the Company more actively into the interior.

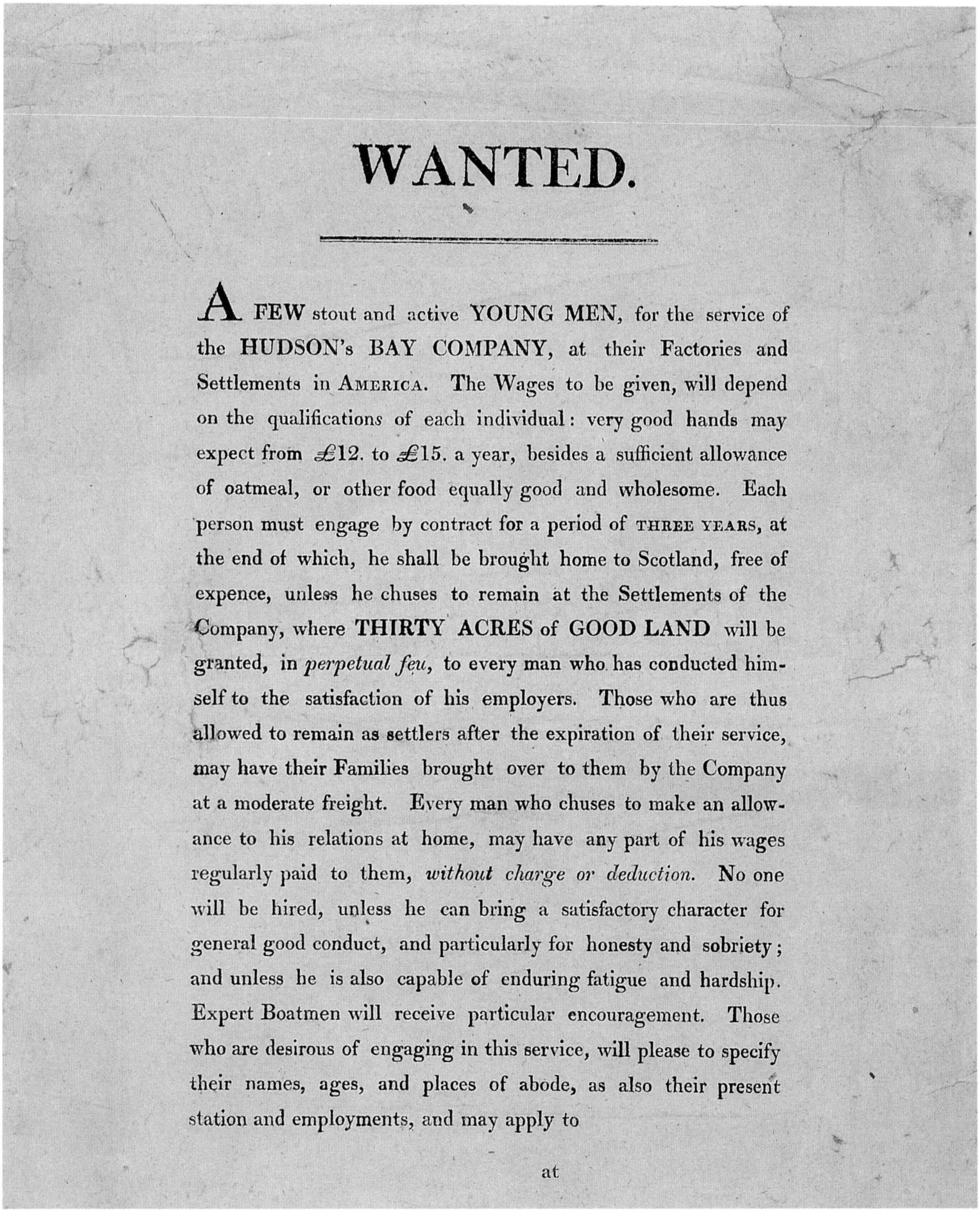

WANTED.

A FEW stout and active YOUNG MEN, for the service of the HUDSON's BAY COMPANY, at their Factories and Settlements in AMERICA. The Wages to be given, will depend on the qualifications of each individual: very good hands may expect from £12. to £15. a year, besides a sufficient allowance of oatmeal, or other food equally good and wholesome. Each person must engage by contract for a period of THREE YEARS, at the end of which, he shall be brought home to Scotland, free of expence, unless he chuses to remain at the Settlements of the Company, where **THIRTY ACRES of GOOD LAND** will be granted, in *perpetual feu,* to every man who has conducted himself to the satisfaction of his employers. Those who are thus allowed to remain as settlers after the expiration of their service, may have their Families brought over to them by the Company at a moderate freight. Every man who chuses to make an allowance to his relations at home, may have any part of his wages regularly paid to them, *without charge or deduction.* No one will be hired, unless he can bring a satisfactory character for general good conduct, and particularly for honesty and sobriety; and unless he is also capable of enduring fatigue and hardship. Expert Boatmen will receive particular encouragement. Those who are desirous of engaging in this service, will please to specify their names, ages, and places of abode, as also their present station and employments, and may apply to

at

Advertisement for recruits for the Hudson's Bay Company. Early nineteenth-century broadside.

National Archives of Canada: Library (Negative no. C-125856).

Eyeball to Eyeball on Cat Lake: Fur Trade Rivalry Intensifies, 1790

This letter, a copy in a fur trade post journal, was written in 1790 by John McNab, the Hudson's Bay Company factor at Albany Fort on Hudson Bay. It dramatizes at a local level the increasingly fierce and sometimes violent competition between the Montreal and the Hudson Bay fur empires. McNab conveys to his colleague the unwelcome news that "an inundation of Canadians encircled our Inland settlements and one sat down within a few yards of one of the stations at Cat Lake. . . ."

Rising costs and depleting fur resources meant the rivals had to expand to survive, and they engaged in a trade war, leap-frogging each other's posts until in the next decade they had pushed through to the Pacific slope. At enormous cost, the Montreal trade won the race. By 1800, the number of furs that passed through Montreal was more than four times the number received by the Hudson's Bay Company.

The Hudson's Bay Company required that detailed journals like this one be kept at all its posts. The journals are now invaluable sources not only for information on the fur trade, but on native peoples, local flora and fauna, diseases, weather and climate, and a host of other topics. Indeed, the Hudson's Bay Company records are the principal source for the early history of the Canadian West. The National Archives of Canada holds microfilm copies of the Hudson's Bay Company records to 1870; most of the originals are in the Provincial Archives of Manitoba.

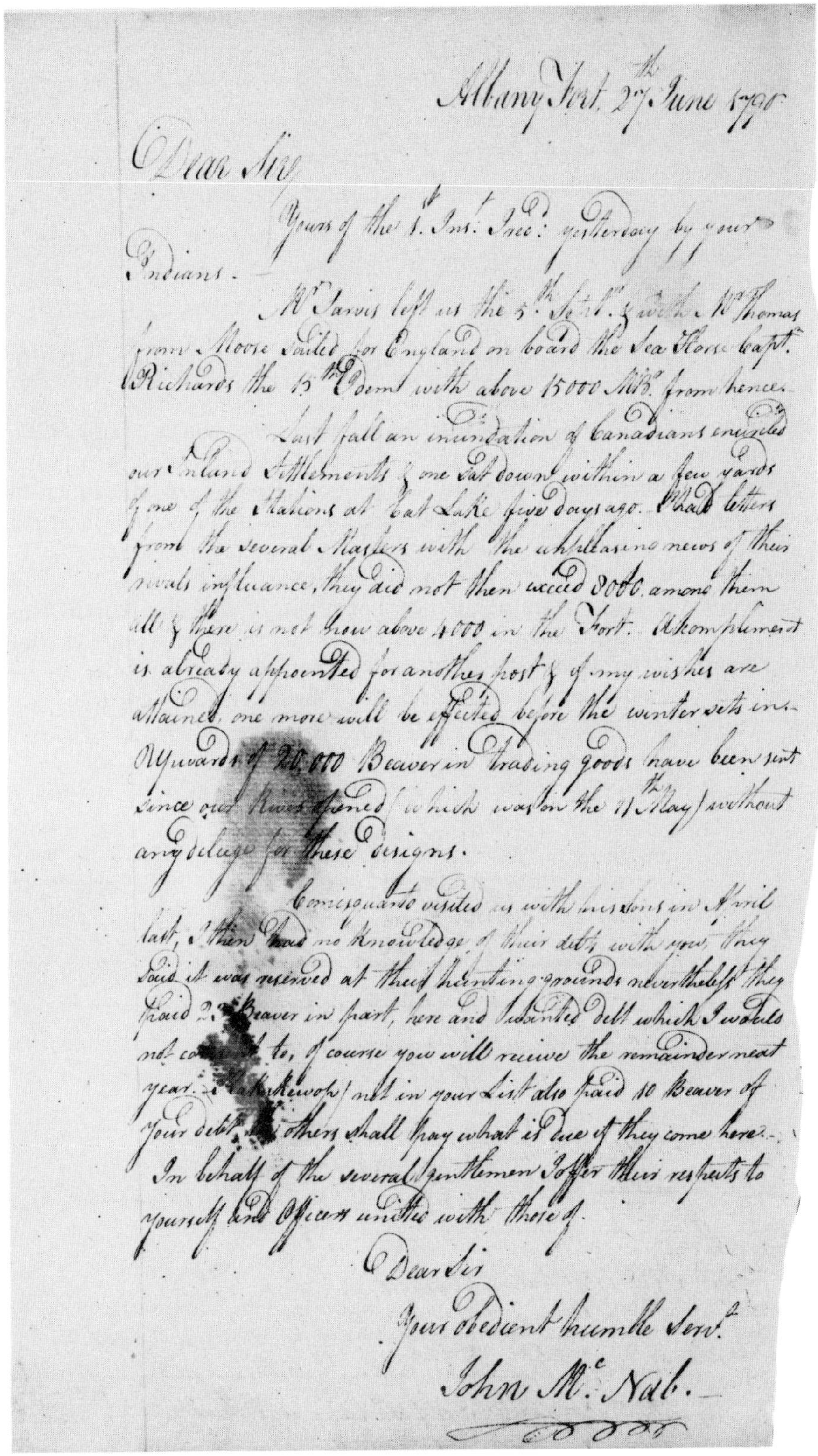

Albany Fort 27th June 1790

Dear Sir

Yours of the 1st Inst. Recd: yesterday by your Indians.

Mr Jarvis left us the 5th Septr. & with Mr Thomas from Moose sailed for England on board the Sea Horse Captn. Richards the 15th Ditto with above 15000 MB. from hence.

Last fall an inundation of Canadians encircled our Inland Settlements & one sat down within a few yards of one of the Stations at Cat Lake five days ago. I had letters from the several Masters with the unpleasing news of their rivals influence, they did not then exceed 8000 among them all & there is not now above 4000 in the Fort. A kompliment is already appointed for another post & if my wishes are attained one more will be effected before the winter sets in. Upwards of 20,000 Beaver in trading goods have been sent since our River opened (which was on the 11th May) without any deluge for these designs.

Comisquarbo visited us with his sons in April last, I then had no knowledge of their debt with you, they said it was reserved at their hunting grounds nevertheless they paid 23 Beaver in part, here and [illegible] debt which I would not co[illegible] to, of course you will receive the remainder next year. Makikewops not in your List also paid 10 Beaver of your debt [illegible] others shall pay what is due if they come here.

In behalf of the several Gentlemen I offer their respects to yourself and Officers united with those of

Dear Sir

Your obedient humble Servt.

John McNab.

Letter, John McNab to John Ballanden, Albany Fort, 27 June 1790, Severn House Journal.

National Archives of Canada: Manuscript Division, MG 19, D 2, vol. 3, unpaginated.

VI

The Founding of the Red River Colony, 1812

Miles McDonnell (1767–1828) penned this letter to his sponsor, Lord Selkirk, just before leaving York Factory on Hudson Bay with a small band of Scottish settlers. These settlers would establish a colony, called Red River, near the junction of the Red and Assiniboine Rivers, from which the modern province of Manitoba would arise. The settlement was a plan of Thomas Douglas, Earl of Selkirk (1771–1820), who had gained a controlling interest in the Hudson's Bay Company.

The Red River Colony, set in the heart of territory that the North West Company considered its own preserve, further increased tensions between the companies.

McDonnell's letter is his personal copy of record that he wrote in his letter book, a practice common until the beginning of the twentieth century.

55

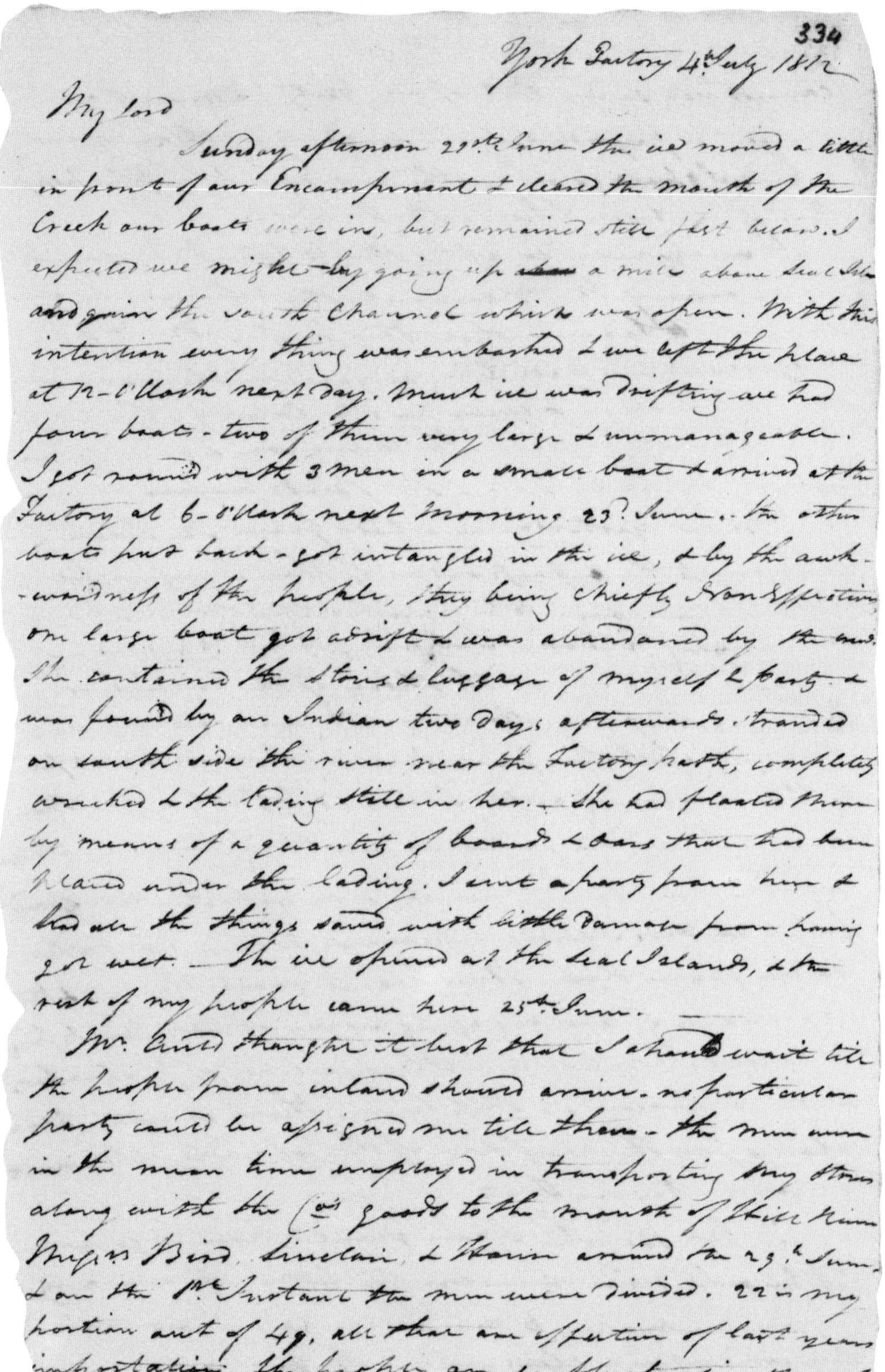
334

York Factory 4th July 1812

My lord

Sunday afternoon 21st June the ice moved a little in front of our Encampment & cleared the mouth of the Creek our boats were in, but remained still fast below. I expected we might by going up ~~above~~ a mile above Seal Islands gain the south Channel which was open. With this intention every thing was embarked & we left the place at 12 o'Clock next day. Much ice was drifting we had four boats - two of them very large & unmanageable. I got round with 3 men in a small boat & arrived at the Factory at 6 o'Clock next morning 23d June. The other boats put back - got intangled in the ice, & by the awkwardness of the people, they being chiefly Iron Sprotin, one large boat got adrift & was abandoned by the men. She contained the Stores & luggage of myself & party & was found by an Indian two days afterwards stranded on south side the river near the Factory path, completely wrecked & the lading still in her. She had floated there by means of a quantity of boards & oars that had been placed under the lading. I sent a party from here & had all the things saved with little damage from having got wet. The ice opened at the Seal Islands, & the rest of my people came here 25th June.

Mr. Auld thought it best that I should wait till the people from inland should arrive - no particular party could be assigned me till then - the men were in the mean time employed in transporting my Stores along with the Co's goods to the mouth of Hill River. Messrs Bird, Sinclair, & Heney arrived the 29th June, & on the 1st Instant the men were divided. 22 is my portion out of 49, all that are effective of last years importation. The people are so fluctuating that I

Letter, Miles McDonnell to the Earl of Selkirk, York Factory, 4 July 1812.

National Archives of Canada, Manuscript Division: McDonnell papers, MG 19, E 4, p. 334.

VI

A "Wooden" Country: New Brunswick, 1784

British North America's early colonists were well aware of the value of her forests, as this petition from the Loyalist inhabitants of St. Andrews, New Brunswick, clearly demonstrates.

All the colonies engaged in lumbering, producing squared timber, boards and planks, and staves and hoops for barrels. The early market for timber, however, was mainly local, and development was small-scale and without much specialization. Two decades later, a major war and greatly increased demand from Great Britain would suddenly and dramatically turn lumbering into a major industry.

This official copy of a petition comes from the papers of Ward Chipman senior and junior. Chipman senior was a Loyalist from Massachusetts who held important posts during the American Revolution. Both father and son held a variety of offices in New Brunswick, and their papers deal with an extensive range of topics.

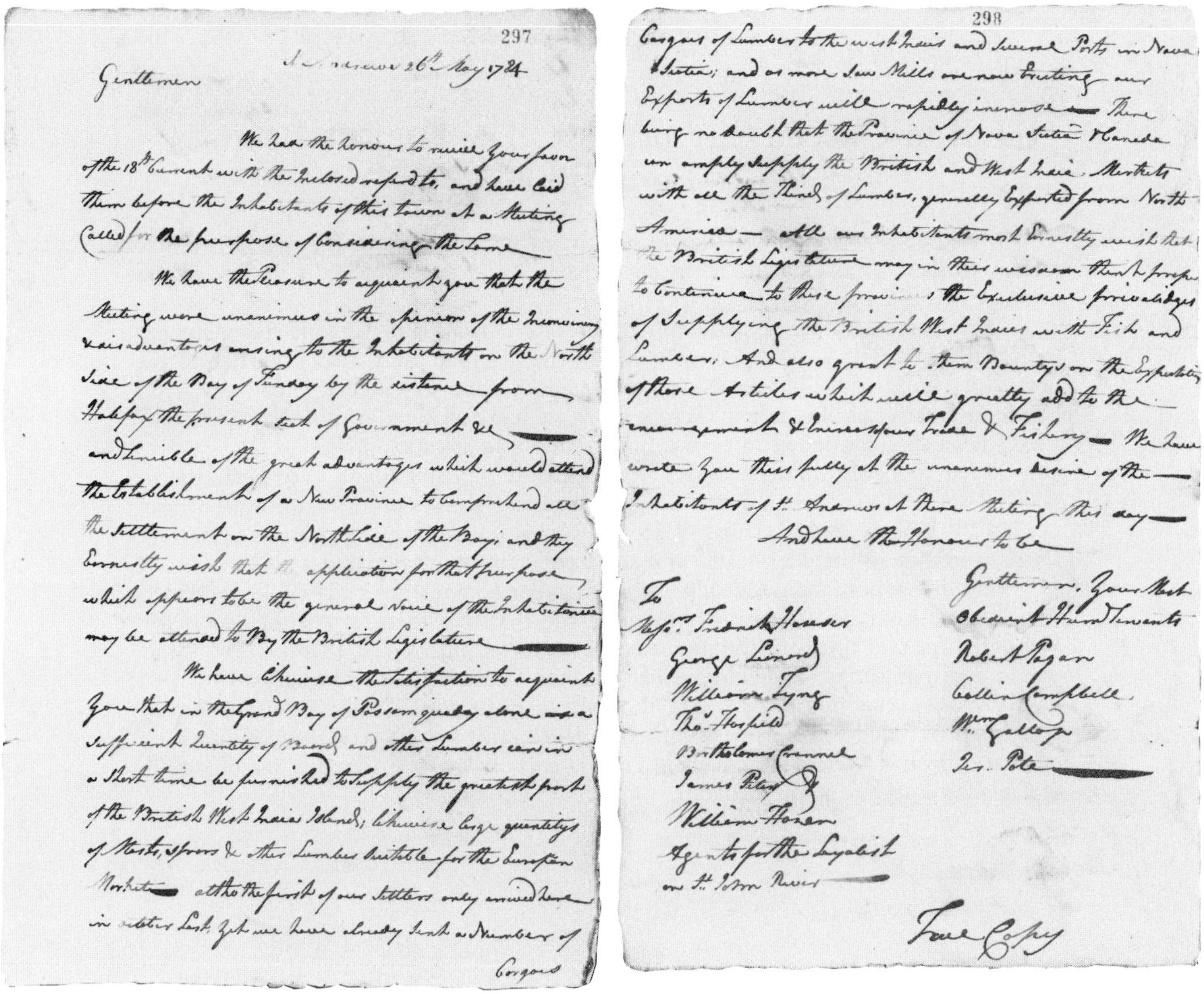
297

St. Andrews 26th May 1784

Gentlemen

We had the Honour to receive Your favor of the 18th Current with the Inclosed respected to, and have laid them before the Inhabitants of this town At a Meeting Called for the purpose of Considering the Same

We have the Pleasure to acquaint you that the Meeting were unanimous in the opinion of the Inconveniency & disadvantages arising to the Inhabitants on the North Side of the Bay of Fundey by the distance from Halifax the present seat of Government &c and sensible of the great advantages which would attend the Establishment of a New Province to comprehend all the settlement on the North Side of the Bay; and they Earnestly wish that the application for that purpose which appears to be the general voice of the Inhabitants may be attended to By the British Legislature

We have Likewise the Satisfaction to acquaint You that in the Grand Bay of Passamquady alone is a sufficient Quantity of Board and other Lumber can in a short time be furnished to supply the greatest part of the British West India Island; Likewise large quantitys of Masts, Spars & other Lumber suitable for the European Market although the first of our Settlers only arrived here in October Last, Yet we have already sent a Number of

Cargoes

298

Cargoes of Lumber to the west Indies and several Ports in Nova Scotia; and as more Saw Mills are now Erecting our Exports of Lumber will rapidly increase — There being no doubt that the Province of Nova Scotia & Canada can amply supply the British and West India Markets with all the Kind of Lumber, generally Exported from North America — All our Inhabitants most Earnestly wish that the British Legislature may in their wisdom think proper to Continue to these Provinces the Exclusive priviledges of Supplying the British West Indies with Fish and Lumber; And also grant to them Bountys on the Exportation of those Articles which will greatly add to the encouragement & Increase of our Trade & Fishery — We have wrote You thus fully at the unanimous desire of the Inhabitants of St. Andrews at their Meeting this day

And have the Honour to be

Gentlemen Your Most Obedient Humble Servants

Robert Pagan
Collin Campbell
Wm. Gallop
Jer. Pote

To
Messrs. Fredrick Houser
George Leonard
William Tyng
Thos. Horsfield
Bartholomew Crannell
James Peters
William Hazen
Agents for the Loyalist on St. John River

True Copy

Representation of Fredrick Houser et al., St. Andrews [New Brunswick], 26 May 1784 [clerical copy].

National Archives of Canada: Manuscript Division, Chipman Family papers, MG 23, D 1, Series 1, vol. 10, pp. 297–298.

VI

Hull to Québec City or Bust: The Lumber Boom is Born, 1806

This little book, although not very impressive at first sight, tells the tale of the first raft of timber to pass down the Ottawa River, bound for Québec City under the pilotage of Philemon Wright (1761–1839).

Wright records that he peddled his wares as he went. On 12 June, for instance, he noted that he sold "450 pces of bords to the priest of South Buck parrish at six dolers per hundred." He had a long and anxious time in Québec City "a-waitin" before he finally sold his raft in October, but he had pioneered a route for timber on the Ottawa that continued to be used until only a few years ago.

What probably induced Wright's venture in the first place were new British tariffs designed to encourage British North American timber production, increasingly needed by Britain in her struggles in the Napoleonic Wars. Even more attractive tariffs were put in place in 1808, and the lumber boom began in earnest.

In 1809, ninety thousand ship-loads of timber — ten ship-loads a day — crossed the Atlantic from British North America. The British American colonies suddenly accounted for two-thirds of the pine timber imported into Great Britain. The totals would continue to rise; the colonies had become Great Britain's lumberyard.

Personal economic records like this one of Philemon Wright — order books, account books, ledgers, business correspondence, and so on — exist in substantial quantities in the National Archives of Canada and can be used to study many aspects of Canada's early economy in detail.

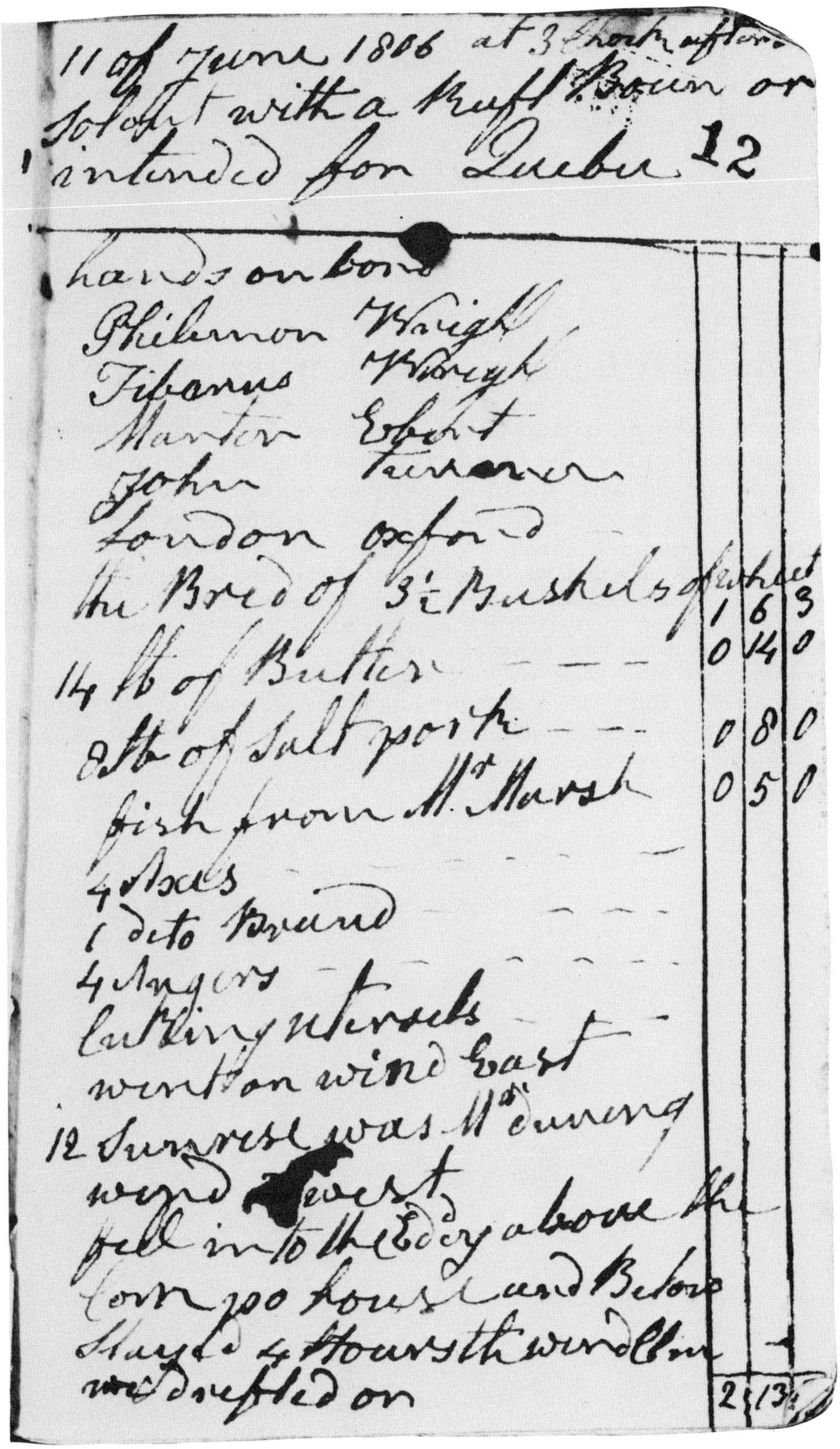
11 of June 1806 at 3 o'clock afternoon
Sot off with a Raft [illegible] or
intended for Quebec 12

hands on bord
Philemon Wright
Tiberius Wright
Martin Ebert
John Turner
London Oxford
the Bred of 3½ Bushels of wheat 1 6 3
14 lb of Butter 0 14 0
8 lb of salt pork 0 8 0
fish from Mr Marsh 0 5 0
4 Axes
1 dito Broad
4 Augers
Cutting utensils
went on wind East
12 Sunrise was [illegible]
wind East
fell into the Eddy above the
Corn [illegible] house and Below
Stayed 4 Hours the wind blew
we drifted on 2 13

Entry for 11–12 June 1806 from Philemon Wright's Raft Book.

National Archives of Canada: Manuscript Division, Wright papers, MG 24, D 8, vol. 114, p. 12.

An Early Concern with Conservation, 1808

British North American colonists often viewed trees simply as giant weeds impeding the cultivation of their land, but even they could be shocked by the wanton devastation caused by the plundering of forests for tall pines suitable for ships' masts. In this petition, some citizens in eastern Upper Canada complained of one firm that had been given a government contract to cut masts:

> Where they have Fallen them large Trees it's like a wind fall and in Turning and Clearing ways to take These Masts away they Destroy many Peoples whole lots . . . Those People . . . have done more damage than can be conceived, by cuting [*sic*] Hundreds of trees down that they do not mean to take away and half cut many others that the Wind will Blow down, and Mostly all as good timber as they take away. . . .

This petition comes from a continuing series of letters and petitions to the government of Upper Canada about a wide variety of daily concerns. Government records, besides telling much of politics, administration and economic development, often throw light on day-to-day life.

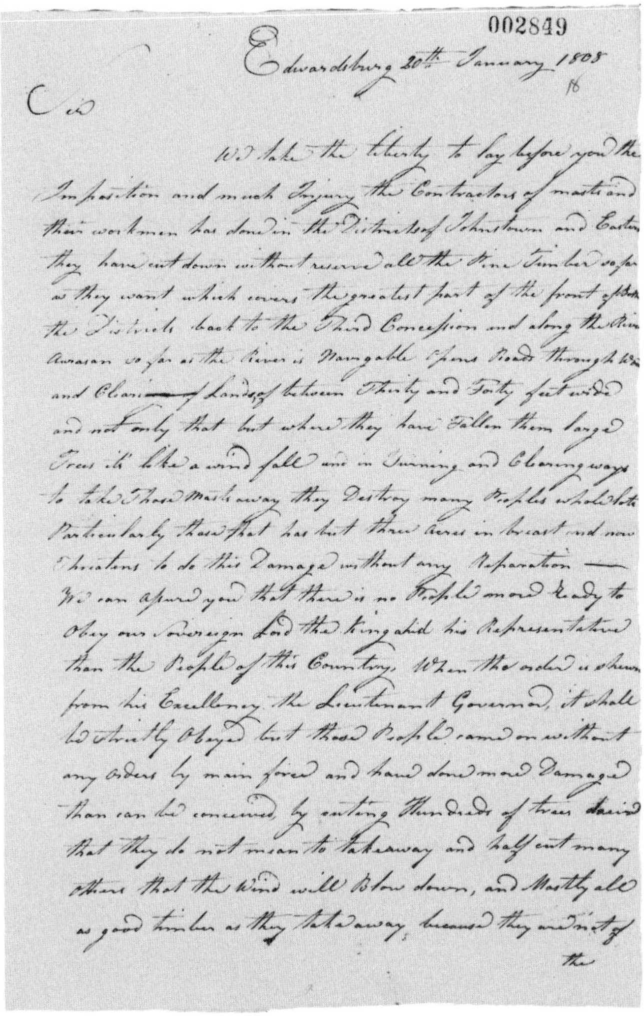

002849

Edwardsburg 20th January 1808

18

Sir

We take the liberty to lay before you the Imposition and much Injury the Contractors of masts and their workmen has done in the Districts of Johnstown and Eastern they have cut down without reserve all the Pine Timber so far as they want which covers the greatest part of the front of both the Districts back to the Third Concession and along the River Awasan so far as the River is Navigable Opens Roads through Woods and Clearing of Lands of between Thirty and Forty feet wide and not only that but where they have Fallen them large Trees it's like a wind fall and in Turning and Clearing ways to take Those Masts away they Destroy many Peoples whole lots Particularly those that has but three acres in breast and now threatens to do this Damage without any Reparation — We can assure you that there is no People more Ready to Obey our Sovereign Lord the King and his Representative than the People of this Country, When the order is shewn from his Excellency the Lieutenant Governor, it shall be strictly Obeyed but those People came on without any orders by main force and have done more Damage than can be conceived, by cutting Hundreds of trees Seized that they do not mean to take away and half cut many others that the Wind will Blow down, and Mostly all as good timber as they take away, because they are not of the

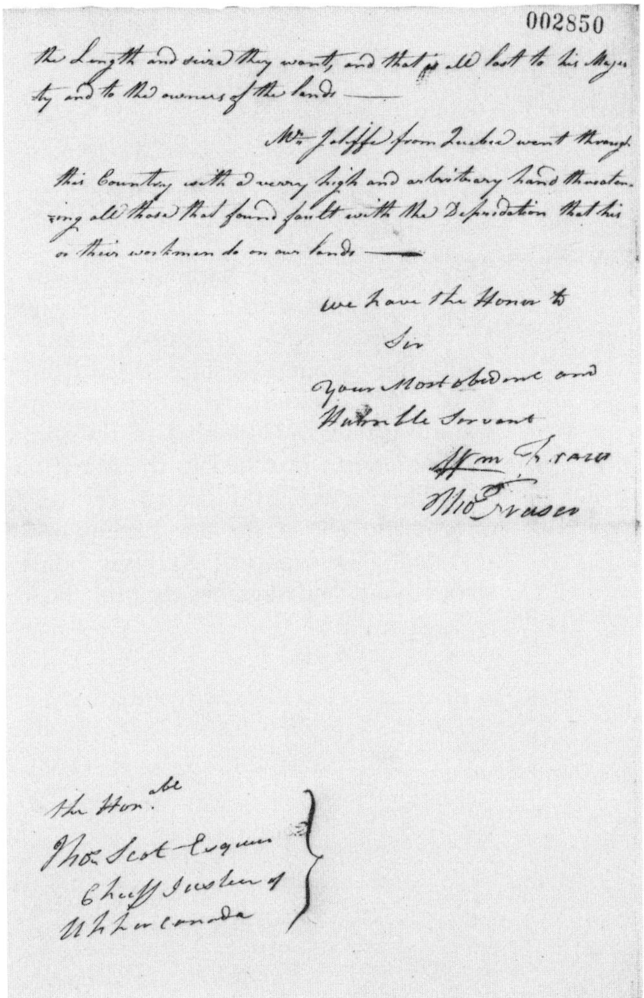

002850

the Length and seize they want, and that [illegible] all lost to his Majesty and to the owners of the lands —

Mr. Jolifte from Quebec went through this Country with a very high and arbitrary hand threatening all those that found fault with the Depredation that his or their workmen do on our lands —

we have the Honor to
Sir
Your Most obedient and
Humble Servant
Wm Fraser
Thos Fraser

The Honble
Thos Scot Esquire
Chief Justice of
Upper Canada

Letter, William and Thomas Fraser to Thomas Scott, Chief Justice of Upper Canada, Edwardsburg, 20 January 1808.

National Archives of Canada: Manuscript Division, Civil Secretary's Correspondence, Upper Canada Sundries, RG 5, A 1, vol. 7, pp. 2849–2850.

Wooden Ships for Wooden Cargoes, circa 1815–1820

This view shows the harbour at Québec City crammed with ships as it would have been most years after 1808. To the right is a large timber raft.

Increased trade in timber meant that more ships were needed to carry it. In 1800, only about 150 ships sailed from Québec City. Ten years later, a peak number of 661 ships manned by 6,600 crew members sailed from the port. The number of ships built locally doubled in the same decade. The growth of Quebec's shipping was more than matched in the Maritimes and Newfoundland.

This view is by Elizabeth Frances Hale (1774–1826), the wife of a government official and one of the few female artists in Canada in this period whose work has survived. The National Archives holds a sketchbook with 51 views as well as 14 watercolours and sketches by Mrs. Hale.

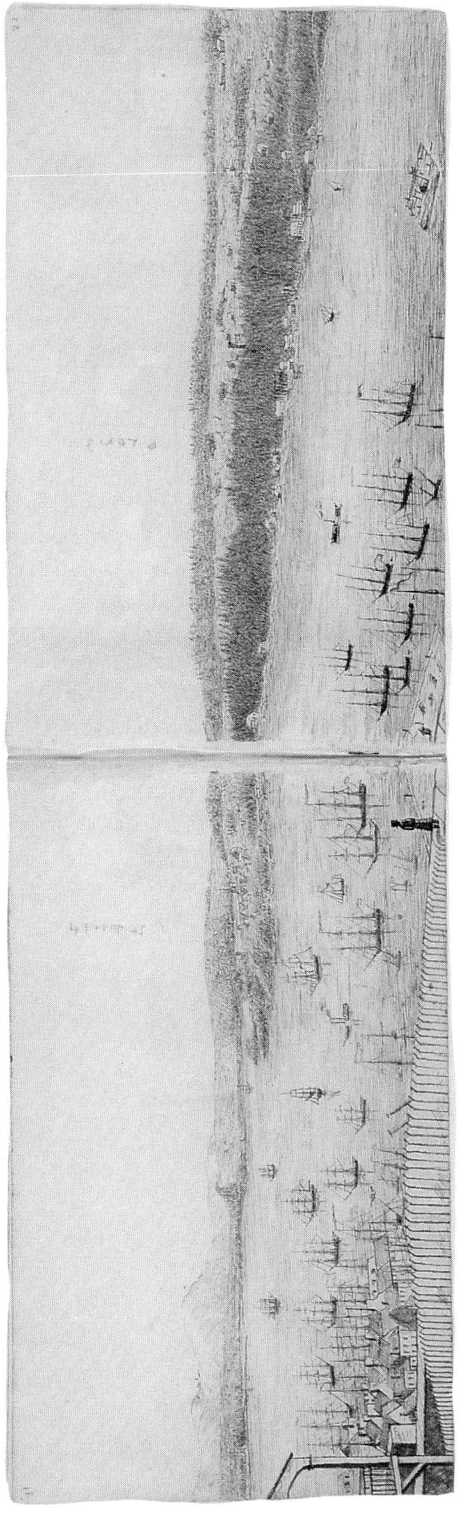

View of part of the lower town and harbour, Québec City. Elizabeth Frances Hale (1774–1826). Pen and ink, early 1800s. 12.8 × 20.6 cm. Folio. *In* Hale Sketchbook.

National Archives of Canada: Documentary Art and Photography Division, Hale Sketchbook, pp. 31–32 (Negative no. C-131287).

VI

The Dawning of the Great Age of Sail, 1760–1815

Ships like these were a common sight in Canadian coastal waters between 1760 and 1815. The large three-masted vessel in the lower view is a fine example of a merchant ship of the mid-eighteenth century. The larger two-masted vessels are schooners, while the smaller vessels are probably shallops, small open or half-decked schooners.

In 1811, an impressive 1,300 vessels were registered as belonging to British North American colonists. Ship-building was generally a cottage industry, with small groups of men constructing a few ships in secure harbours or bays. These ships were used for fishing or coasting (short distance trade) between the colonies. Although the timber trade and growing commerce with the West Indies were a stimulant to larger-scale ship-building, most exports were still carried in British-built ships. For the Maritimes, the great age of sail was just beginning.

These two magnificent hand-coloured engravings depict ships at Sable Island, Nova Scotia, and on the shore westward of the Saint John River, New Brunswick, respectively. They are from DesBarres' *Atlantic Neptune* (see Item 8). In addition to its cartographic value, *The Atlantic Neptune* met high artistic standards.

60

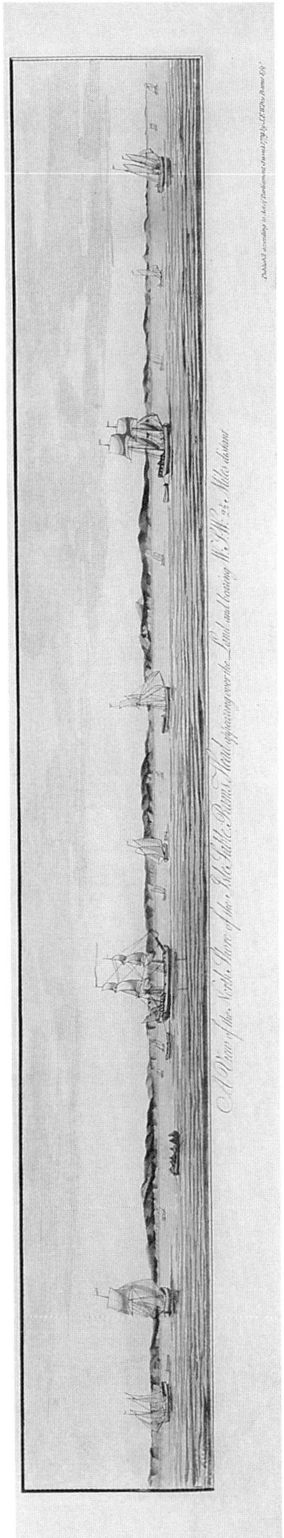 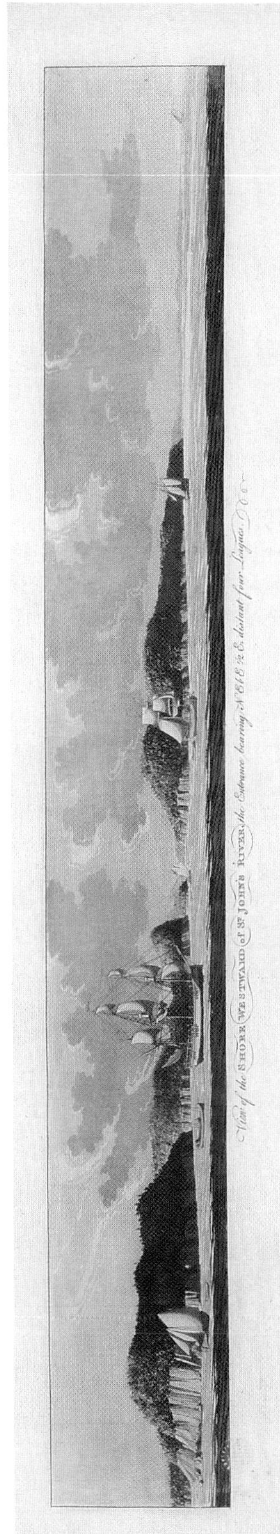

A View of the North Shore of the Isle Sable Rams Head appearing over the Land and bearing W.S.W. 2½ Miles distant. J.F.W. DesBarres. London: J.F.W. DesBarres, 1 June, 1779. Aquatint with hand colouring. 13.3 × 72.0 cm.

Originally on sheet of five views of the Isle of Sable (East End). London, 1 June 1779.

View of the Shore Westward of the St. John's River the Entrance bearing NEbE½E distant four Leagues. London: J.F.W. DesBarres. Aquatint with hand colouring. 15.5 × 74.0 cm.

Originally on undated sheet of three views, circa December 1780. Earlier state of view appeared as one of five views on sheet dated 26 July 1777.

In J.F.W. DesBarres. *Surveys of North America Entitled The Atlantic Neptune* . . . . London: J.F.W. DesBarres, 1775–1781.

National Archives of Canada: Documentary Art and Photography Division (Negative nos. C-40972 and C-40973).

VI

Making the Atlantic Coast Safe for Canadian Commerce, 1806

In this chart a British naval squadron stalks enemy French warships off the coast of North America. Britain's wars both aided and impeded British North America's maritime commerce. Under British protection and encouragement, the Maritimes had tried with limited success to build up a trade with the West Indies after the American Revolution. The outbreak of the Napoleonic Wars with France induced Britain to allow the United States into the West Indies trade, a move that quickly decimated the trade of the Maritimes and Newfoundland.

Because of its aid to France, however, after 1808, Britain excluded the United States from the West Indies trade. This lack of competition as well as new British inducements, which had begun as early as 1803, made trade from British North America to the West Indies very attractive and profitable.

This manuscript chart plots the track of the *Hero*, one ship in a Royal Naval squadron patrolling between Barbados and Newfoundland. The chart marks locations where neutral vessels were boarded, and the known positions of the French squadron.

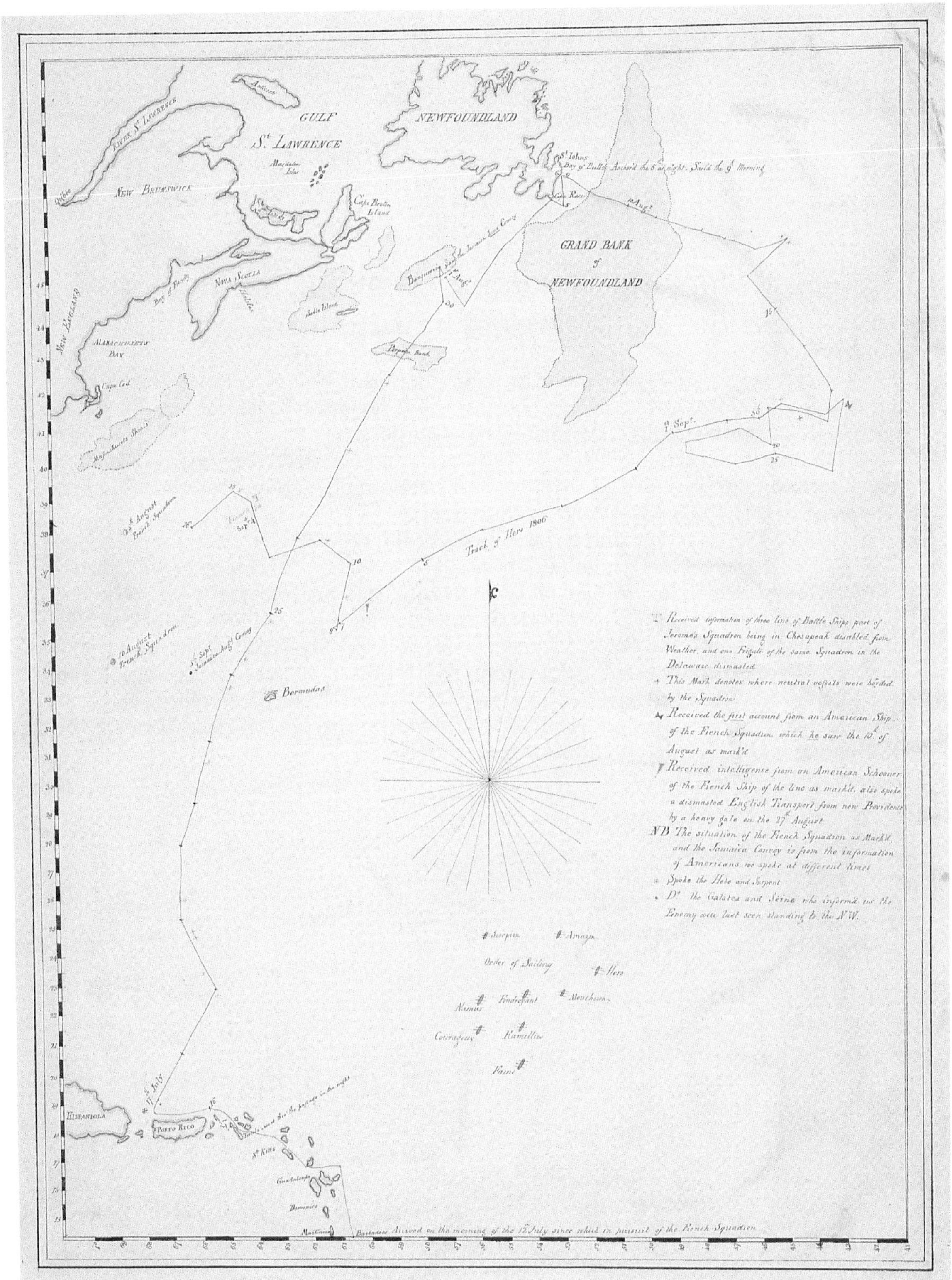

Chart of the track of the *Hero*, 1806.
Cartographer unknown. Map:
manuscript, hand-coloured, circa 1806.
47.0 × 34.8 cm.

National Archives of Canada:
Cartographic and Architectural Archives
Division (NMC 6752).

VI

A Busy Shipping Season for Liverpool, Nova Scotia, and the Beginnings of a Millionaire, 1811

From this register, a clear picture of the shipping trade of a moderate-sized port — Liverpool, Nova Scotia — emerges. The register provides information on the ships, their size, crews, ownership, destinations and cargoes.

The majority were small ships, locally built and owned. Trade was chiefly with the West Indies in fish (used as cheap food for slaves on plantations there) and lumber. The local coastal trade was second in importance.

One of the Liverpool shipowners (number 12 on the first list), Enos Collins (1774–1871), was reputed at his death in 1871 to be the richest man in Canada, with an estate worth six million dollars. Collins was one of twenty-six children. Lacking much formal education, he went to sea at an early age as a cabin boy. He was captain of a schooner before he was twenty and quickly became part-owner of a number of vessels trading out of Liverpool. With profits he made from shipping in the War of 1812, Collins invested in a number of other business enterprises.

Registers such as this one were kept in ports by customs officials to aid in the calculation and collection of customs duties.

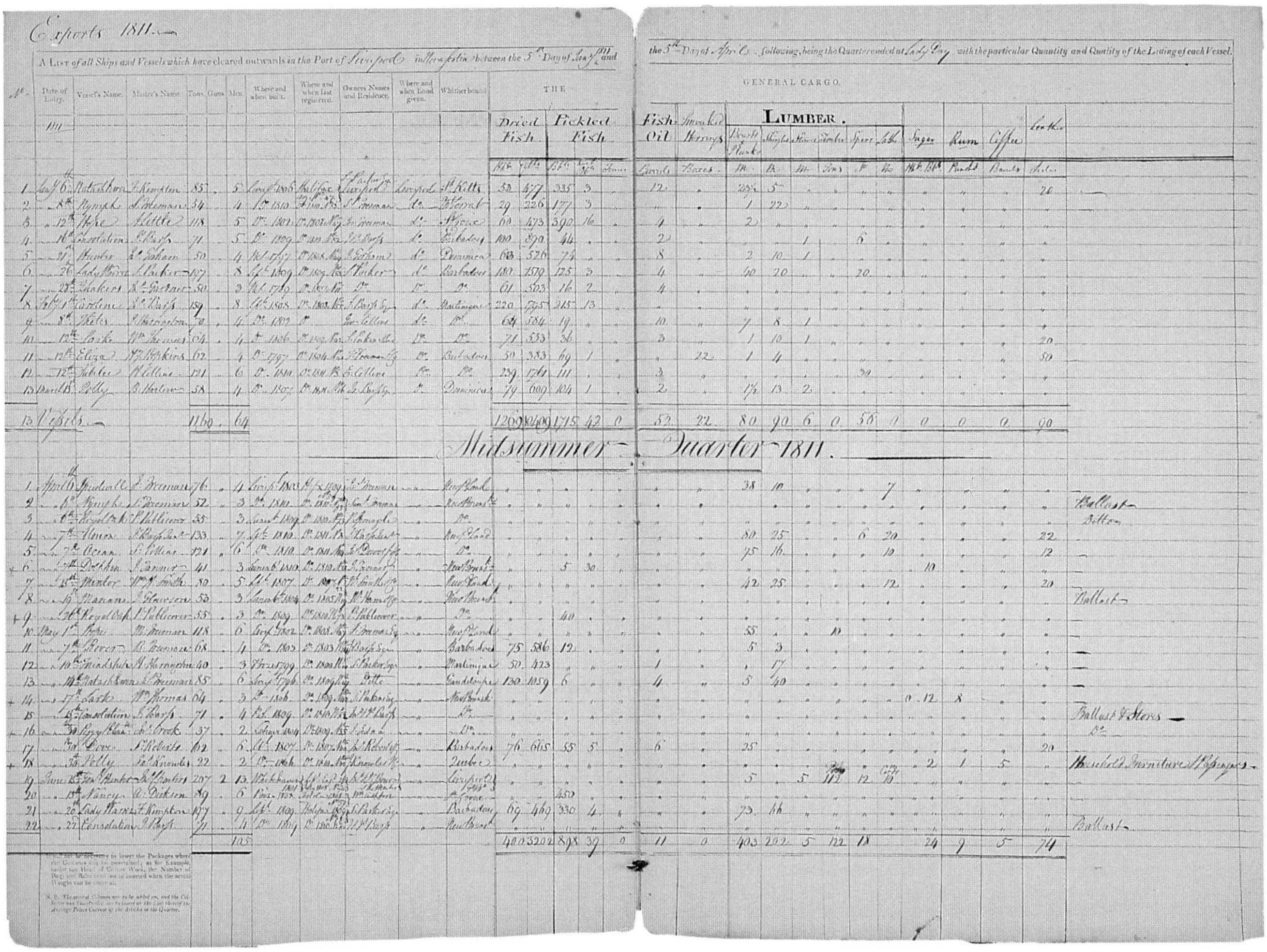
Exports 1811.

A List of all Ships and Vessels which have cleared outwards in the Port of Liverpool

the 5th Day of April following, being the Quarter ended at Lady Day with the particular Quantity and Quality of the Lading of each Vessel.

GENERAL CARGO.

Dried Fish | Pickled Fish | Fish Oil | Smoked Herrings | LUMBER. | Sugar | Rum | Coffee

Midsummer Quarter 1811.

List of Vessels Cleared Outwards from Liverpool, Nova Scotia, 5 January–5 April 1811. Entry in Liverpool, Nova Scotia, Customs Register.

National Archives of Canada: Government Archives Division, Records of the Department of National Revenue, RG 16, A 2, vol. 525, unpaginated.

Cod Makes Newfoundland North American, 1810

The fisheries were Newfoundland's primary economic activity. Cod was the main catch, and it was marketed chiefly in the Catholic countries of the Mediterranean and in the West Indies.

A significant change occurred in the fisheries — and in Newfoundland — in this period. Up to 1800, most fishing was done from trans-Atlantic "Bankers" that returned to Britain at the end of the season. In 1788, there were 20,000 men involved in the fishery, of whom 12,000 returned to Britain with the fishing fleet. The difficulties and dangers of the Napoleonic Wars plus the fact that Newfoundland could now process and sell fish more cheaply than the trans-Atlantic fishing fleet spelled the end of the Bankers. The importance of the local schooners can be seen from the return displayed here. Newfoundland was now more definitely an integral part of North America than a fishing outpost of Great Britain.

This return of the fisheries and inhabitants for Conception Bay in 1810 comes from the papers of Sir John Duckworth (1748–1817), who was from 1810 to 1813 both Governor of Newfoundland and Commander-in-Chief of the Newfoundland squadron. His papers contain much relating to his official business in that period. In addition to original papers, the National Archives has assembled extensive microfilm copies of Duckworth's papers in the Provincial Archives of Newfoundland and Labrador; the Douglas Archives of Queen's University, Kingston; the National Maritime Museum, Greenwich, England; and papers in the possession of Justice R.S. Furlong of St. John's, Newfoundland.

A Return of the Fishery and Inhabitants for the District of Conception Bay for the year 1810

03603

Numbers	Shipping	No. Tons	No. Guns	No. Men	No. Passengers	Quintals of Fish	Tons of Cod Oil	Tons of Seal Oil	Tons of Blubber		Names of the Harbors: Carbonear	Hr. Grace	Portugal Cove	Total
	Fishing Ships not Bankers									Nil				
	Bankers European													
	Ditto Island													
	Sack Ships	9815	14	557							35	28	5	68
No. of	Ships from the British colonies 14	1159		171										
	United States 2	419	6	23										
	West Indies 1	176	3	17										
	Coasters 5	150		23							1	2	2	5
72	Vessels on the Northern Coast	3431												
	From England — included in the Number of Sack Ships													
No. of	Passengers from Ireland				31									
	from Jersey													
	Fishing Ships													
No. of	Boats kept by Boatmen													
	Inhabitants													650
No. men employed in the Fishery	In Ships or vessels on the Northern Coast	fishermen / shoremen		432 / 216		45200	169							
	Boats and Shallops			1278			603							
	as Shore men			540										
Quintals Fish made by	Fishing Skiffs — included in the Number of Boats													
	Bankers European													
	Island													
	By Boatmen													
	Inhabitants					127800								
Fish exported to	Spain Portugal Italy					6600								
	British Europe					42376								
	West Indies					1670								
	British America					718								
	United States													
Tierces of	Salmon carried to Market													
Barrels of	Herring ditto													21
Tons of Train Oil made by	Fishing Skiffs													15
	Bankers European													
	ditto Island						372							
	By Boatmen													
Price of	Fish Merchantable 14/6 per Quintal													
	Salmon per Tierce 55/													
	Train Oil per Ton £25													
	Seal Oil per ditto £25													
No. of	Seal skins													
Tons of	Seal Oil made							635.3						66354
Value of	Furs taken by Inhabitants													
	Truck with Indians													
No. of	Stages													
	Train Vats													440
No. of	Acres of Land improved — This Article has never been ascertained													1160
No. of	Private Houses													
	Publick Houses													1165
	Masters													20
	Mistresses													1140
	Men Servants													1110
	Women Servants													1810
	Children													469
	Dieters													5020
No. of	Protestants													
	Roman Catholicks													7840
No. of	Persons in the district													2405
	Born										79	129	169	10245 377
	Died										29	33	20	82

Return of the Fishery and Inhabitants of Conception Bay, Newfoundland, 1810.

National Archives of Canada: Manuscript Division, Duckworth papers, MG 24, A 45, p. 3603.

VI

A Fishing Station on the St. Lawrence River, 1809

Elsewhere, off south-western Nova Scotia, in New Brunswick's Bay of Fundy, and up the St. Lawrence River, fishing for a variety of species was also important. Large fish-curing and schooner-owning firms such as the St. John's firms and the Robin interests mixed with smaller enterprises.

A moderate-sized enterprise in the Gaspé owned by two brothers from the Island of Jersey and operated since 1792 is shown in the plan reproduced here. The plan shows in detail the layout and operation of a fishing station. "Stages" were docks and "flakes" were racks on which fish were laid out for drying.

The plan was part of a petition to government for a grant of land — a further demonstration of the wide range of information often contained in government documents.

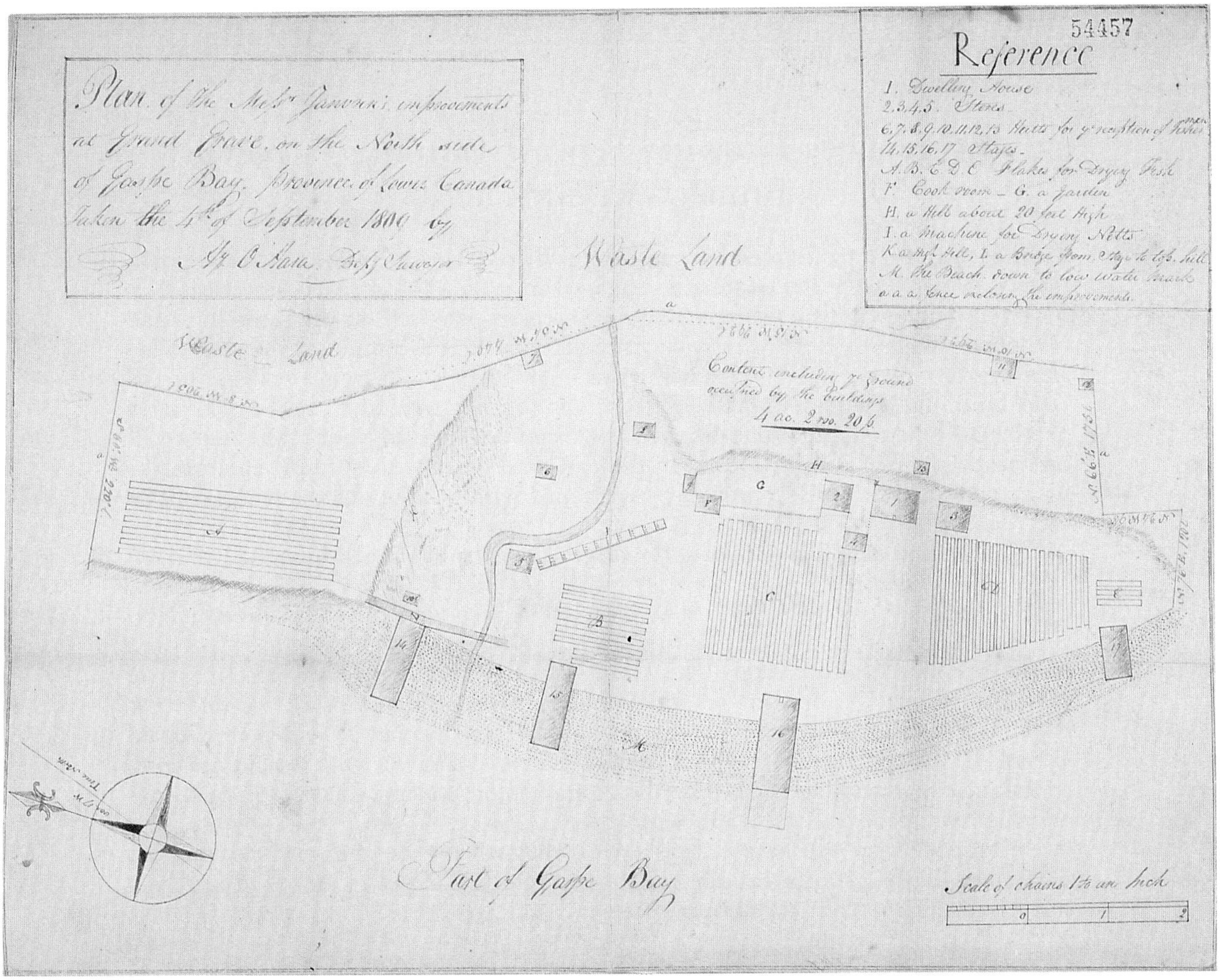

Plan of Messrs. Janvrins' Improvements of Grand Cove, Gaspé. Hy. O'Hara Deputy Surveyor. Pen and ink, 4 September 1809.

National Archives of Canada: Manuscript Division, Lower Canada. Land Petitions and Related Records, 1657–1842. RG 1, L 3 L, vol. 111, p. 54457.

Were They Growing Fences? Farming in New Brunswick, circa 1790

Farming was the most common occupation in British North America, with approximately 80 per cent of the population engaged in it on a full or part-time basis.

This engraving demonstrates farming methods practised on the Saint John and Nashwaak Rivers in New Brunswick in the 1790s. It is a composite showing many elements of typical English-Canadian farms of the period. There is a realistic line of farm buildings, ranging from a settler's first log hut (see Item 14) to a country gentleman's mansion (see Item 8) with associated out-buildings for crops and stock, backed by the ever-present forest. In front, a field beset with stumps left from the first stages of clearing is improbably partitioned with a variety of the fences then in use.

This print is an illustration in the original edition of Patrick Campbell's *Travels in the Interior Inhabited Parts of North America in the Years 1791 and 1792* (Edinburgh, 1793). Patrick Campbell (fl. 1760–1823) was a Scot who travelled through New Brunswick, Quebec and Upper Canada as far as Niagara, as well as through portions of the northern United States. The greatest part of the *Travels* is a description of New Brunswick. The drawing on which the print was primarily based was undoubtedly made locally — possibly by Campbell's talented nephew, Lieutenant Dugald Campbell. The print is a composite from at least two sources, with a field drawn as a rectilinear plan without perspective dividing the more realistic line of farm buildings and the river scene.

Campbell may well have had a sketch by himself inserted between two sections of a more finished sketch in order to show the various types of fences in use — a matter of much interest to European farmers.

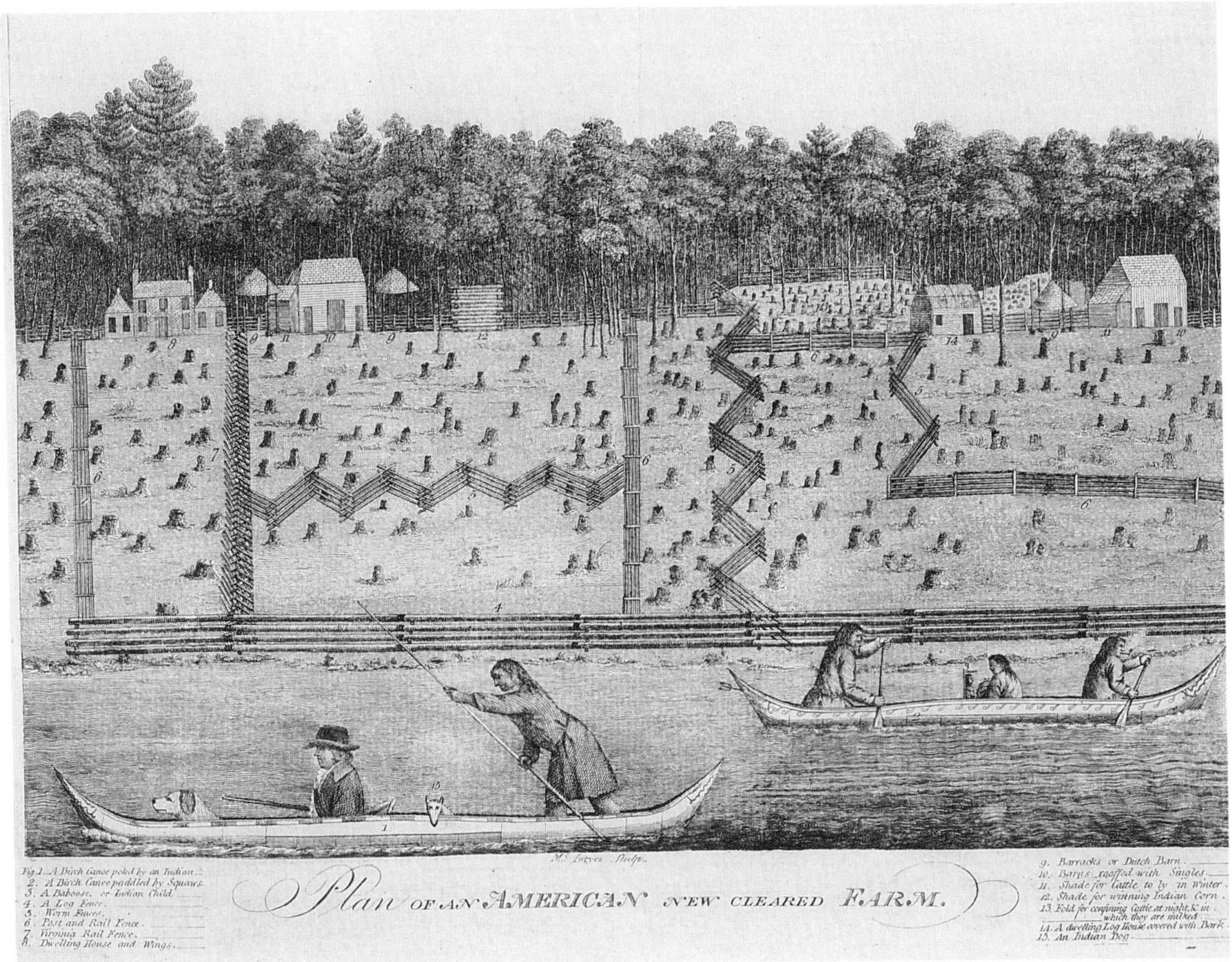

Plan of an American New Cleared Farm. Attributed to Dugald Campbell. Engraved by McIntyre. Plan: engraved, 1793. 33.0 × 24.5 cm.

In Patrick Campbell, *Travels in the Interior Inhabited Parts of North America in the Years 1791 and 1792.* Edinburgh: 1793, facing p. 86.

National Archives of Canada: Library (Negative no. C-130548).

Patterns on the Land: French-Canadian Agriculture, 1795

In Quebec, wheat was the main crop, matching fur in export value by 1800. In this plan of 1795, the French-Canadian land system can be seen in the seigneury of Sorel, with its long narrow farms arranged in ranges along rivers and streams.

Land under cultivation in Quebec expanded rapidly, especially after 1795 when British markets opened to Canadian produce. Agricultural exports, however, dropped sharply in the early nineteenth century, and wood rapidly replaced wheat as the chief export. There is much controversy about whether this drop represents a decline in agricultural production caused by unsuitable farming methods or a shift to supplying expanding internal markets because of an unstable international market.

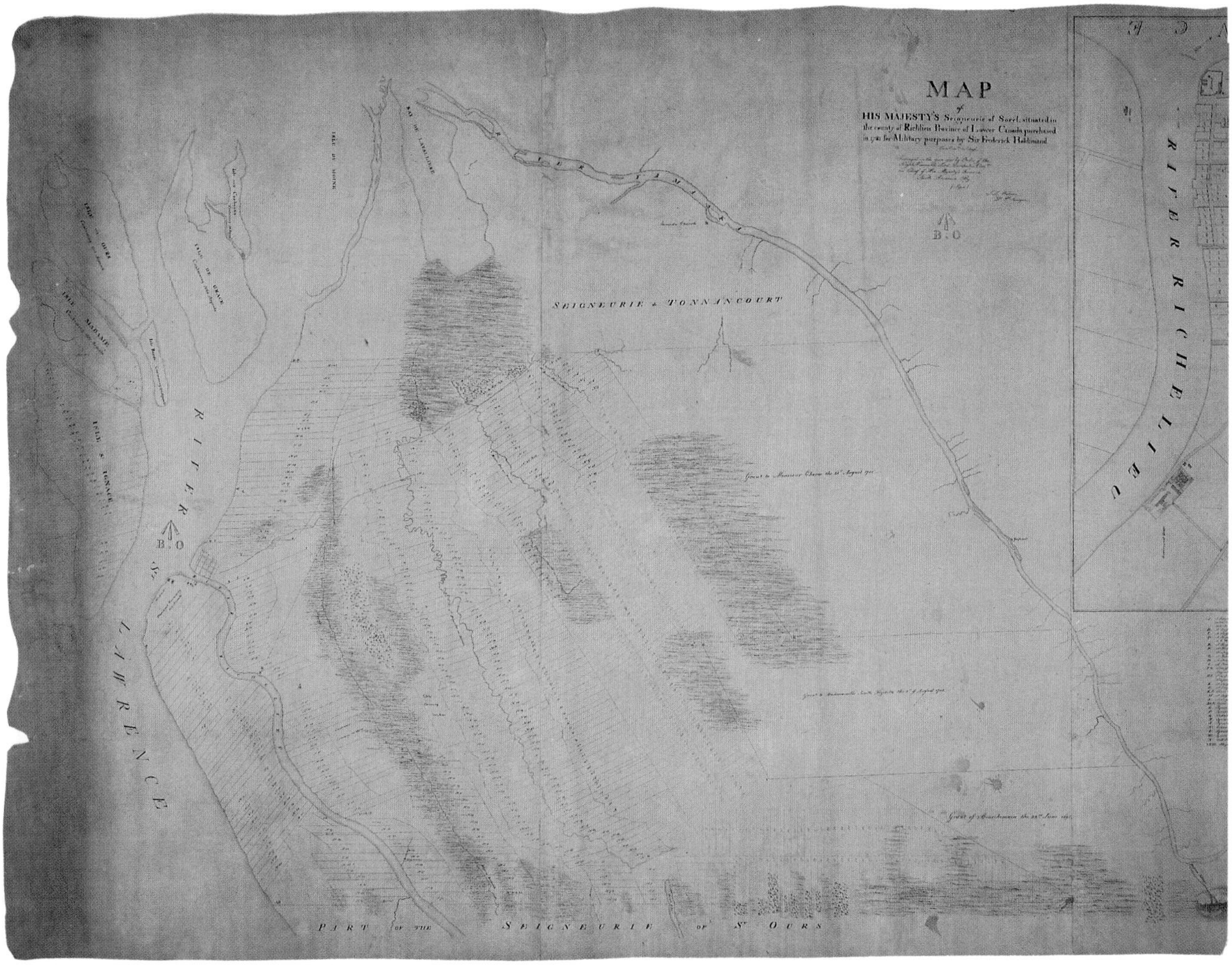

"Map of His Majesty's Seigneurie of Sorel, situated in the county of Richelieu Province of Lower Canada . . . Surveyed in the year 1795 . . ." S.Z. Watson, Deputy Provincial Surveyor. Copy. E.J. Ford. Lieut. Royal Engineers Office, Québec. 26 February 1838. 130.0 × 225.5 cm.

National Archives of Canada: Cartographic and Architectural Archives Division (NMC 26944).

Merchant Shops in Québec City, 1806

These adjoining shops on St. John's Street (rue Saint-Jean), Québec City, were on the edge of the upper town, possibly in the new St. John suburb beyond the city walls. Both shops display their goods: the tanner has his hides strung on a line, while the general merchant exhibits his wares on his window ledge and shutters.

One general merchant advertising his stock in the *Quebec Mercury* for 30 June 1806 listed, among other items for sale, "loaf sugar and teas, muscatal and sun raisins, almonds and nuts, sauces and florence oil, single and double Gloucester cheese, hardware, stationery and perfumery . . . Dartford gun powder and patent shot & c. & c."

Merchants often lived above their shops or — as in the case of the tanner, as an inscription on this work indicates — rented upstairs rooms to others. Expanding agriculture, burgeoning exports and the resulting growth of towns and cities meant that these shops would increasingly have their equivalents across central and eastern British North America.

The artist, Sempronius Stretton (1781–1842), served in Canada between 1803 and 1806 with the 49th and the 40th Regiments of Foot. His pictures include views of York (Toronto), Lake Erie, Queenston and Quebec City. He executed many studies of Canadian birds — the earliest known — and of costume. The National Archives holds five watercolours by Stretton and a sketchbook with forty-three works, including the one displayed here.

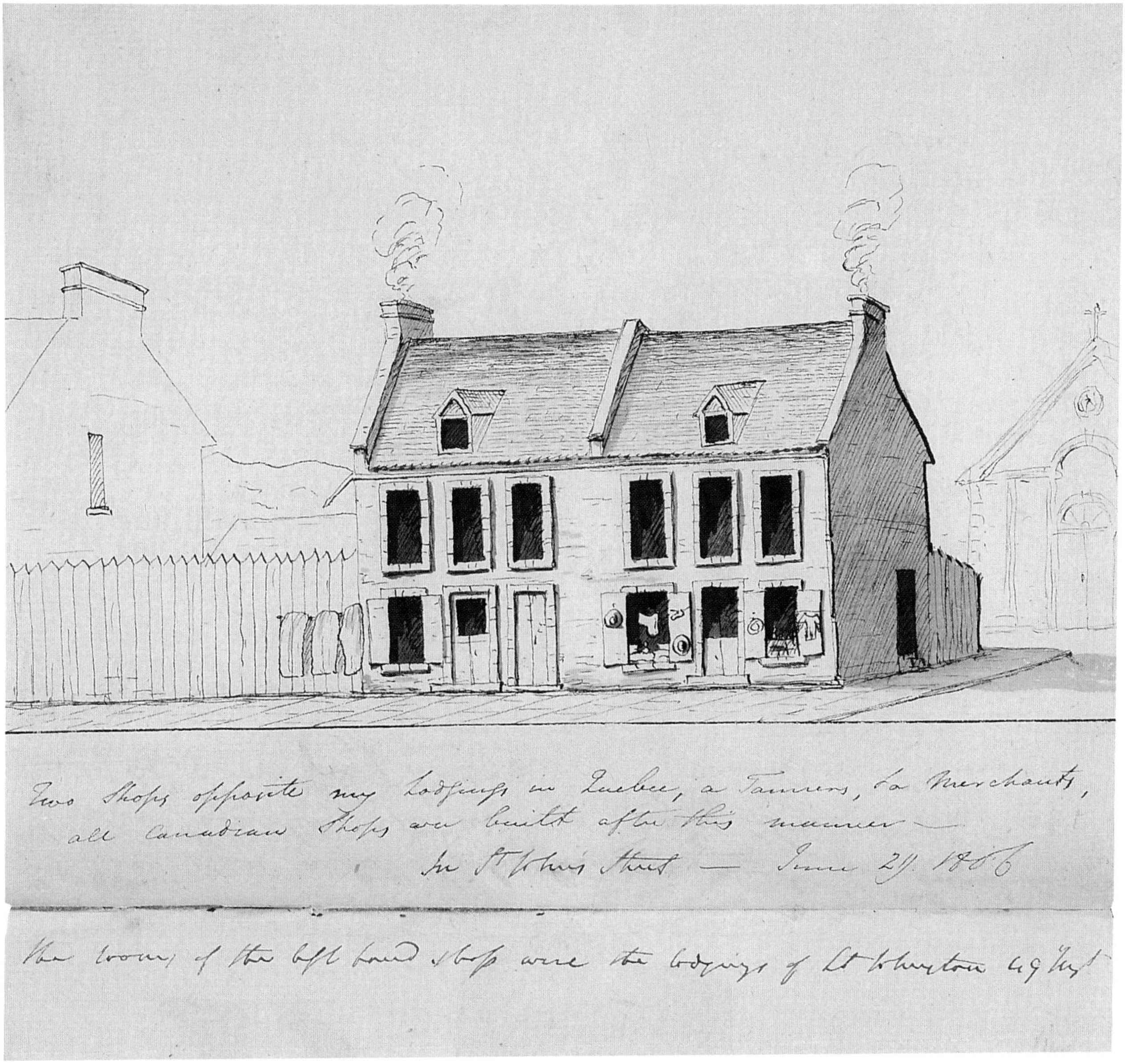

"Two Shops opposite my Lodgings . . . "
Sempronius Stretton (1781–1842). Pen and ink with grey wash, 29 June 1806. 16.0 × 20.0 cm. Folio.

National Archives of Canada: Documentary Art and Photography Division, Stretton Sketchbook, vol. 1, p. 36 (Negative no. C-14834).

A Mill at Dartmouth, Nova Scotia, circa 1801

Growing population and increasing prosperity encouraged the production of such varied products as soap, paper, hats, metals, ships and flour, especially in or near major towns. The *Royal Gazette* published in Halifax, 5 September 1797, announced that Davis and Barker had erected a grist mill on the Dartmouth side opposite the naval hospital. They would be ready to receive grain by September. Barker left the business shortly thereafter.

Interesting details of the scene recorded by George Isham Parkyns (1750–1820) include the long trough constructed to lead water into the second storey of the mill to power the mill machinery and the two men to the right using a sawpit to cut planks by hand.

This print is "before letters," meaning it was produced to test the quality of the image before lettering was placed on the printing plate. Such an early impression from a plate yields the strongest and clearest image. The National Archives also holds a copy of this print done "after letters."

View of Halifax from Davis' Mill. George Isham Parkyns (1750–1820). London: April, 1801. Hand-coloured aquatint, in blue ink. 32.4 × 53.0 cm.

National Archives of Canada: Documentary Art and Photography Division (Negative no. C-985).

Child Slavery? An Apprentice's Indenture, 1785

In this indenture, a standard printed form with manuscript additions, William Dedham, son of a labourer, aged fourteen years, commits himself to Andrew Doe of Québec City in 1785 as an apprentice for seven years. In return for his labour, Dedham is to receive room and board, five pounds towards a new set of clothes at the end of his apprenticeship, and instruction in the "Art, Trade and Mystery" of shoemaking.

This indenture has more to say about the apprentice's morals than his duties. He is not to play at "Cards, Dice or any other unlawful Game," nor is he to "haunt Ale-houses, Taverns or Play-houses." With their long periods of unpaid labour, and their virtual lack of restrictions on the powers of the master, apprenticeship indentures of this period have been called little more than a form of slavery.

Other indentures, contracts, partnership agreements, and the like scattered through the collections of the National Archives tell much about conditions of labour and social relations in this period.

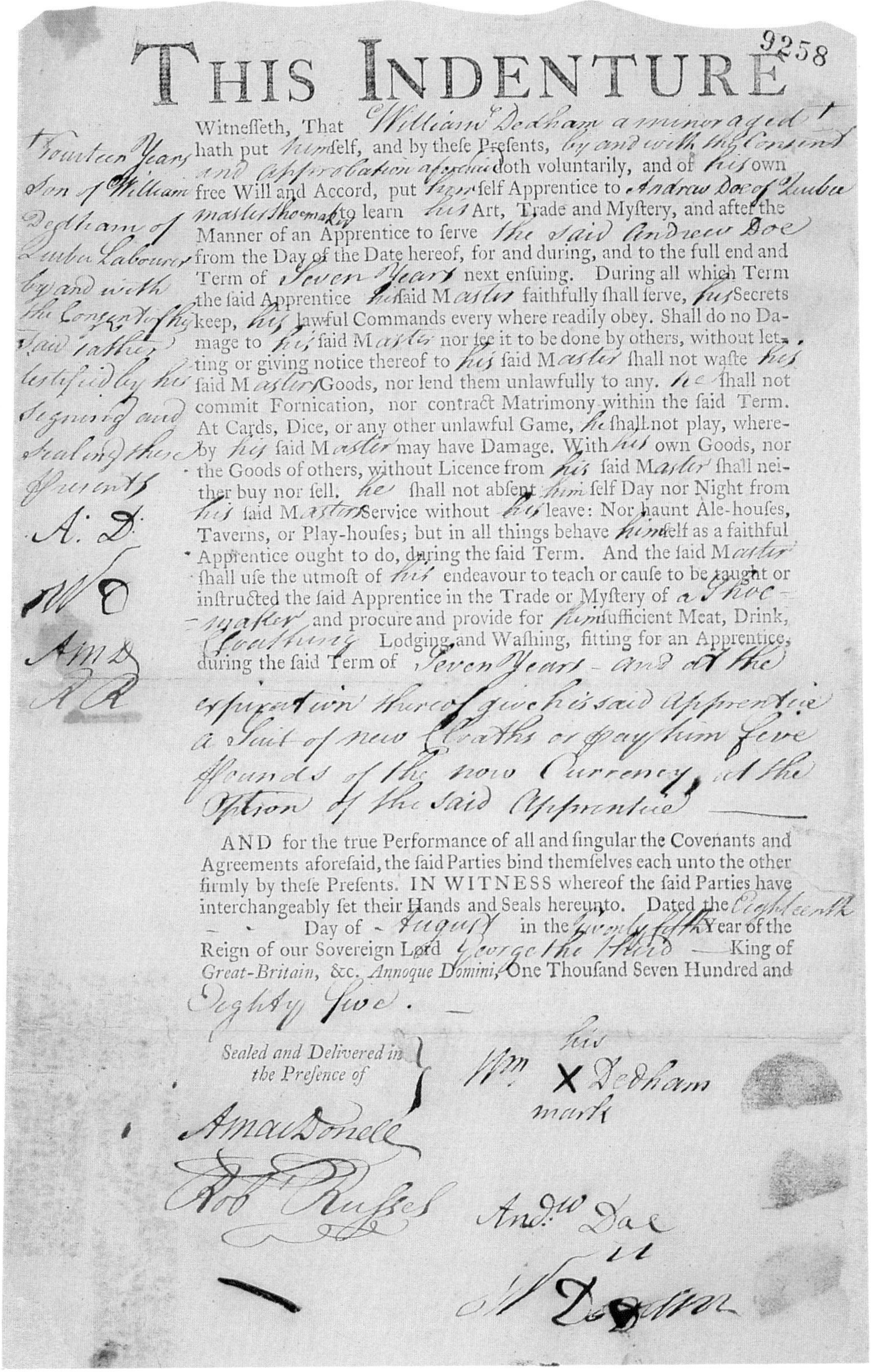

9258

THIS INDENTURE

Witnesseth, That William Dedham a minor aged Fourteen Years Son of William Dedham of Quebec Labourer hath put himself, and by these Presents, by and with the Consent and Approbation aforesaid doth voluntarily, and of his own free Will and Accord, put himself Apprentice to Andrew Doe of Quebec master Shoemaker to learn his Art, Trade and Mystery, and after the Manner of an Apprentice to serve the said Andrew Doe from the Day of the Date hereof, for and during, and to the full end and Term of Seven Years next ensuing. During all which Term the said Apprentice his said Master faithfully shall serve, his Secrets keep, his lawful Commands every where readily obey. Shall do no Damage to his said Master nor see it to be done by others, without letting or giving notice thereof to his said Master shall not waste his said Masters Goods, nor lend them unlawfully to any. he shall not commit Fornication, nor contract Matrimony within the said Term. At Cards, Dice, or any other unlawful Game, he shall not play, whereby his said Master may have Damage. With his own Goods, nor the Goods of others, without Licence from his said Master shall neither buy nor sell. he shall not absent himself Day nor Night from his said Masters Service without his leave: Nor haunt Ale-houses, Taverns, or Play-houses; but in all things behave himself as a faithful Apprentice ought to do, during the said Term. And the said Master shall use the utmost of his endeavour to teach or cause to be taught or instructed the said Apprentice in the Trade or Mystery of a Shoe-maker and procure and provide for him sufficient Meat, Drink, Cloathing Lodging and Washing, fitting for an Apprentice, during the said Term of Seven Years – and at the expiration thereof give his said Apprentice a Suit of new Cloaths or pay him five Pounds of the now Currency, at the Option of the said Apprentice —

by and with the Consent of the said Father testified by his signing and sealing these Presents

A. D.

W D

A M D

R R

AND for the true Performance of all and singular the Covenants and Agreements aforesaid, the said Parties bind themselves each unto the other firmly by these Presents. IN WITNESS whereof the said Parties have interchangeably set their Hands and Seals hereunto. Dated the Eighteenth Day of August in the twenty fifth Year of the Reign of our Sovereign Lord George the Third King of *Great-Britain*, &c. *Annoque Domini*, One Thousand Seven Hundred and Eighty five. —

Sealed and Delivered in the Presence of

A MacDonell

Robt Russel

Wm his X mark Dedham

Andw Doe

W Dedham

Apprenticeship Indenture of William Dedham, 18 August 1785. Printed form with manuscript additions.

National Archives of Canada: Manuscript Division, Civil and Provincial Secretary, Lower Canada. "S" Series. RG 4, A 1, vol. 28, p. 9258.

VII

Religion

Outside of Roman Catholic Quebec, British North America in the period after the Conquest presented a picture of great religious variety, with many denominations ministering to the souls of the colonists. All the churches faced a common problem — too few resources to meet the demands for solace and guidance that were placed upon them. How the various denominations and church leaders tried to cope with that problem provides a perspective on documents relating to religion in the period.

Congregational Meeting House, St. John's, Newfoundland, circa 1789

Even in matters of religion, Newfoundland remained Britain's neglected colony. Missionary priests from Ireland succeeded in winning masses of converts to Roman Catholicism, but they were too few to minister effectively to their flocks. Protestant dissenters relied largely on lay preachers; the Church of England was virtually inactive.

This Congregational church was founded by John Jones (1737–1800), a converted British soldier. Jones's small congregation originally met secretly on the "Barrens" outside St. John's because of British regulations against Dissenters. The situation was eased in 1784 by a proclamation granting freedom of worship in Newfoundland. The meeting house pictured here was built in 1789 and incorporated quarters for a charity school for all denominations, which Jones had begun with his own army pension. By 1794, Jones had a congregation of 400.

Despite Jones's success in St. John's, Congregationalism, with its lack of organization beyond the individual congregation and its appeal to the middle classes, did not take a strong hold in Newfoundland.

The skill evident in the execution of this plan as well as Jones's military background suggests this plan was prepared by an army officer. The plan's depiction of the Sunday dress of the relatively well-to-do in about 1790 is particularly charming. The plan itself is a very early example of the 200,000 plans and architectural drawings held by the National Archives.

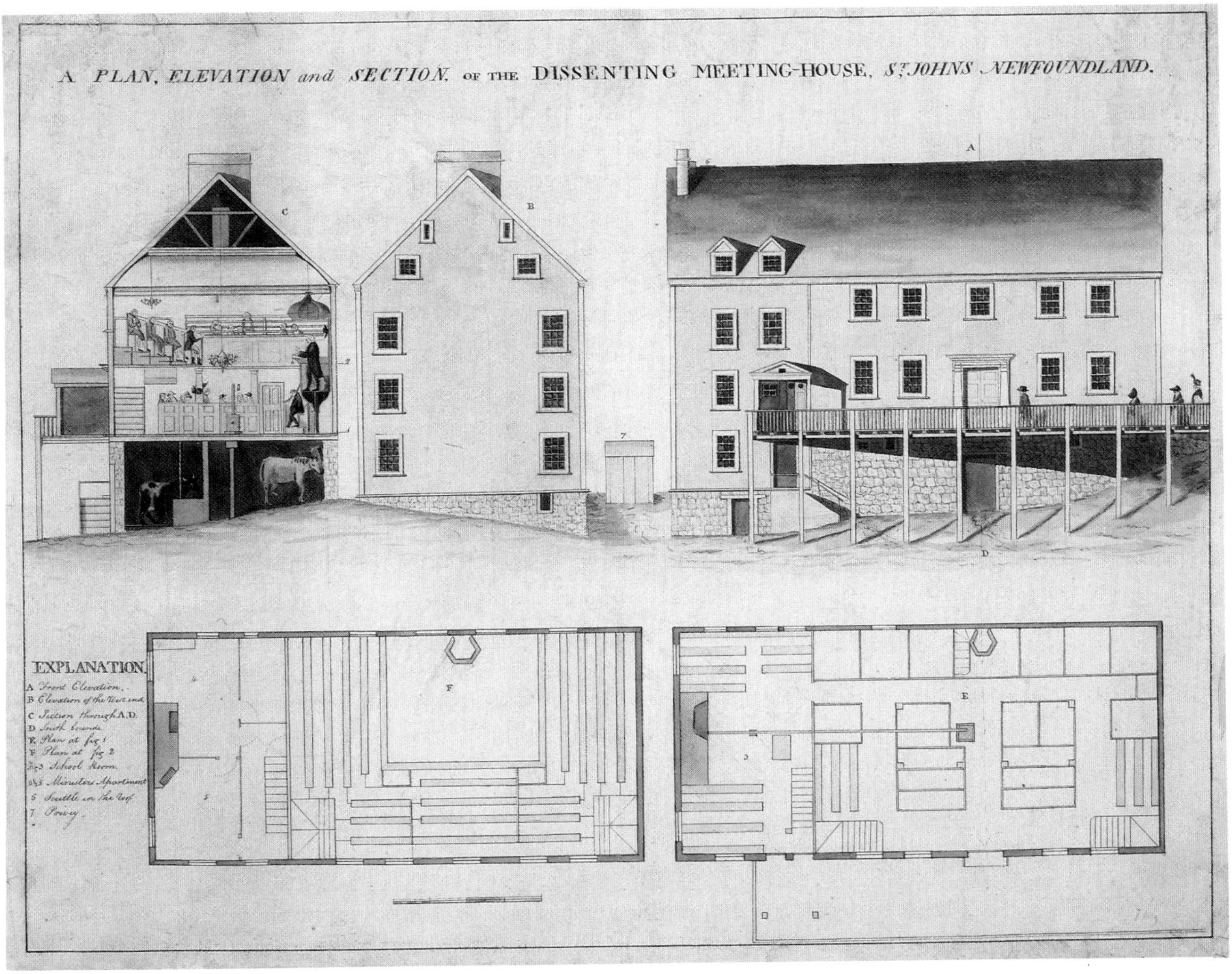

"A Plan, Elevation and Section of the Dissenting Meeting-House, St. Johns, Newfoundland." Artist unknown. Pen and ink with watercolour, circa 1789. 31.1×41.9 cm.

National Archives of Canada: Documentary Art and Photography Division (Negative no. C-3374).

VII

The "New Light" in Nova Scotia, 1775–1784

The Great Awakening or New Light revival was the major popular movement — religious, social, or political — of its time in Nova Scotia, and Henry Alline (1748–1784) was its first leader. Alline was also a gifted writer, and his *Life and Journal* gives remarkable insight into his tortured and mystical soul.

Born in Newport, Rhode Island, and raised in Falmouth, Nova Scotia, Alline felt oppressed by the strict Calvinism and limited opportunities of his environment. After years of doubt and guilt, he came to an assurance of conversion in 1775, just at the outbreak of the American Revolution.

Preaching an emotional brand of modified Calvinism that balanced God's love for mankind with His terrible condemnation of sinners, Alline travelled through most of Nova Scotia and the settled parts of what are now New Brunswick and Prince Edward Island. He found his greatest acceptance in rural and frontier Nova Scotia — especially those areas settled by "Yankees" experiencing both economic hardship and the psychological anxiety of rootlessness, heightened after the Revolution had forced the breaking of their ties with New England. The revival did not distract people from sympathy with the American rebellion, but served as an emotional outlet for those unable to act politically. It did help to produce a primitive form of local patriotism based on Nova Scotia's "mission" in North America.

Alline died in 1784, leaving no formal organization behind him. Most of his followers were absorbed into the strong Baptist fellowship that became an important religious ingredient in Maritime life.

In addition to his posthumously published journal, Alline left a volume on his theology, a book of sermons, and another of his hymns, some of which remained in use throughout the nineteenth century.

71

THE

REV. MR. HENRY ALLINE'S

LIFE, &c.

CHRIST is the fountain of life, the source of happiness, the glory of angelic realms, and the triumph of Saints, and I trust is the life of my soul, the joy of my life, my present and everlasting portion. I therefore desire, and intend by his grace that his name should be my theme, until the last period of my days. And O may his blessed Spirit be breathed into all my endeavours, may his love sweeten all my trials, invigorate all my labours; may his name fill up every period of my life, when in private, and every sentence, when in public: and hoping that he will cause me to write and leave amongst the rest of my writings this short account of my life. And as that is my design, I shall not overburden the reader with a relation of many passages that would be of no benefit, but shall only relate that, which may be worth the readers perusal.

I WAS born in Newport, in the government of Rhode-Island, in North America, on the 14th day of June, 1748, of William and Rebecca Alline, who were born and brought up in Boston, who gave me an early instruction in the principles of the christian religion. I was early sent to school, and was something forward in learning; was very early moved upon by the spirit of God, though I knew not then what ailed me.

THE first moving I remember was, when about eight years of age, by some discourse between my father and my eldest sister, in a thunder-storm, when I heard her say, that she had reason to be so distressed, that if she should

The Life and Journal of the Rev. Mr. Henry Alline. Henry Alline. Boston, 1806, p. 3.

National Archives of Canada: Library (Negative no. C-130546).

VII

The Pious Habitant? 1810

There is a tendency to assume that French Canadians throughout the nineteenth century were devoutly pious and meekly obedient to the Roman Catholic Church.

How, then, to explain this *mandement* (order) in which the Bishop of Quebec complains that, despite his frequent warnings, habitants were turning local saints' day festivities into excuses for drunken brawls and debauchery? Some enterprising souls even seem to have become professional patron saint celebrators, wandering merrily from one parish to another in a seemingly endless spree. The bishop notes that he had already suppressed saints' day celebrations in twenty parishes, and gives warning to others. Such problems occurred frequently in the first quarter of the nineteenth century.

The Roman Catholic Church shared a problem with all the Canadian churches of the period — shortage of clergy. The Conquest and European wars had virtually cut off European supplies of priests. The few recruits found locally received a poor quality of theological education, and, because of the urgent need, were often sent out to the parishes too young and ill-prepared. Even the best of the clergy were overwhelmed by the sheer numbers of their parishioners: in 1805, there were 186 priests to serve 200,000 faithful in the Maritimes and Upper and Lower Canada. The resulting lack of effective spiritual guidance often led to arrogant independence, hostility and immorality among the laity. The church required determined and forceful leadership to reassert its control.

The frequent *mandements* issued by the bishops to their flocks (see also Items 87 and 97) give much insight into the concerns and reactions of the Roman Catholic hierarchy.

1810

MANDEMENT concernant les Fêtes Patronales de Paroisses.

JOSEPH OCTAVE PLESSIS,

Par la miséricorde de Dieu et la grace du S. Siège Apostolique Evêque de Québec, &c. &c. A nos très chers frères en Notre Seigneur, les Curés et Missionaires de notre Diocèse, Salut et Bénédiction.

DEPUIS longtemps, NOS TRES CHERS FRERES, les désordres introduits à l'occasion des fêtes patronales des paroisses, sont devenus pour vos évêques un objet d'amertume et de sollicitude, comme vous en pouvez juger par les divers moyens qu'ils ont mis en œuvre pour y remédier. Ces jours vénérables, destinés dans leur première institution à nourrir la piété et la sainte joie des fidèles, en leur remettant plus particulièrement sous les yeux les circonstances du Mystère ou les vertus du Saint en l'honneur duquel leur église étoit dédiée, sont devenus, par le malheur des temps, des jours de tristesse et de deuil pour la religion, des jours de promenades et de débauches, des jours de querelles et d'ivrognerie, des jours de blasphêmes et de batailles, dont la pluspart d'entre vous ont entendu les affligeans récits, lorsqu'ils n'en ont pas été personellement témoins. Nos Illustres Prédécesseurs ont essayé de toute manière de prévenir ces désordres, d'abord en déclarant que ces fêtes ne seroient plus que de dévotion, puis en transférant quelques-unes au dimanche suivant, ensuite en les faisant célébrer dans des saisons moins favorables aux rassemblemens, enfin en supprimant tout à fait celles qui étoient l'occasion d'excès plus scandaleux.

LES choses en étoient là lorsque nous avons pris la conduite de ce diocèse. Sur les remontrances de plusieurs d'entre vous et d'après les informations prises dans nos visites, nous avons aussi ordonné la suppression totale de la fête du Patron dans une vingtaine de paroisses, comme le seul remède qui pût y arrêter efficacement le mal. Mais ce remède prive certaines ames pieuses d'un grand sujet de consolation et excite en elles une sorte de jalousie contre ceux dont les fêtes patronales subsistent encore, quoique non exemptes de tous les abus qui ont fait supprimer les leurs.

DESIRANT donc adopter un systême qui mît toutes les fêtes patronales sur le même pied, et sincèrement touchés de l'aspect affligeant de tant d'églises privées d'honorer solemnellement leurs saints patrons, nous avons

Mandement of Joseph-Octave Plessis, Bishop of Quebec, concerning the observance of saints' days, 1810. Pamphlet, p. 1.

National Archives of Canada: Library (Negative no. C-130541).

VII

A Defender of the Faith

Joseph-Octave Plessis (1763–1825), Bishop of Quebec, 1806–1825, was one of the most significant Roman Catholic clergymen of this period. Described as ambitious, methodical and a realist with a flair for diplomacy, Plessis concentrated his considerable powers on sustaining and strengthening his Church and managing its relations with the state. A decided opponent of the French Revolution and all it stood for, he saw Britain as a defender of traditional and established values. He was highly suspicious of democratic movements in French Canada. Plessis cooperated with the British authorities in civil matters while resisting their efforts to weaken the Church. He opposed a plan for state-controlled education, but encouraged the establishment of Catholic primary education. Faced with a serious shortage of clergy, Plessis channelled a significant number of young ecclesiastics into classical education, a policy that eventually halted the decline in recruitment. At his death in 1825, he left a Church much stronger than he had found it in 1806.

JOSEPH OCTAVE PLESSIS.
NÉ EN 1763,
CONSACRÉ EVÊQUE DE CANATHE EN 1801
& Evêque Titulaire de l'Eglise Catholique du Canada depuis 1806;

Joseph Octave Plessis. Attributed to William Berczy (1744–1813). Hand-coloured aquatint, early 1800s. 25.5 × 20.3 cm.

National Archives of Canada: Documentary Art and Photography Division (Negative no. C-99308).

VII

A Manuscript of Possibly the Oldest Preserved Canadian Composition, circa 1756–1791

This manuscript volume from the parish church at Ste. Foy contains words in Latin and music for hymns sung at vespers, a complete "Mass and Office of the Holy Family," and a complete "Passion of Our Lord Jesus Christ According to St. Matthew for Palm Sunday." Because this music was not part of the unchangeable portion of the Mass, the volume was probably used infrequently. The manuscript was prepared for François-Xavier Borel, a Frenchman, who was the priest at Ste. Foy from 1756 to 1774 and 1786 to 1791, for his own use from the pulpit.

The "Prose" part of the "Mass of the Holy Family," a portion of which is illustrated here, may have been composed by Charles-Amador Martin (1648–1711), the second Canadian-born priest. If so, it may also be the oldest preserved Canadian composition. First printed in 1801, the "Prose" was chanted at the Québec Cathedral on the Holy Family feast day until the 1950s.

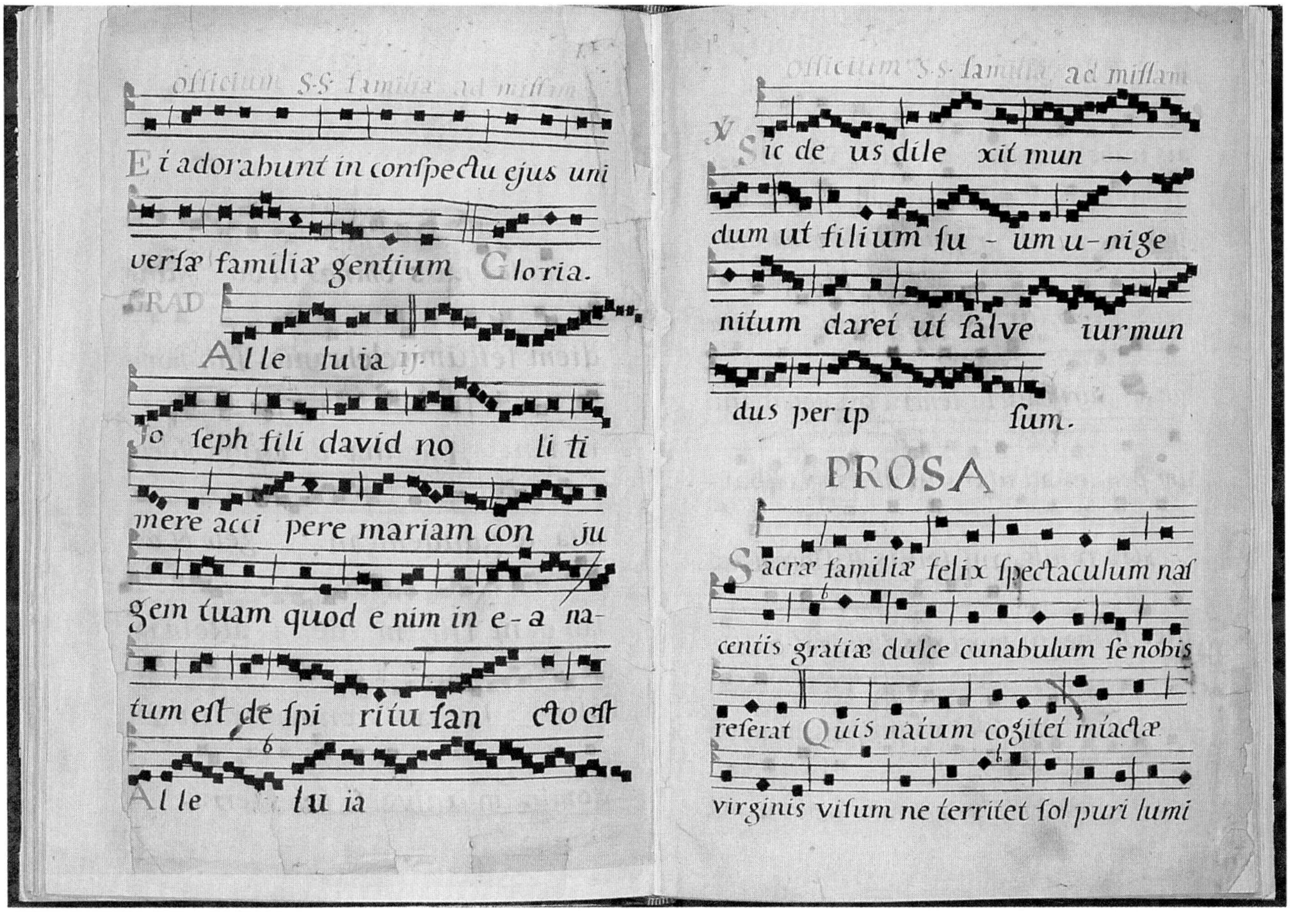

Volume of religious music and liturgy. Author unknown. Manuscript, circa 1756–1791.

National Archives of Canada: Manuscript Division, François-Xavier Borel papers, MG 18, E 21, unpaginated.

VII

"The Most Valuable Baptist Document in Ontario," 1805

The minute book of the Baptist Church in Boston, Ontario (near present-day Simcoe, inland from Lake Erie) has been called "the most valuable Baptist document in Ontario," both for its early date (1804–1830) and for the extensive picture it gives of congregational life in pioneer days. The entries exhibited deal with the original organization of the church when it began in 1805 with seven members. The entries make clear that like many pioneer churches, the Baptists relied on lay members to preach and administer the sacraments. The Boston Church, as mentioned in the entries, joined the Baptist Shaftesbury Association centred in Vermont, which sent ordained ministers on tours to local congregations without clergy.

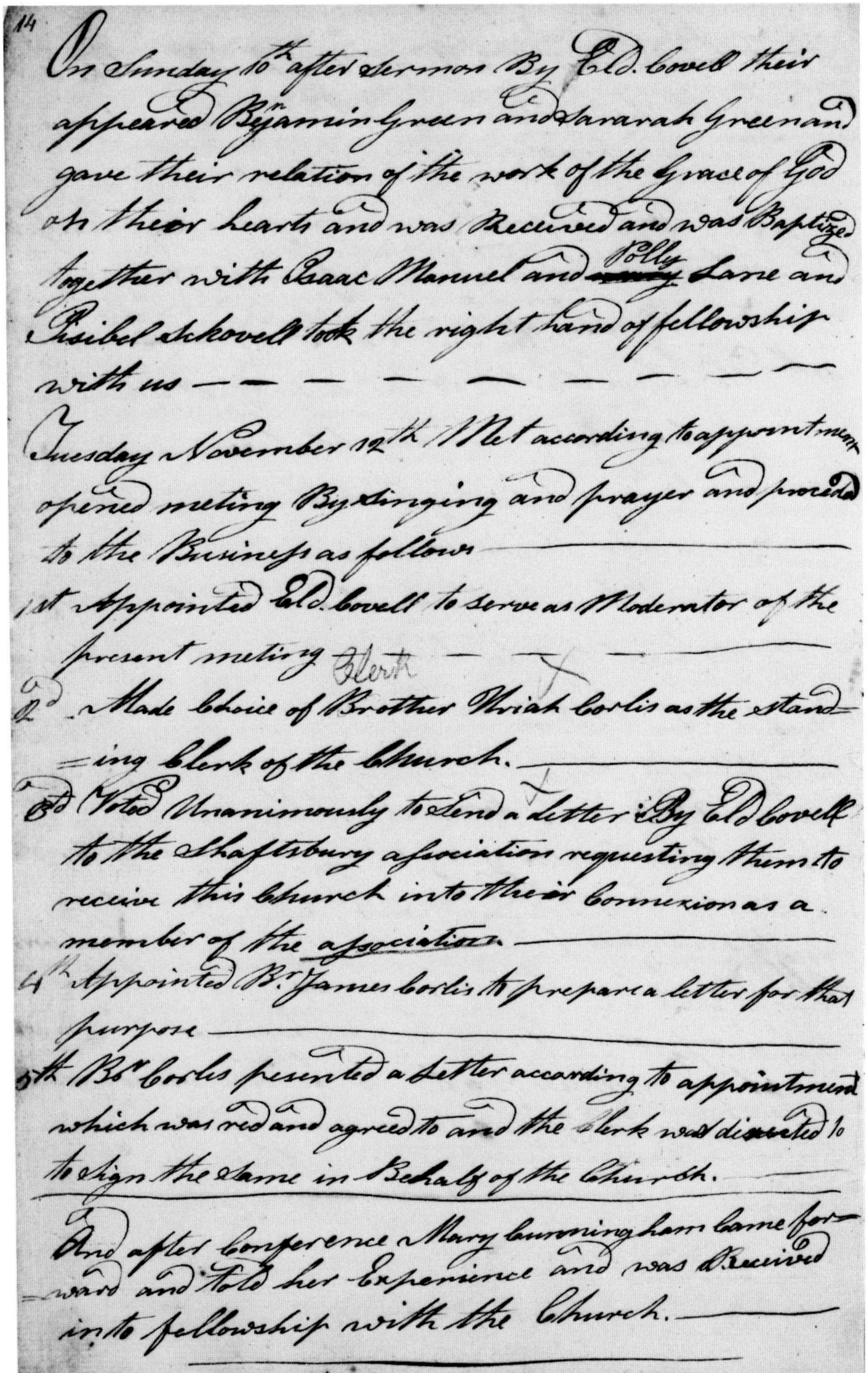
14
On Sunday 10th after Sermon By Eld. Covell their
appeared Benjamin Green and Sararah Green and
gave their relation of the work of the Grace of God
on their hearts and was Received and was Baptized
together with Isaac Mannel and Polly Lane and
Psibel Schovell took the right hand of fellowship
with us — — — — — — — —
Tuesday November 12th Met according to appointment
opened meting By singing and prayer and proceded
to the Business as follows ——
1st Appointed Eld. Covell to serve as Moderator of the
present meting — — ——
2d Made Choice of Brother Uriah Corlis as the stand-
-ing Clerk of the Church. ——
3d Voted Unanimously to send a Letter By Eld Covell
to the Shaftsbury association requesting them to
receive this Church into their Connexion as a
member of the association. ——
4th Appointed Br. James Corlis to prepare a letter for that
purpose ——
5th Br. Corlis presented a Letter according to appointment
which was red and agreed to and the Clerk was directed to
to sign the same in Behalf of the Church. ——
And after Conference Mary Cunningham Came for-
-ward and told her Experience and was Received
into fellowship with the Church. ——

Boston Baptist Church Minute Book.
Manuscript, 1804–1830.

National Archives of Canada: Manuscript
Division, MG 9, D 7-2, p. 14.

VIII

Society and Culture

The period between the Conquest and the end of the War of 1812 marked a watershed for fine arts, literature and science in British North America.

On the one hand, in pioneer communities with limited resources to devote to high culture, there was no great outpouring of prose, poetry, music or drama. Popular leisure activities were simple and often geared to physical or outdoor activity. Folk songs and stories flourished, but were very seldom recorded. Folk art was not often preserved. Practical publications such as newspapers and almanacs put down sturdy roots, while nascent scientific interest concentrated on the natural and practical spheres.

On the other hand, prosperity, immigration and increasingly concentrated settlement were providing immigrant and native writers and artists with a base on which to begin to build a distinctive Canadian culture whose products before 1815 included Canada's first novel, poetry, plays, a growing travel and religious literature, and a golden age of French-Canadian painting.

VIII

The First Novel Written in North America, 1763–1768

Most figures noted for making a major contribution to British North America's development in the late eighteenth and early nineteenth century were men. Few individuals indeed made their mark in the spheres of literature or high culture. It is striking then to encounter a writer who was both a woman and Canada's (as well as North America's) first novelist.

Dramatist, essayist, librettist, theatre manager and novelist Frances Brooke (d. 1789) was a noted figure in literary and theatrical circles in London. In 1763, she sailed for Québec to join her husband, who was military chaplain there. During her stay, which lasted until 1768, she wrote *The History of Emily Montague* (1769). The novel was structured as a series of fictionalized letters, based on Brooke's life at Québec and containing her witty and perceptive comments on politics, religion, society and nature. The grace and style of the narrative assured it would become required reading for travellers to Canada.

It is remarkable that the artist of Mrs. Brooke's portrait was also a woman, the Scottish-born Catherine Read (1723–1778), a fashionable London portraitist of the day who, in an age dominated by male artists, specialized in painting women. The two women were close friends, which may account for the warm informality of the portrait, so different from the convention of the day.

Portrait of Frances Brooke. Catherine Read (1723–1778). Oil on canvas, 1771. 71.6 × 59.4 cm.

National Archives of Canada: Documentary Art and Photography Division (Negative no. C-11373).

An English Canadian Poem, circa 1806

Closer to the generality of literary production in English-speaking Canada at this period are William Robe's two epic poems, "Quebec Winter" and "Quebec Summer." In this passage from "Summer," Robe discusses (as virtually every writer did) the poor condition of Canada's roads and, more unusually, the local diet at Québec City as winter turned to spring. Although rather pedestrian as poetry, Robe's observations were perceptive and often ranged well beyond conventional poetic interests to include, for example, the plight of the unemployed in winter, the police, and the flies in summer. Written on paper watermarked 1806, the poems are not known to have been published.

Before 1815, Canadian literature was very much in the pioneer stages of its development. Many could not write, and those who could were too busy to do so or did not have the inclination or literary skill to put their thoughts on paper. In English, much writing was in the form of published diaries and journals or letters of soldiers and inhabitants, the most remarkable being Alexander Henry's *Travels and Adventures in Canada . . .* (1809) (see Item 13). Closely related were travel accounts by British and European tourists. Both forms tell us much about general conditions and the thought of people at the time. Religious writings were prominent and in Nova Scotia included *The Life and Journal of the Rev. Mr. Henry Alline* (1806) (see Item 71). Poetry was more common as a literary form than prose.

The period was important in the main for laying the foundations of future literary development.

William Robe (1765–1820), an officer of the Royal Artillery, served in Canada 1794–1795, in 1799 and again circa 1800–1806. Robe designed the Anglican cathedral at Québec City and supervised its construction.

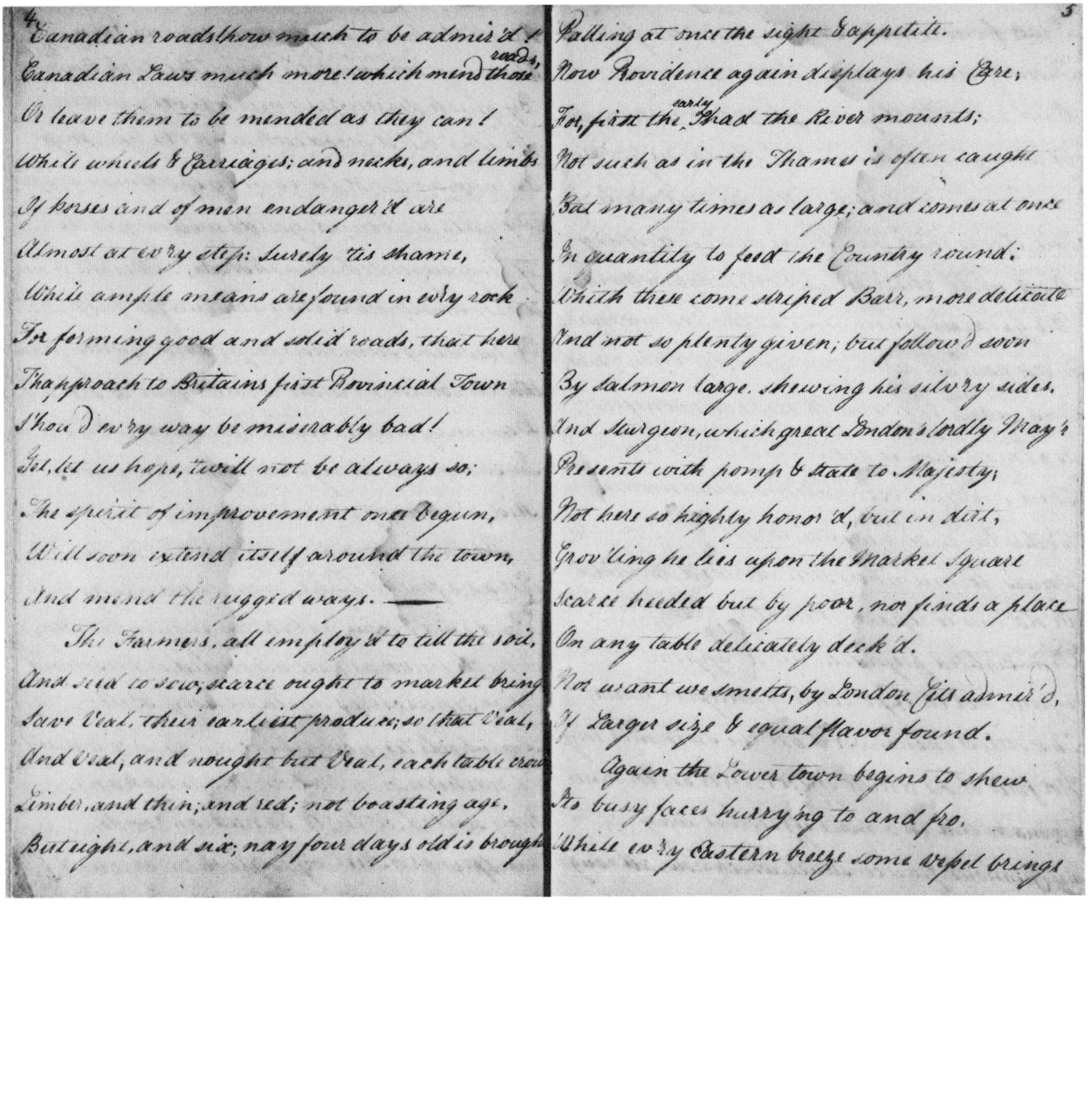

4

Canadian roads! how much to be admir'd!
Canadian Laws much more! which mend those roads,
Or leave them to be mended as they can!
While wheels & Carriages; and necks, and limbs
Of horses and of men endanger'd are
Almost at ev'ry step: Surely 'tis shame,
While ample means are found in ev'ry rock
For forming good and solid roads, that here
Th'approach to Britains first Provincial Town
Shou'd ev'ry way be miserably bad!
Yet, let us hope, 'twill not be always so;
The spirit of improvement once begun,
Will soon extend itself around the town,
And mend the rugged ways. —
The Farmers, all employ'd to till the soil,
And seed to sow; scarce ought to market bring
Save Veal, their earliest produce; so that Veal,
And Veal, and nought but Veal, each table crow[ns]
Limber, and thin; and red; not boasting age,
But eight, and six; nay four days old is brough[t]

5

Palling at once the sight & appetite.
Now Providence again displays his Care;
For, first the early Shad the River mounts;
Not such as in the Thames is often caught
But many times as large; and comes at once
In quantity to feed the Country round:
With these come striped Barr, more delicate
And not so plenty given; but follow'd soon
By salmon large, shewing his silv'ry sides.
And Sturgeon, which great London's lordly May'r
Presents with pomp & state to Majesty;
Not here so highly honor'd, but in dirt,
Grov'ling he lies upon the Market Square
Scarce heeded but by poor, nor finds a place
On any table delicately deck'd.
Nor want we smelts, by London Cits admir'd,
Of Larger size & equal flavor found.
Again the Lower town begins to shew
Its busy faces hurry'ng to and fro,
While ev'ry Eastern breeze some vessel brings

"Quebec Summer." William Robe (1765–1820). Manuscript, circa 1806.

National Archives of Canada: Manuscript Division, Lawrence M. Lande collection, MG 53, 189, pp. 4–5.

A Poem by French Canada's Most Significant Contemporary Writer

This manuscript for "Le Dépit ridicule ou le Sonnet perdu" was written by Joseph Quesnel (1746–1809), the most significant literary figure of his day in French Canada. A Frenchman who had been captured on a French privateer during the American Revolution, Quesnel settled in Quebec in 1779. A versatile writer, he composed songs, plays and poetry. His play *Colas et Colinette, ou le Bailli dupé*, a comic opera in three acts with fourteen songs, was first produced by the Théâtre de Société (which Quesnel helped to found) in Montreal in 1789–1790.

Another of his plays was entitled *L'Anglomanie, ou le Dîner à l'anglaise*, a satire ridiculing the seigneurs' infatuation with English fashion. Some of his poems appeared in newspapers, and his music was performed locally.

Other French Canadians composed songs and poems, which they often published in newspapers. Indeed, newspapers themselves were significant vehicles of French Canadian culture. *Le Canadien*, founded in 1806, first gave voice to the nationalist tone that has marked Québécois literature ever since. Joseph-Octave Plessis, Bishop of Quebec, was the foremost orator of his day, and many of his pronouncements were published (see Items 73 and 97).

Still, as in English Canada, formal culture was thin. No novels were published. A vigorous folk tradition of songs and stories flourished, but very little was written down in this period. Quesnel expressed his frustration at the lack of artistic development through the wry humour of "Le Dépit ridicule." The poet complains to his wife "What is the good of the trouble I take for rhyming / If no one ever has time to listen to my verse." She, more practical, responds: "I see you every day writing or dreaming / Whilst I must bring up your children." The poet then announces his great project to her — to lock his friends in a room and read to them "all the lines of my last work."

The National Archives holds twenty-four manuscript poems by Joseph Quesnel in the Lande collection, as well as other of his family papers relating to his business and personal affairs.

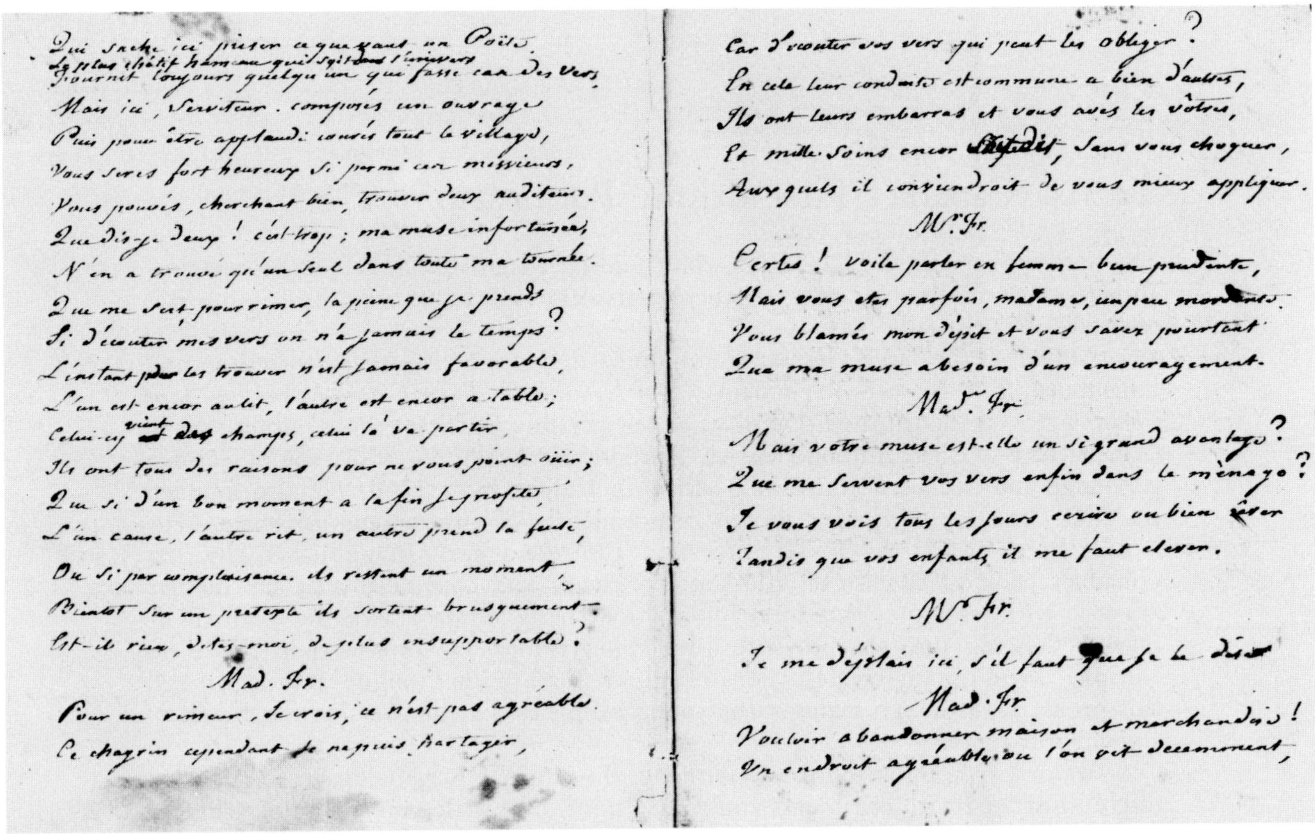

Qui sache ici priser ce que vaut un Poëte.
Le plus chétif hameau qui soit dans l'univers
Fournit toujours quelqu'un qui fasse cas des Vers.
Mais ici, Serviteur. composés un ouvrage
Puis pour être applaudi courés tout le village,
Vous serés fort heureux si parmi ces messieurs,
Vous pouvés, cherchant bien, trouver deux auditeurs.
Que dis-je deux ! c'est trop ; ma muse infortunée,
N'en a trouvé qu'un seul dans toute ma tournée.
Que me sert pour rimer, la peine que je prends
Si d'écouter mes vers on n'a jamais le temps ?
L'instant pour les trouver n'est jamais favorable,
L'un est encor au lit, l'autre est encor à table ;
Celui-cy vient des champs, celui là va partir,
Ils ont tous des raisons pour ne vous point ouïr ;
Que si d'un bon moment à la fin je profite,
L'un cause, l'autre rit, un autre prend la fuite,
Ou si par complaisance ils restent un moment,
Bientot sur un prétexte ils sortent brusquement.
Est-il rien, dites-moi, de plus insupportable ?
Mad. Fr.
Pour un rimeur, je crois, ce n'est pas agréable.
Ce chagrin cependant je ne puis partager,
Car d'écouter vos vers qui peut les obliger ?
En cela leur conduite est commune à bien d'autres,
Ils ont leurs embarras et vous avés les vôtres,
Et mille soins encor ~~[illegible]~~, sans vous choquer,
Auxquels il conviendroit de vous mieux appliquer.
Mr. Fr.
Certes ! voila parler en femme bien prudente,
Mais vous êtes parfois, madame, un peu mordante.
Vous blamés mon dépit et vous savez pourtant
Que ma muse a besoin d'un encouragement.
Mad. Fr.
Mais votre muse est-elle un si grand avantage ?
Que me servent vos vers enfin dans le ménage ?
Je vous vois tous les jours écrire ou bien rêver
Tandis que vos enfants il me faut élever.
Mr. Fr.
Je me dépitais ici, s'il faut que je le dise
Mad. Fr.
Vouloir abandonner maison et marchandise !
Un endroit agréable où l'on vit décemment,

"Le Dépit ridicule ou le Sonnet perdu."
Joseph Quesnel (1746–1809).
Manuscript, n.d.

National Archives of Canada: Manuscript Division, Lawrence M. Lande collection, MG 53, 177, unpaginated.

Canada's First Ethnic Publication, 1787

The literary diet of most Canadians who could read consisted largely of newspapers, almanacs, hand bills and posters — those practical publications of greatest immediate relevance to their daily lives.

Aimed at the large German community in Nova Scotia that centred around Lunenburg, this Nova Scotia almanac *Der Neuschottländische Calender Auf das Jahr Christi 1789*, is the third edition of what was possibly the first ethnic publication in Canada. Its publisher, Anthon Henrich (Anthony Henry) (1734–1800) was of German parentage and had been active in printing in Halifax from 1760. He also founded the first Canadian newspaper to run independently of government patronage (The *Nova Scotia Chronicle and Weekly Advertiser*, 1769) and in 1776 published the first Canadian book to contain an illustration. Henry was convinced that his modest almanac with its appropriate local information could compete with the German almanacs flooding into the province from Pennsylvania. He promised in the 1788 edition, "I will use my greatest endeavour to keep our mother tongue current through this press . . . although many of the young people declare an aversion for it, out of a wonderful conceit."

Set in a type imported from Germany, the almanac is well composed and profusely illustrated with ornaments and zodiac signs. The little book contains standard almanac information on phases of the moon, zodiac charts, tables of historic dates, lists of local government and military officials, court days and the like. It must have enjoyed considerable success, as it continued to be published annually beyond 1800.

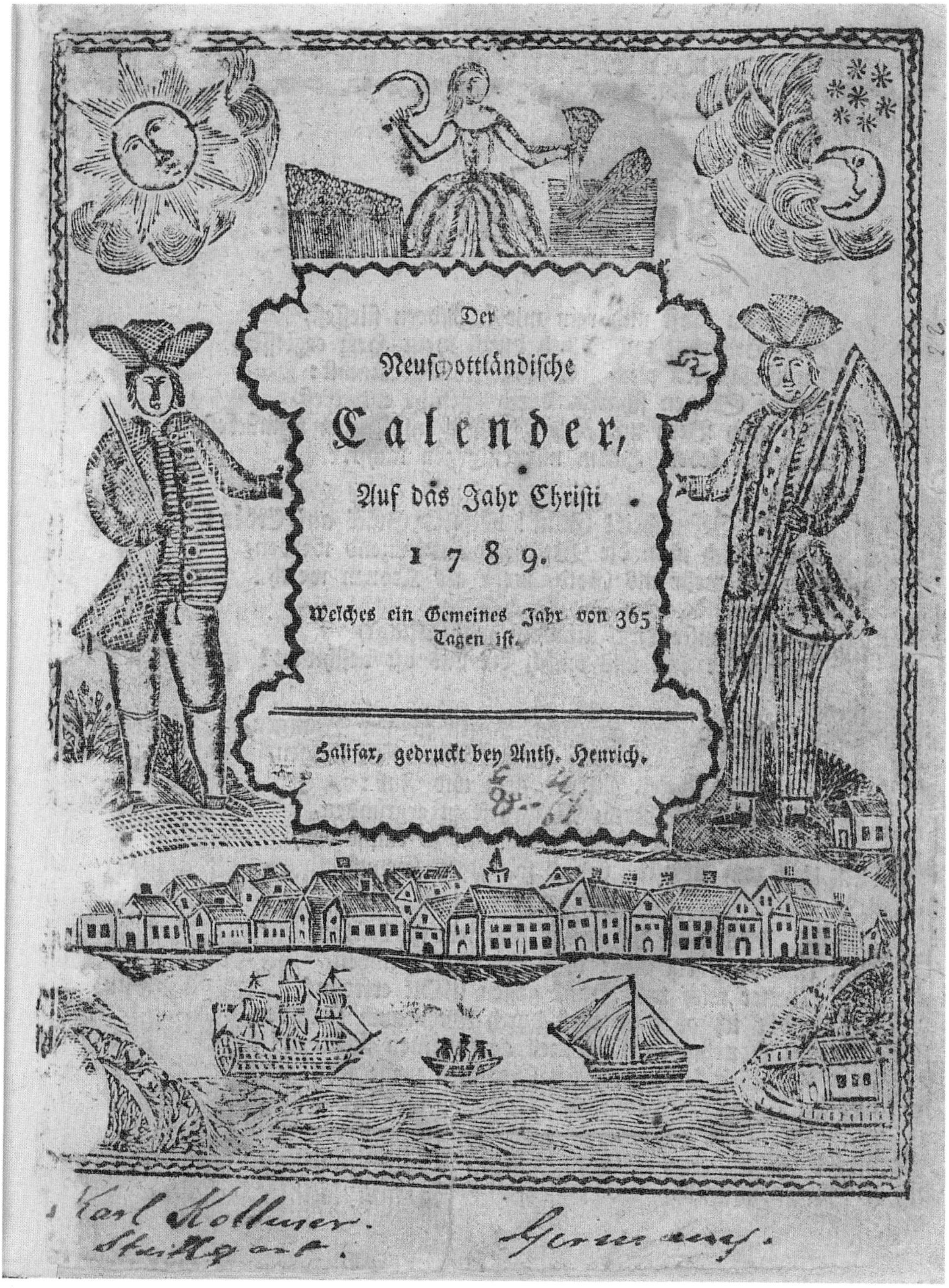
Der

Neuschottländische

Calender,

Auf das Jahr Christi

1789.

Welches ein Gemeines Jahr von 365 Tagen ist.

Halifax, gedruckt bey Anth. Henrich.

Der Neuschottländische Calender Auf das Jahr Christi 1789. Halifax: Anthony Henry, 1788. Title page.

National Archives of Canada: Library (Negative no. C-105286).

French-Canadian Portraiture, circa 1800

This portrait is an example of the most significant development in Canadian fine arts of the period — the beginnings of a golden age of French Canadian painting that would stretch forward to the 1850s. Growing urban communities and increasing prosperity created a demand for painters, especially those specializing in portraiture. Painters like Robert Field in Halifax and William Berczy, who spent a portion of his career in Upper Canada, benefited from this demand, but the effects were most noticeable where the concentration of population was highest — in Quebec. Louis Dulongpré, creator of this portrait, was credited in his obituary with 3,500 oil and pastel portraits, an output almost beyond that of any other Canadian painter. Religious canvases provided some income for Quebec artists as well, but little inspiration. The tastes of the clergy were traditional and conservative.

French-Canadian painters created a distinctive Canadian portrait style, unique because it evolved when Quebec artists, cut off from study in France by the French Revolution and the Napoleonic Wars, pursued their own path. Beginning with the ornate rococo heritage of the French court, the Canadian style was tempered by sober thoughts of war and revolution in Europe, as well as threats of American invasion at home. The style combined a provincial naiveté with the sophistications of a European style to produce portraits that are alert, lively, and very much linked to their Canadian roots.

Louis Dulongpré (1754–1843) was a Frenchman who had studied in France and settled in Montreal after fighting in the American Revolution. He began painting portraits and religious works in the 1790s. The subject of this portrait, Joseph Papineau, was the father of the orator and politician, Louis-Joseph Papineau. Dulongpré executed four copies of it.

Joseph Papineau. Attributed to Louis Dulongpré (1754–1843). Oil on canvas, n.d. 74.3 × 61 cm.

National Archives of Canada: Documentary Art and Photography Division (Negative no. C-95591).

VIII

Seeds for Sale, circa 1764–1773

Like literature and the fine arts, science was in its infancy in Canada before 1815. One area of considerable amateur and professional interest was botany. Many letters of the period refer to seeds being sent abroad to relatives and friends. Here, on a more ambitious scale, John Wright offers to sell exotic Canadian seeds to interested gardeners in Britain. Wright was the gardener to the Governor of Quebec. As early as 1764, he was gathering large quantities of seeds to send home to "Noblemen & Gentlemen of the Society of Edinburgh," who, as he notes in this handbill, presented him with a gold medal for his efforts.

By 1767, Wright was offering to send to Britain seeds of up to 400 different species individually parceled with the proper botanical name and the soil each plant required marked on the package. Wright also imported and sold British vegetable and flower seeds as well as fruit trees and roses, thus also encouraging the acclimatization of British plants to Canada. Wright returned to Britain in late 1772 or 1773.

All the available information on Wright comes from various advertisments in the official government newspaper, the *Quebec Gazette*. The National Archives holds an extensive subject and nominal index for the *Gazette*, 1764 to 1823.

2336

A

CATALOGUE

OF

TREES, SHRUBS, FLOWERS and HERBS,

DISCOVERED IN

CANADA, in NORTH-AMERICA,

By JOHN WRIGHT, GARDINER and SURVEYOR of his MAJESTY's Cardens, in the CITY of QUEBEC. Collector of American Seeds, for a Society of Noblemen and Gentlemen in Scotland, and Sold by him, on the cheapest Terms, at QUEBEC.

TREES and SHRUBS.

PLANTS.

N. B. Noblemen, Gentlemen and others wanting any of the above Plants or Seeds, may depend on being served on the most reasonable Terms: and whatever new Discoveries he may make in America, shall always think it his greatest Ambition to serve the Curious. Commissions are taken in only at the New-York Coffee-House, Sweeting's-Alley, Cornhill, London: in Scotland, by Mr. Wright, Nursery-Man, at Leith; and at Quebec by the above John Wright.---He will establish a Correspondent in London, to whose Care he will entrust such Seeds and Plants as may be ordered for Ireland, or any Part of England. It will be most proper to send Orders as early as possible, that there may be sufficient Time to procure the Seeds or Plants required. Mr. Wright has been several Years in America collecting Seeds for a Society of Noblemen and Gentlemen, who have testified their Approbation of his Care by making him a Present of a Gold Medal. As he intends pursuing farther Discoveries, he hopes the Curious will, as they see his Merit deserve, give him their Orders, which will be attended to with the utmost exactness.

A Catalogue of Trees, Shrubs, Flowers and Herbs Discovered in Canada . . . . John Wright. [London], circa 1764–1772. Broadside.

National Archives of Canada, Manuscript Division, Dartmouth papers, MG 23, A 1, vol. 2, p. 2336.

Fishing on the Montmorency River, 1782

Except for native games, very little in the way of organized team sports existed in Canada before 1815. Summer activities consisted mainly of picnicking, hunting and fishing — and as the habitants' wealth of fish in this watercolour suggests, fine clothes and fancy equipment did not always lead to the best catch.

One young British soldier fishing for salmon very near to Montmorency in 1815 recounted the sentiments that have led generations of Canadians to brave sunburn, heat and mosquitoes in search of fish:

> At last — never shall I forget that moment — in a sweeping eddy, almost under a rock, I had a splendid rise — hooked my fish and away he went. . . he had run me out about five-and-twenty yards of line, when he leaped out of the water, and tried all sorts of manoeuvres to disengage himself. . . . I succeeded in killing my fish. . . . It weighed nearly ten pounds, and, as may be imagined, I was not a little elated at my success . . . to a youngster as I then was, and passionately fond of fishing withal, the sensation I experienced on taking my first fish is scarcely to be defined. . . . Never to my latest breath shall I cease to remember this eventful day.[1]

This view, with its delicate shading and striking luminosity, is perhaps the finest surviving example of James Peachey's work.

[1]Frederick Tolfrey, *The Sportsman in Canada*, 2 vols. (London: 1845), I, pp. 82–83.

A View on Montmorenci River.... James Peachey (fl. 1773–1797). Hand-coloured etching, 1782. 42.8 × 61.0 cm.

National Archives of Canada: Documentary Art and Photography Division (Negative no. C-2024).

A Dance in the Château St. Louis, 1801

Many travellers remarked that British North America had only two seasons — summer and winter. Winter was the prime time for leisure activities, and no region was more fond of skating, sleighing and partying than French Canada. In this view, warmed by fireplaces and lit by candlelight, a "danse à la ronde" is performed amidst the rich surroundings of the Château St. Louis, the Governor's residence where soirées were held once or twice a week in winter. The dancers, in a mixture of elegant dress (fashion was only about a year behind London and Paris) and local costume, present a study in contrast as do the observers in the background, many of whom are in habitant dress. Music is provided by a country fiddler and tambourines. Similar if more modest gatherings occurred at all levels of British North American society, with dancing, card playing and feasting.

George Heriot (1759–1839) sketched extensively during his travels as Deputy Postmaster-General of British North America. His works, a number of which accompany his classic, picturesque *Travels through the Canadas* (1807), are a valuable record of early Canadian life. The National Archives holds seventy-three Heriot watercolours and wash drawings, including a sketch book, as well as many aquatints and engravings after his works.

Dance in the Château St. Louis. George Heriot (1759–1839). Watercolour, 1801. 24.6 × 37.6 cm.

National Archives of Canada: Documentary Art and Photography Division (Negative no. C-40).

IX

Social Conditions

Perhaps in no area of life did the late eighteenth and early nineteenth century differ more from our own time than in its attitude to the provision of health and welfare systems. Available services were much more limited and less effective. Social problems like alcoholism, inadequate health care, violence and social disorder, however, were as great or greater a concern, relative to the scale of society, as in our own time.

IX

Lottery Tickets, 1781

In eighteenth-century and early nineteenth-century Canada, it was not seen as the role of government to build schools, hospitals, orphanages or other community facilities. Their creation relied largely upon the churches and individual charity — often in the form of lotteries.

Now exceptionally rare, these first-class tickets in the 1781 Halifax Public School Lottery sold for 20 shillings (about $2.50) each. They could win up to 4,250 pounds ($10,500). The sponsors were attempting to raise 750 pounds ($1,875).

Halifax Public School Lottery Tickets, 1781.

National Archives of Canada: Manuscript Division, MG 9, B 9-23.

A Mutual Insurance Club, circa 1805

Destitution due to serious illness, old age or the death of a bread-winner were terrifying threats to many Canadians before 1815 and indeed for more than a century thereafter. Provision for sickness or death were a heavy burden borne almost entirely by the individual. One solution was for individuals (almost invariably men) to band together in "friendly societies," pooling their funds for mutual aid.

The Quebec Benevolent Society, whose general regulations are exhibited here, was founded in Québec City in 1789 with twenty members. It grew to 238 by 1808. Candidates for membership had to be between twenty-one and forty-five years old and in good health. They paid an initiation fee and monthly dues. In return, they received modest benefits of 20 shillings ($2.50) per week for the first twelve weeks of illness or disability and half that rate thereafter. Lump sums of £10 ($25.00) were paid on the death of a member's wife or for a member's funeral. A widow and her family could receive £50 ($125.00) on a vote of the membership.

The society drew its members from both the French and English communities in Québec City and was proud of its role in reducing the increasing tensions between the two groups.

Although the society claimed to draw its members from "all ranks of society," only the financially comfortable could have afforded to join it. Such societies were rare and unlikely to exist outside urban areas. Beyond their own resources and those of their kin, the vast majority of people would have had little or no protection in the face of serious illness or death.

Then, as now, advertising was important to insurance services. This manuscript copy of the Quebec Benevolent Society's regulations, written about 1805, comes from the papers of John Neilson, proprietor of the *Quebec Gazette*. He probably used this manuscript to typeset a pamphlet of which he produced 400 copies for the society. The order books of the printing firm are in the Neilson collection at the National Archives. They are a valuable source to historians and to students of literature who use them to study ephemeral publications — pamphlets, official notices, advertisements, playbills — for many of which no copies now survive.

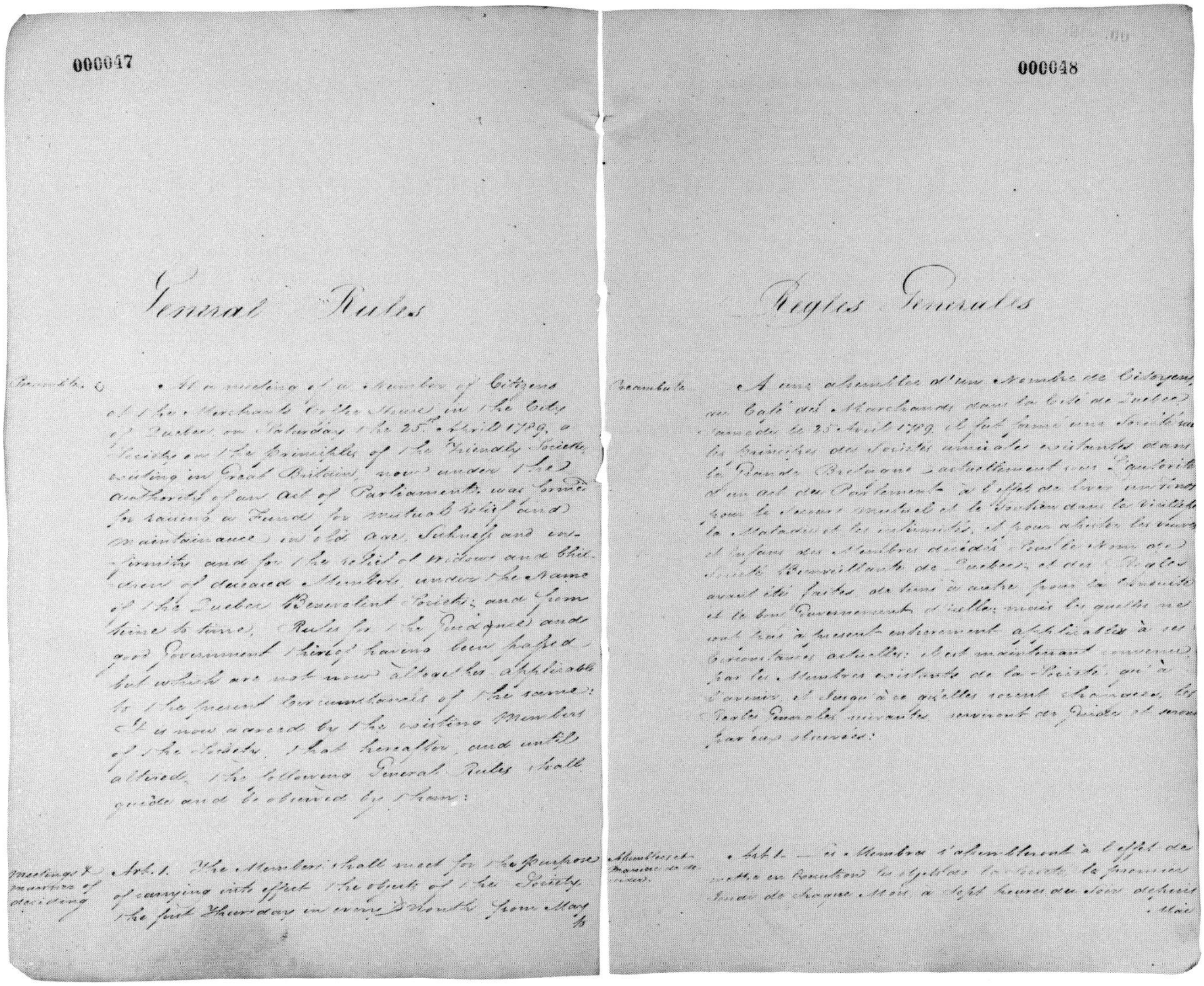

000047

General Rules

Preamble. At a meeting of a Number of Citizens at the Merchants Coffee House, in the City of Quebec, on Saturday the 25th April 1789, a Society on the principles of the Friendly Societies existing in Great Britain, now under the authority of an Act of Parliament, was formed for raising a Fund for mutual relief and maintainance in old age, Sickness and infirmity and for the relief of widows and children of deceased Members under the Name of the Quebec Benevolent Society; and from time to time, Rules for the guidance and good Government thereof having been passed but which are not now altogether applicable to the present circumstances of the same: It is now agreed by the existing Members of the Society, that hereafter, and until altered, the following General Rules shall guide and be observed by them:

Meetings & manner of deciding. Art. 1. The Members shall meet for the purpose of carrying into effect the objects of the Society the first Thursday in every Month from May to

000048

Règles Générales

Preambule. A une assemblée d'un Nombre de Citoyens au Café des Marchands dans la Cité de Québec samedi le 25 Avril 1789, il fut formé une Société sur les principes des Sociétés amicales existantes dans la Grande Bretagne, actuellement sous l'autorité d'un acte du Parlement, à l'effet de lever un fonds pour le secours mutuel et le soutien dans la vieillesse la Maladie et les infirmités, et pour assister les veuves et enfans des Membres décédés, sous le Nom de Société Bienveillante de Québec; et des Règles ayant été faites de tems à autre pour la conduite et le bon Gouvernement d'icelle, mais lesquelles ne sont pas à present entièrement applicables à ses circonstances actuelles: Il est maintenant convenu par les Membres existants de la Société, qu'à l'avenir, et jusqu'à ce qu'elles soient changées, les Règles Générales suivantes servent de Guide et soient par eux observées:

Assemblées et manière de décider. Art. 1. — Les Membres s'assembleront à l'effet de mettre en exécution les objets de la Société, le premier Jeudi de chaque Mois, à sept heures du Soir, depuis Mai

Quebec City Benevolent Society Membership Book. John Neilson (1776–1848). Manuscript volume, 1789–1808.

National Archives of Canada: Manuscript Division, Neilson papers, MG 24, B 1, vol. 26, pp. 47–48.

IX

The Inmates of a Hospital at Montreal, 1814–1815

More than in our own day, hospitals were the last refuge of the impoverished, the very old and the abandoned. In the first list of hospital inmates, the number of elderly is very noticeable, while the "salle de refuge" is not an area we would associate with a modern hospital. The young boys listed are all five years old or younger. The second list of young children entering the hospital in 1814 and 1815 seems particularly shocking: 57 per cent of them died within a few months of admission.

Various lists for hospitals, orphanages, insane asylums and prisons of this period are scattered through official and private papers at the National Archives. They provide rare insights into these early social and charitable institutions.

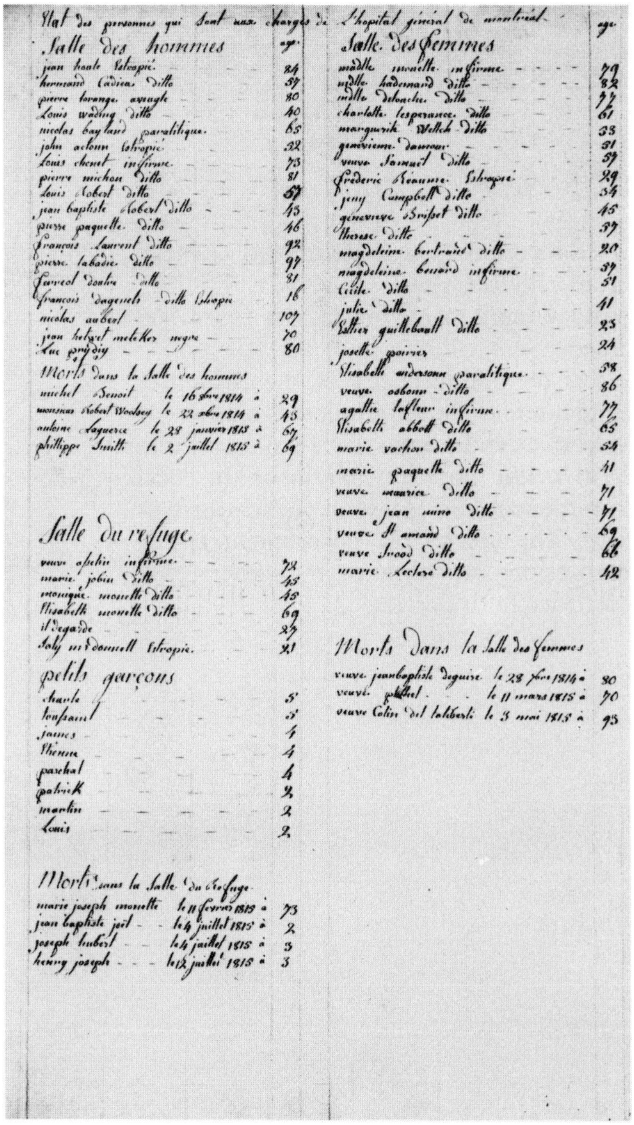

Etat des personnes qui sont aux charges de l'hopital général de montréal

Salle des hommes	age
jean haule estropié	84
hermenegilde Cadieux ditto	57
pierre lorange aveugle	80
Louis wading ditto	40
nicolas bayland paralitique	65
john acleum estropié	32
Louis chenet infirme	73
pierre michon ditto	81
Louis Robert ditto	57
jean baptiste Robert ditto	45
pierre paquette ditto	46
françois Laurent ditto	92
pierre labadie ditto	97
Ferreol Dontre(?) ditto	81
françois dagenets ditto estropie	16
nicolas aubert	107
jean helzet melcher negre	70
Luc prydiy(?)	80

Morts dans la salle des hommes

michel Benoit le 16 9bre 1814 à	29
monsieur Robert Woolsey le 22 xbre 1814 à	45
antoine Laguerre le 28 janvier 1815 à	67
phillippe Smith le 2 juillet 1815 à	69

Salle du refuge	
veuve aselin infirme	72
marie jobin ditto	45
monique monette ditto	45
Elisabeth monette ditto	69
il degarde	27
Saly mcdonnell estropie	21

petits garçons	
charle	5
constant	5
james	4
etienne	4
paschal	4
patrick	3
martin	2
Louis	2

Morts dans la salle du refuge

marie joseph monette le 11 fevrier 1815 à	73
jean baptiste joel le 4 juillet 1815 à	2
joseph hubert le 4 juillet 1815 à	3
henry joseph le 12 juillet 1815 à	3

Salle des femmes	age
madlle monette infirme	79
madlle hudonnard(?) ditto	82
madlle delorche(?) ditto	77
charlotte lesperance ditto	61
marguerite Welch ditto	33
genevieve dameau(?)	31
veuve Samuel ditto	57
Frederic Beaume estropie	29
jeny Campbell ditto	34
genevieve Brisset ditto	45
therese ditto	37
magdeleine bertrand ditto	20
magdeleine benard infirme	37
Cecile ditto	51
julie ditto	41
Esther guillebeault ditto	23
josette poirier	24
Elisabeth anderson paralitique	58
veuve osborn ditto	86
agathe lafleur infirme	77
Elisabeth abbott ditto	65
marie vachon ditto	54
marie paquette ditto	41
veuve maurice ditto	71
veuve jean mire ditto	71
veuve St amand ditto	69
veuve Frood ditto	66
marie Leclere ditto	42

Morts dans la salle des femmes

veuve jeanbaptiste deguire le 28 9bre 1814 à	80
veuve gibbel(?) le 11 mars 1815 à	70
veuve Colin del Lalberti(?) le 3 mai 1815 à	93

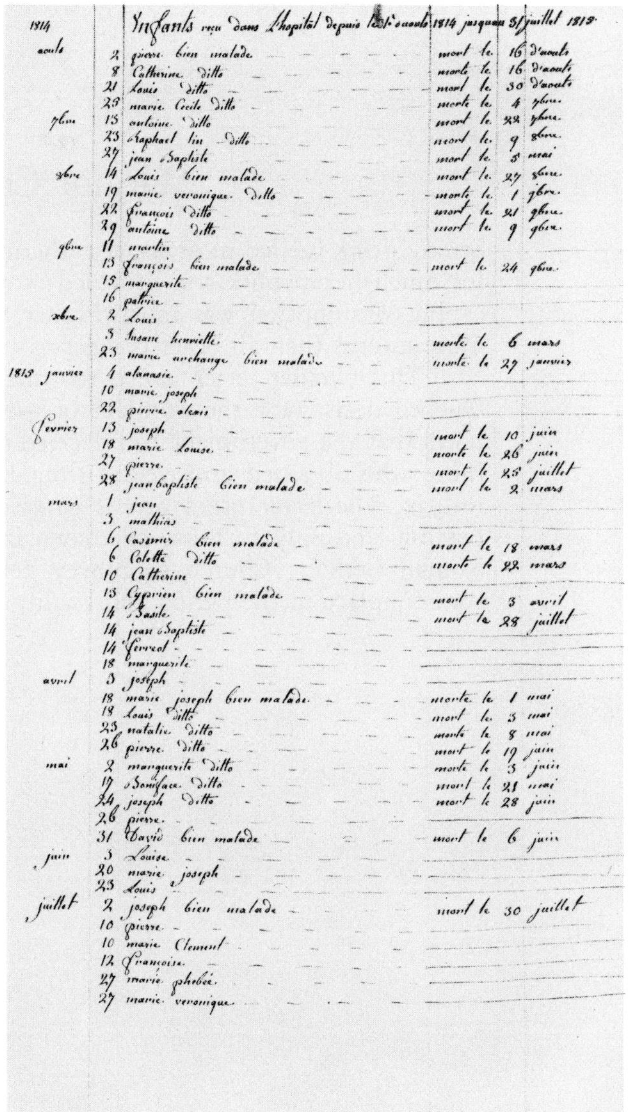

1814		Enfants reçu dans l'hopital depuis le 1er aout 1814 jusqu'au 31 juillet 1815	
aout	2	pierre bien malade	mort le 16 d'aout
	8	Catherine ditto	morte le 16 d'aout
	21	Louis ditto	mort le 30 d'aout
	25	marie Cecile ditto	morte le 4 7bre
7bre	15	antoine ditto	mort le 22 7bre
	23	Raphael lin ditto	mort le 9 8bre
	27	jean Baptiste	mort le 5 mai
8bre	14	Louis bien malade	mort le 27 8bre
	19	marie veronique ditto	morte le 1 9bre
	22	françois ditto	mort le 21 9bre
	29	antoine ditto	mort le 9 9bre
9bre	11	martin	
	13	françois bien malade	mort le 24 9bre
	15	marguerite	
	16	patrice	
xbre	2	Louis	
	5	Susanne henriette	morte le 6 mars
	23	marie archange bien malade	morte le 29 janvier
1815 janvier	4	alanasie	
	10	marie joseph	
	22	pierre alexis	
fevrier	13	joseph	mort le 10 juin
	18	marie Louise	morte le 26 juin
	27	pierre	mort le 25 juillet
	28	jean baptiste bien malade	mort le 2 mars
mars	1	jean	
	3	mathias	
	6	Casimir bien malade	mort le 18 mars
	6	Colette ditto	morte le 22 mars
	10	Catherine	
	13	Cyprien bien malade	mort le 3 avril
	14	Basile	mort le 28 juillet
	14	jean Baptiste	
	14	Ferreol	
	18	marguerite	
avril	3	joseph	
	18	marie joseph bien malade	morte le 1 mai
	18	Louis ditto	mort le 3 mai
	23	natalie ditto	morte le 8 mai
	26	pierre ditto	mort le 19 juin
mai	2	marguerite ditto	morte le 3 juin
	17	Boniface ditto	mort le 21 mai
	24	joseph ditto	mort le 28 juin
	26	pierre	
	31	David bien malade	mort le 6 juin
juin	3	Louise	
	20	marie joseph	
	23	Louis	
juillet	2	joseph bien malade	mort le 30 juillet
	10	pierre	
	10	marie Clement	
	12	françoise	
	27	marie phebee	
	27	marie veronique	

Montreal Hospital Returns, 1815.

National Archives of Canada: Manuscript Division, Executive Council: Lower Canada. Board of Audit of the Provincial Public Accounts, 1759–1841, RG 1 5A, vol. 292, unpaginated.

IX

Liquor Control, 1787

Strong drink fuelled most social gatherings of this period. It was considered essential for much heavy work and provided escape from the dreariness of everyday life. Per capita consumption was much higher than today, and many towns and cities had more taverns than all other businesses combined.

This circular letter issued to parish priests on the authority of the Bishop of Quebec deals with the problem of over-abundant and under-regulated taverns. It notes that the government had decreed that tavern licences were to be issued only to those who obtained attestations from the local priest and the captain of the local militia. The letter urges priests to give recommendations to as few individuals as possible and only to those of known integrity. The use by the government of the Roman Catholic Church to convey new instructions and enforce regulations was commonplace in the period and readily accepted by both parties.

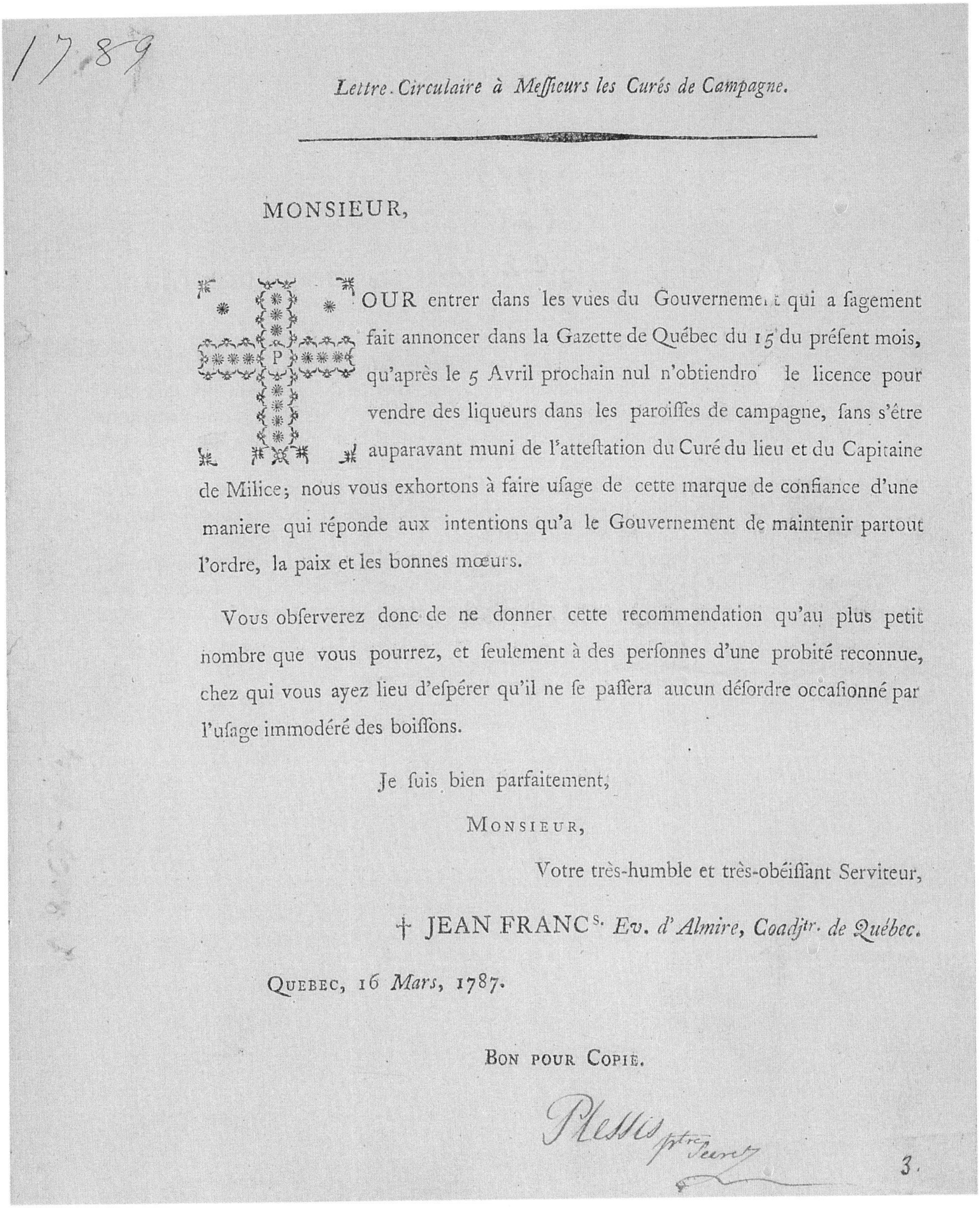

1789

Lettre Circulaire à Meſſieurs les Curés de Campagne.

MONSIEUR,

POUR entrer dans les vues du Gouvernement qui a ſagement fait annoncer dans la Gazette de Québec du 15 du préſent mois, qu'après le 5 Avril prochain nul n'obtiendroit le licence pour vendre des liqueurs dans les paroiſſes de campagne, ſans ſ'être auparavant muni de l'atteſtation du Curé du lieu et du Capitaine de Milice; nous vous exhortons à faire uſage de cette marque de confiance d'une maniere qui réponde aux intentions qu'a le Gouvernement de maintenir partout l'ordre, la paix et les bonnes mœurs.

Vous obſerverez donc de ne donner cette recommendation qu'au plus petit nombre que vous pourrez, et ſeulement à des perſonnes d'une probité reconnue, chez qui vous ayez lieu d'eſpérer qu'il ne ſe paſſera aucun déſordre occaſionné par l'uſage immodéré des boiſſons.

Je ſuis bien parfaitement,

MONSIEUR,

Votre très-humble et très-obéiſſant Serviteur,

† JEAN FRANC^S. *Ev. d'Almire, Coadj^tr. de Québec.*

QUEBEC, 16 *Mars*, 1787.

BON POUR COPIE.

Plessis ptre Secret.

3.

Circular letter to parish priests, March 1787. Broadside.

National Archives of Canada: Library (Negative no. C-130539).

IX

The Petition of a Thief Against the Branding of His Hand, 1795

Justice was often ineffective in early British North America and partially because of that, extremely harsh. Colonists often petitioned their local governments that they did not have enough law-enforcement officers, that prisons were non-existent or decrepit and that lawlessness was rampant and unchecked. At times, the only way to stop crime seemed to be to issue stern, even brutal, sentences.

Here a petty criminal, sentenced to six months for stealing a modest amount of woolen cloth, petitions for remission of the second part of the sentence — that he be branded on the hand. He was granted a pardon by Lord Dorchester.

Historians and social scientists have recently begun to study crime and punishment in early British North America using court records and related material like this petition in an attempt to better understand social disorder and its causes.

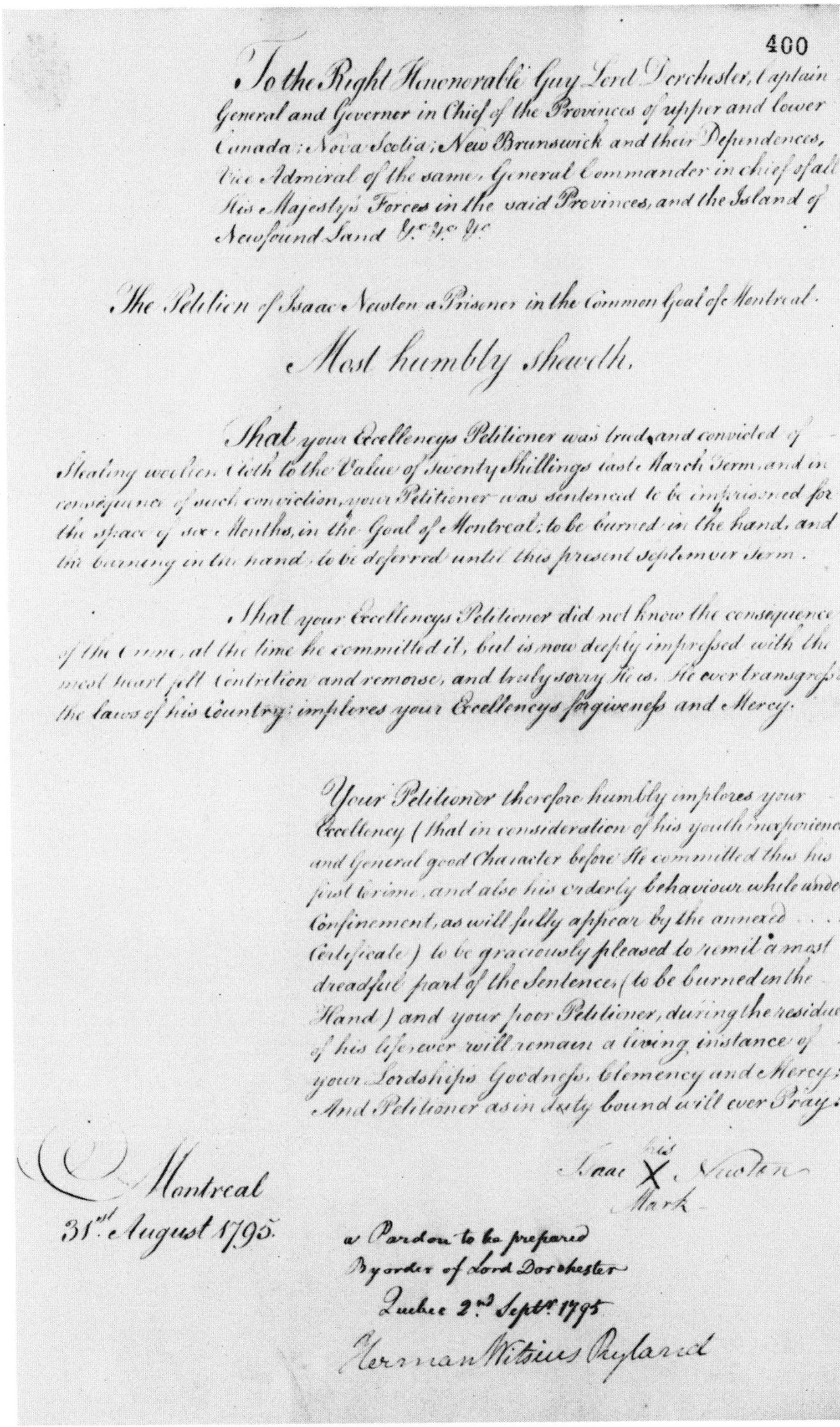
400

To the Right Honorable Guy Lord Dorchester, Captain General and Governor in Chief of the Provinces of upper and lower Canada; Nova Scotia; New Brunswick and their Dependences, Vice Admiral of the same, General Commander in chief of all His Majesty's Forces in the said Provinces, and the Island of Newfound Land &c. &c. &c.

The Petition of Isaac Newton a Prisoner in the Common Goal of Montreal.

Most humbly sheweth.

That your Excellencys Petitioner was tried, and convicted of Stealing woollen Cloth to the Value of twenty Shillings last March Term, and in consequence of such conviction, your Petitioner was sentenced to be imprisoned for the space of six Months, in the Goal of Montreal; to be burned in the hand, and the burning in the hand to be deferred until this present September Term.

That your Excellencys Petitioner did not know the consequence of the Crime, at the time he committed it, but is now deeply impressed with the most heart felt Contrition and remorse, and truly sorry He ev. He ever transgressed the laws of his Country; implores your Excellencys forgiveness and Mercy.

Your Petitioner therefore humbly implores your Excellency (that in consideration of his youth inexperience and General good Character before He committed this his first Crime, and also his orderly behaviour while under Confinement, as will fully appear by the annexed Certificate) to be graciously pleased to remit a most dreadful part of the Sentence (to be burned in the Hand) and your poor Petitioner, during the residue of his life, ever will remain a living instance of your Lordships Goodness, Clemency and Mercy; And Petitioner as in duty bound will ever Pray.

Montreal
31st. August 1795.

Isaac his X Mark Newton

a Pardon to be prepared
By order of Lord Dorchester
Quebec 2nd Septr. 1795
Herman Witsius Ryland

Petition of Isaac Newton against the burning of his hand, 1795.

National Archives of Canada: Manuscript Division, Provincial and Civil Secretaries' Offices, Lower Canada. Applications for Pardons or Clemency, 1767–1857. RG 4, B 20, vol. 1, p. 400.

X

Native Peoples

In eastern and central British North America, the presence of European colonists had become an established fact for native peoples, and much of their energies were focused on coping with the complications arising from that situation. Further west and in the North, where the white presence was less dominating, native cultures continued much more to follow their own rhythm. Native societies of this period generated little documentation that has been placed in modern archives; surviving white documentation, however, often contributes substantially to understanding their cultures.

X

An Important Fragment in the Beothuk Puzzle, 1768

The final result of contact with whites for small and weak Indian tribes could be extinction.

Having occupied areas of the island of Newfoundland for more than 1,000 years, the Beothuks by the eighteenth century had retreated into the sparsely populated area of Notre Dame Bay. Continuing white pressures and violence wiped them out completely by 1829. They disappeared almost without a trace; their habitations disintegrated and their sites were destroyed by new settlements or washed away. Very few artifacts have survived. This lack of archaeological evidence gives very special significance to the maps and accounts of Captain John Cartwright R.N. (1740–1824), which were based on an expedition he undertook in 1768 at the request of Governor Palliser of Newfoundland to make contact with the Beothuk.

This map, along with two others and a lengthy report on his excursion, were sent by Cartwright in 1773 to the Earl of Dartmouth, Secretary of State for the Colonies, in the vain hope of eliciting aid for the Beothuks. The map is packed with information — it shows the position of the Beothuk wigwams and square dwellings along the Exploits River, Indian "deer foils" (caribou fences), and areas with "sewels." Figures from 1 and 6 along the river mark the positions of Cartwright's party at the end of each day of travel, and hand-written notes contain geological observations.

Scholars have used the number of dwellings on the map to estimate the Indian population in 1768 — about 350. Equally important are the illustrations, the most detailed depictions of Beothuk artifacts now in existence. They include a distinctive canoe and paddle, a summer *mamateek* (wigwam), a bow and arrow, quivers, rectangular and round containers, an axe and "sewels" (sticks with bark tassels used to extend deer fences where tree cover was sparse). It is little enough left of a people who prior to white contact numbered more than 1,000.

The National Archives holds two other maps, (a general one of Newfoundland and a map of Triton Island and surrounding area in Notre Dame Bay) and the manuscript report "Remarks on the Situation of the Red Indians, natives of Newfoundland . . . taken on the spot in the year 1768," sent by Cartwright to Dartmouth. It is perhaps not surprising, given his sympathy for the weak and downtrodden, that Cartwright in the 1790s became a famous radical leader in British politics.

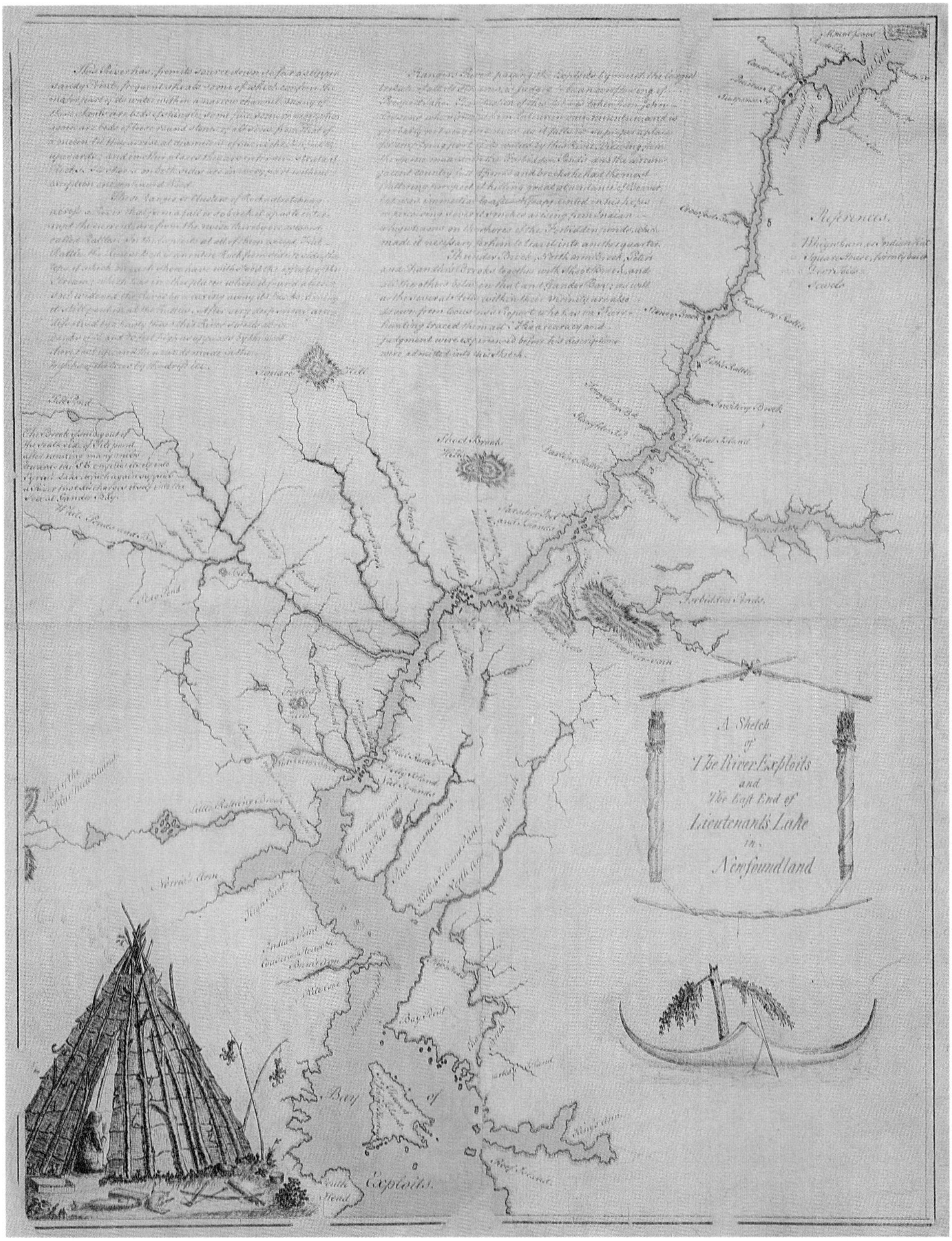

Map of the Exploits River. John Cartwright (1740–1824). Map: manuscript, hand-coloured, circa 1773. 38.8 × 30.2 cm.

National Archives of Canada: Cartographic and Architectural Archives Division (NMC 27).

X

A Symbol of Micmac Resistance, circa 1804

This Micmac catechism and grammar, written on alternate pages in Micmac and French, was transcribed by Joseph Gueguen (1741–1825) — who had himself laboured among the Micmac before the Conquest — for a new French missionary, Father Jean Mande Sigogne (1763–1844), who had arrived in 1799.

Roman Catholicism had flourished for the forty years after the Conquest, even though the Micmac had been without priests. The Micmac themselves had maintained manuscripts of what they called simply "the book" — a collection of biblical passages, a catechism, some psalms, hymns and prayers. Written in hieroglyphs on birchbark, it was copied as required.

The Micmacs were the first North Americans to come into contact with Europeans, and they had two hundred years of experience behind them when the British arrived. The gradualness of white penetration into their homeland had allowed them to come to terms with change, accept what they could and reject what they could not. They had reached an agreeable compromise with the French and they resisted the coming of the English. They maintained their band structure and clung to their Catholicism.

The Micmacs' religion was an act of defiance, commemorating their ties with the French. From the first, the Micmacs had incorporated their own beliefs into Christianity, a tendency that had been accentuated by a long absence of priests. Their religion had a strong native element, and they saw it as part of themselves. Catholicism continued to define them as a group distinct from the colonists around them, and their beliefs stiffened their will to fight assimilation.

Although the book illustrated has been a part of the Indian Affairs records in the National Archives since 1885, its significance has only recently been recognized. Native studies researchers and linguists are presently studying it in order to understand the degree to which religious terminology was assimilated into the Micmac language by the turn of the eighteenth century.

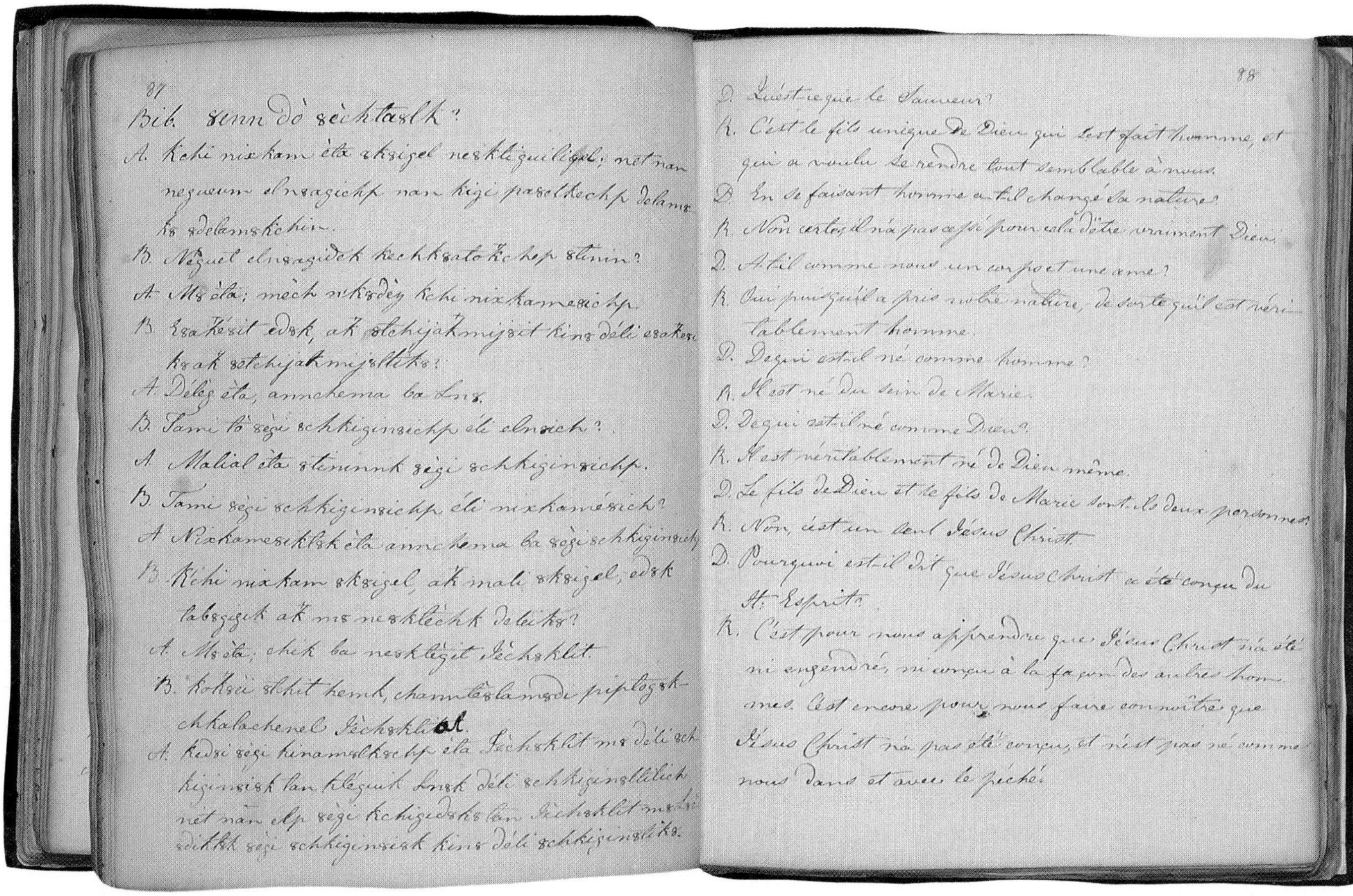
88

D. Qu'est-ce que le Sauveur?

R. C'est le fils unique de Dieu qui s'est fait homme, et qui a voulu se rendre tout semblable à nous.

D. En se faisant homme a-t-il changé sa nature?

R. Non certes, il n'a pas cessé pour cela d'être vraiment Dieu.

D. A-t-il comme nous un corps et une ame?

R. Oui puisqu'il a pris notre nature, de sorte qu'il est véritablement homme.

D. De qui est-il né comme homme?

R. Il est né du sein de Marie.

D. De qui est-il né comme Dieu?

R. Il est véritablement né de Dieu même.

D. Le fils de Dieu et le fils de Marie sont-ils deux personnes?

R. Non, c'est un seul Jésus Christ.

D. Pourquoi est-il dit que Jésus Christ a été conçu du St. Esprit?

R. C'est pour nous apprendre que Jésus Christ n'a été ni engendré, ni conçu à la façon des autres hommes. C'est encore pour nous faire connaître que Jésus Christ n'a pas été conçu, et n'est pas né comme nous dans et avec le péché.

Micmac Catechism and Grammar. Transcription attributed to Joseph Gueguen (1741–1825). Manuscript volume, circa 1804.

National Archives of Canada: Government Archives Division, Records of the Department of Indian Affairs, RG 10, vol. 738, pp. 87–88.

The Iroquois: Brother Against Brother, 1780

The Iroquois League, the most organized and powerful native grouping in northeastern North America, had its homeland in upper New York State. When the American Revolution broke upon it, the League was dismayed and puzzled by the spectacle of Englishman fighting Englishman; most Iroquois attempted to maintain an uneasy neutrality. In 1777, gifts and constant pressure finally ripped apart the "Longhouse" (as the Iroquois called their confederacy). Some supported the rebels; most remained loyal to the Crown.

These poignant speeches, recorded on the spot in Mohawk, represent a last, futile attempt to restore unity. Little Abraham (d. 1780), an elderly Mohawk leader who had remained a true neutral, led a delegation of rebel Iroquois to the British stronghold at Fort Niagara in 1780. There he and the others begged the loyal Iroquois to lay down their arms and return home, to live in peace with the Americans. The speech shown runs in part:

> We have heard one another's words once more, we who were formerly of the Long House. What has happened to us is calamitous! There is now no Long House where you and I can safely tell each other our fears . . . You, who went away, should reconsider the policy of the Long House . . . so that all our people will live again upon our former firesides and plantations, and smoke will rise again from our former cabins and all will enjoy the lordship of their lands again. This is our mind.

But it was already too late. The Americans, the previous summer, had pillaged the Iroquois lands, levelling the settlements. There was no going home again.

Little Abraham was thrown into a windowless, unheated stone vault where he died, a disillusioned man. The loyal Iroquois fought on to the end of the war, when they were granted new land by the British at Grand River and Deseronto, Ontario. There, the gradual incursion of white settlement would radically alter their way of life.

The text of this speech comes from the Claus Family papers, which date from 1755 to 1886. Several members of the family were important officials in the Indian Department both before and after the American Revolution, and the papers contain correspondence, journals, accounts, and other records of the Clauses and other Indian Department officials relating to Canada's native peoples. Because of their high informational value, the papers have undergone extensive conservation and have been microfilmed.

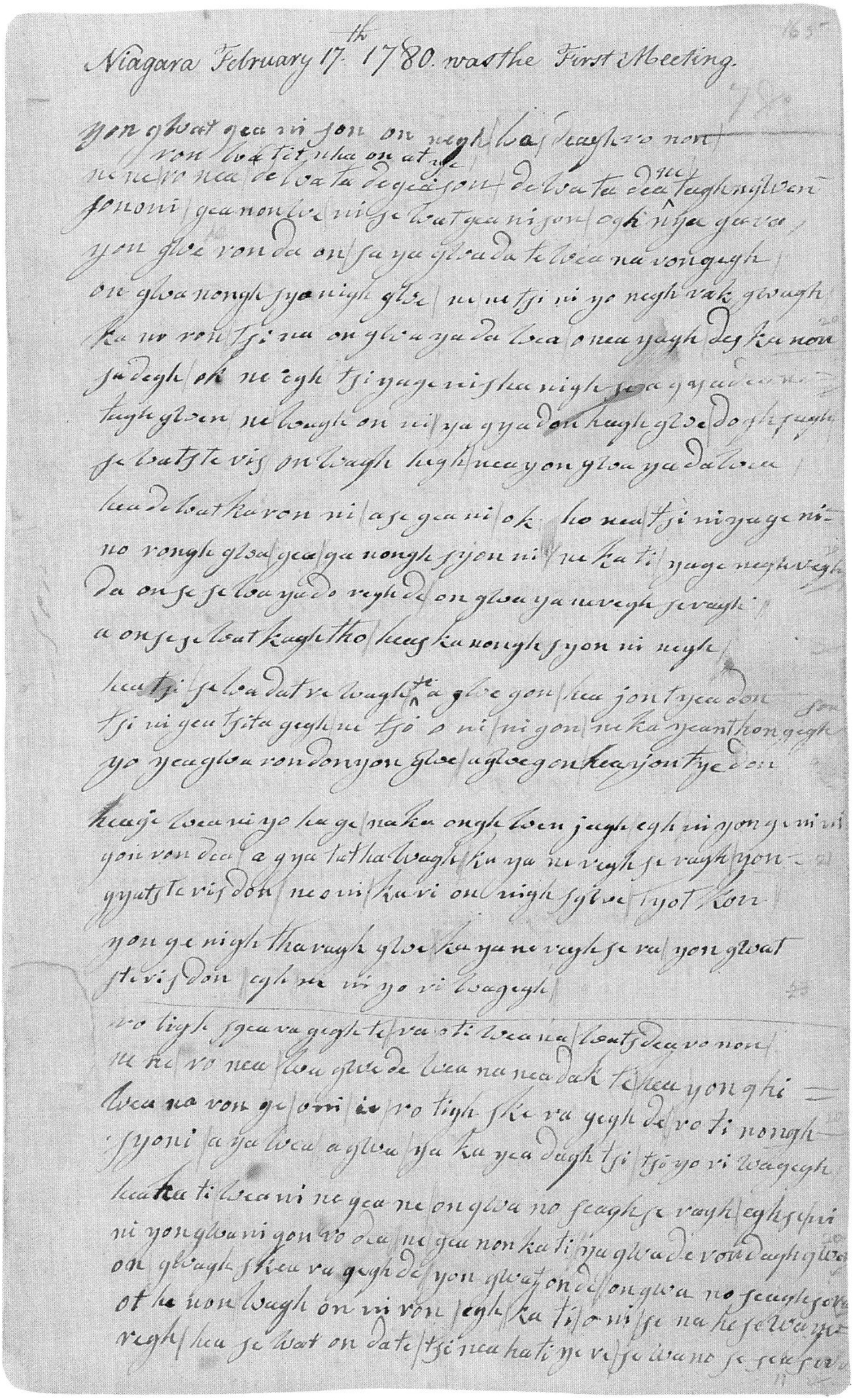
Niagara February 17th 1780 was the First Meeting.

Record of Proceedings of an Iroquois Council at Fort Niagara, 17 February 1780.

National Archives of Canada: Manuscript Division, Claus Family papers, MG 19, F 1, vol. 2, p. 165.

X

Western Indians: Dependants of the Fur Trade? 1776

Further west, the pressures of white civilization were weaker, and natives maintained their independence more easily than in the East. This contemporary copy of a letter in a fur trading post journal hints that the fur trade was as dependent upon the Indians as they were upon it. Fur traders relied upon the Indians as couriers and suppliers of provisions — two of the many basic tasks white traders could not easily accomplish on their own. Giving presents to the Indians was an accommodation by Europeans to the culture of the native peoples. Basically, the traders were dependent upon the natives for furs. If this was "a leisure time for Indians," then it was perforce a leisure time at the trading posts. The letter mentions efforts and "inducements" to "retrieve and increase" trade. In part, this was because of rivalry among fur trading companies, but even more because at this period the Indians' demands for goods were inelastic. An Indian would trap enough to satisfy his basic needs, with some left over for entertainment. So, competitive terms and lavish gifts did not increase the demand for supplies; they simply caused natives to hunt less since they could bring in fewer furs to obtain what they wanted. This is not to suggest that natives were never exploited by the fur trade, but clearly native people could still demand and receive a system of trade that in certain basic procedures conformed to their own way of life.

Like the letter exhibited as Item 54, this one is a copy of record in a fur journal.

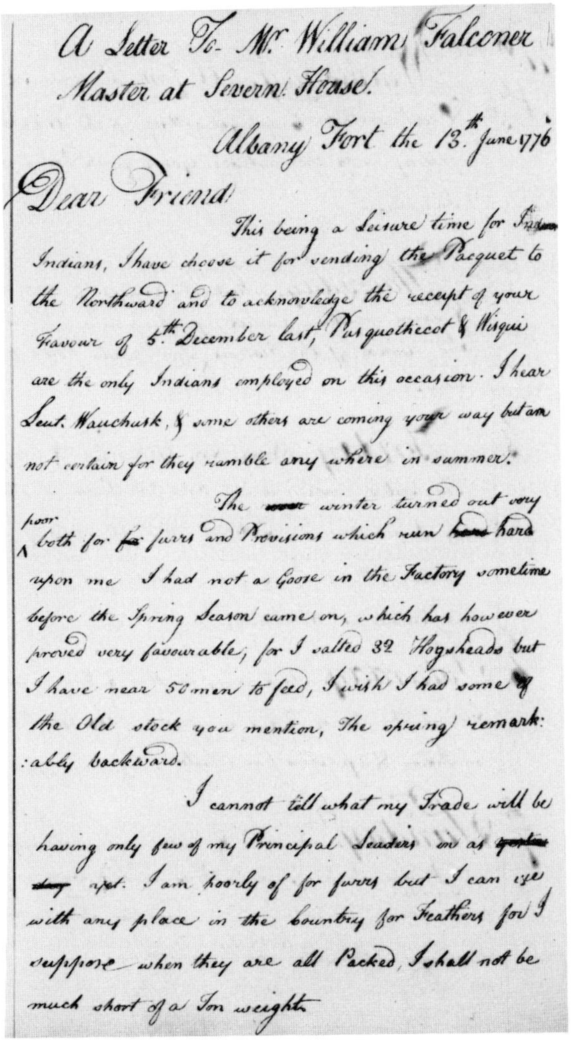

A Letter To Mr William Falconer
Master at Severn House.

Albany Fort the 13th June 1776

Dear Friend

This being a Leisure time for Indians, I have choose it for sending the Pacquet to the Northward and to acknowledge the receipt of your Favour of 5th December last, Pusquothicot & Wisqui are the only Indians employed on this occasion. I hear Lieut. Wauchusk, & some others are coming your way but am not certain for they ramble any where in summer.

The winter turned out very poor both for furrs and Provisions which run hard upon me I had not a Goose in the Factory sometime before the Spring Season came on, which has however proved very favourable; for I salted 32 Hogsheads but I have near 50 men to feed, I wish I had some of the Old stock you mention, The spring remark:ably backward.

I cannot tell what my Trade will be having only few of my Principal Leaders in as yet. I am poorly of for furrs but I can vie with any place in the Country for Feathers for I suppose when they are all Packed, I shall not be much short of a Ton weight.

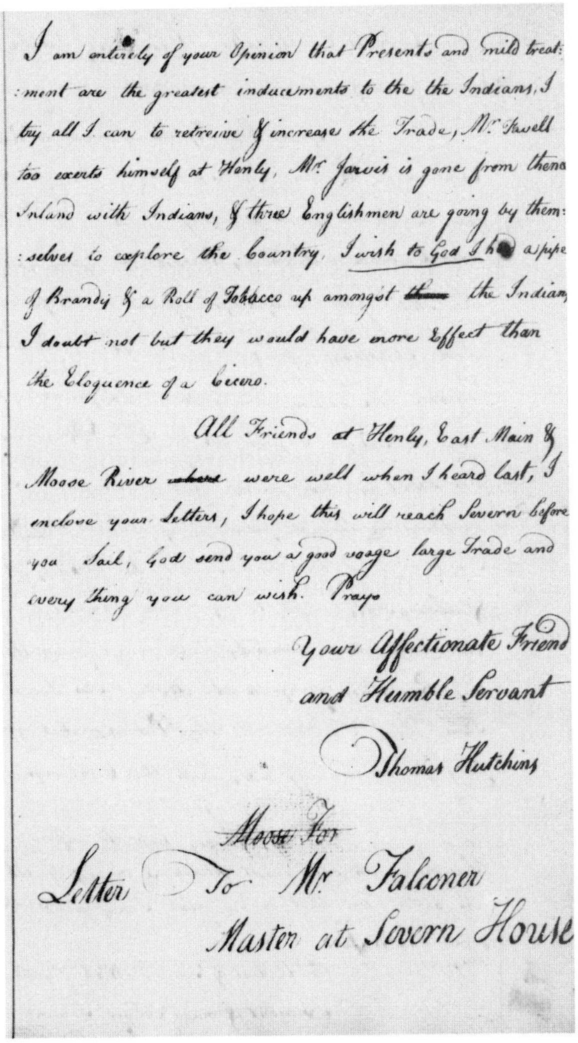

I am entirely of your Opinion that Presents and mild treat:ment are the greatest inducements to the the Indians, I try all I can to retrieve & increase the Trade, Mr Favell too exerts himself at Henly, Mr Jarvis is gone from thence Inland with Indians, & three Englishmen are going by them:selves to explore the Country, I wish to God I had a pipe of Brandy & a Roll of Tobacco up amongst the Indians I doubt not but they would have more Effect than the Eloquence of a Cicero.

All Friends at Henly, East Main & Moose River were well when I heard last, I enclose your Letters, I hope this will reach Severn before you Sail, God send you a good voyage large Trade and every thing you can wish. Prays

Your Affectionate Friend
and Humble Servant

Thomas Hutchins

~~Moose For~~

Letter To Mr Falconer
Master at Severn House

Letter, Thomas Hutchins to William Falconer, Albany Fort, 13 June 1776.

National Archives of Canada: Manuscript Division, Severn House Journal, MG 19, D 2, vol. 2, unpaginated.

The Pacific Coast, 1778

In this sketch of a Nootka communal house, the only indication of the white man's influence is the sketch itself. The building is constructed of massive cedar planks and support beams from the local forest. The planks were of great value, handed down through generations. Clothing, hats and rugs were locally made, as the loom attests. Fish, the major food supply, are being roasted and suspended on horizontal poles above a fire for drying and smoking.

Contact with white civilization for Pacific Coast natives was quite limited. When they did trade, West Coast natives rapidly acquired a reputation for their discrimination and their ability to drive a hard bargain. The confidence the Indians showed in their trading was indicative of their power. The Indians could have destroyed any of the trading vessels that visited their villages.

This pencil sketch was probably executed by John Webber on the spot during Cook's visit to Nootka in 1778 (see Item 2).

Interior of Communal House with Women Weaving, Nootka. John Webber (1751–1793). Grey wash and pencil, March-April 1778. 19.1 × 14.6 cm.

National Archives of Canada: Documentary Art and Photography Division (Negative no. C-2821).

An Extraordinary Painting of an Inuit Costume, circa 1768–1781

The Inuit, at this period the almost exclusive inhabitants of the Arctic, experienced very little contact with Europeans. The first sustained contact came between Moravian missionaries and Labrador Inuit in the 1770s. Except for this and fleeting trade at other locations, white culture had almost no impact upon them.

Rarity of contact makes information about the Inuit very valuable and gives this oil painting an exceptional ethnographic value. Among depictions of the time relating to native peoples, the work is unusual for its large size and the fact that it is an oil. The latest research suggests, moreover, that this painting is an accurate study of an authentic Labrador or Baffin Island Inuit costume modelled by a European woman in London between 1768 and 1781. The desire for thoroughness is evidenced by the presentation of both a front and a back view to capture the full costume. So great was the attention to detail that it is possible to identify the material from which the clothing was made. The wide, high boots are of special interest. The style appears to have died out in the nineteenth century, and no specimens of the boots exist today.

The artist, Angelica Kauffman (1741–1807), was a Swiss portrait painter who lived in London between 1766 and 1781. The National Archives also holds a companion oil of an Inuit man's costume.

Woman in Inuit Clothing, circa 1768–1781. Angelica Kauffman (1741–1807). Oil on canvas. 91.5 × 71.3 cm.

National Archives of Canada: Documentary Art and Photography Division (Negative no. C-95201).

XI

War of 1812

On 18 June 1812, at the height of the Napoleonic conflict, the United States declared war on Great Britain and struck at the British possessions on the continent. The immediate cause was British action on the high seas — searching American ships for goods destined for enemy ports and impressment of American sailors.

The main battles of the war took place near the international boundary in modern Ontario and Quebec. Although now half-forgotten, the war posed a serious threat that the United States would capture and absorb Canada. Many colonists — with good reason — feared the American boast that taking Canada would be "a mere matter of marching."

A Letter that Gave the British a Vital Warning, 1812

Through their commercial grapevine, the Canadian fur traders of the North West Company learned in June 1812 that the United States had declared war on Great Britain and her colonies in Canada. The merchants conveyed this electrifying news to British officials in Canada long before official channels brought word of hostilities.

A copy of this letter (this version is the British army's official deposit copy) was despatched immediately to Captain Charles Roberts, commander at St. Joseph's Island in Lake Huron, the most westerly British military post. The fur traders had worked quickly; Roberts also heard the news from a messenger from Amherstburg (Windsor) and via a letter from Major-General Isaac Brock.

As a result of the warning, the American garrison at nearby Mackinac Island awoke on the morning of 16 July to find the astonishing sight of 45 determined British redcoats, 180 voyageurs and fur traders, and 400 war-like Sioux, Chippewa, Winnebago, Menominee and Ottawa, backed by two six-pound brass cannons, demanding immediate surrender of the garrison. The dazed Americans did not even know there was a war on! They surrendered without a shot. The bloodless victory, along with the taking of Detroit, gave the British early control of the Michigan territory and the Upper Mississippi — as well as a sharp psychological edge over the supposedly "wily" Yankees.

The National Archives of Canada holds approximately 2,000 volumes of the records of the British army in Canada, which the British government agreed to leave after the army's withdrawal. They are a treasure trove of information not only on Canada's military history, but on her social and economic history as well.

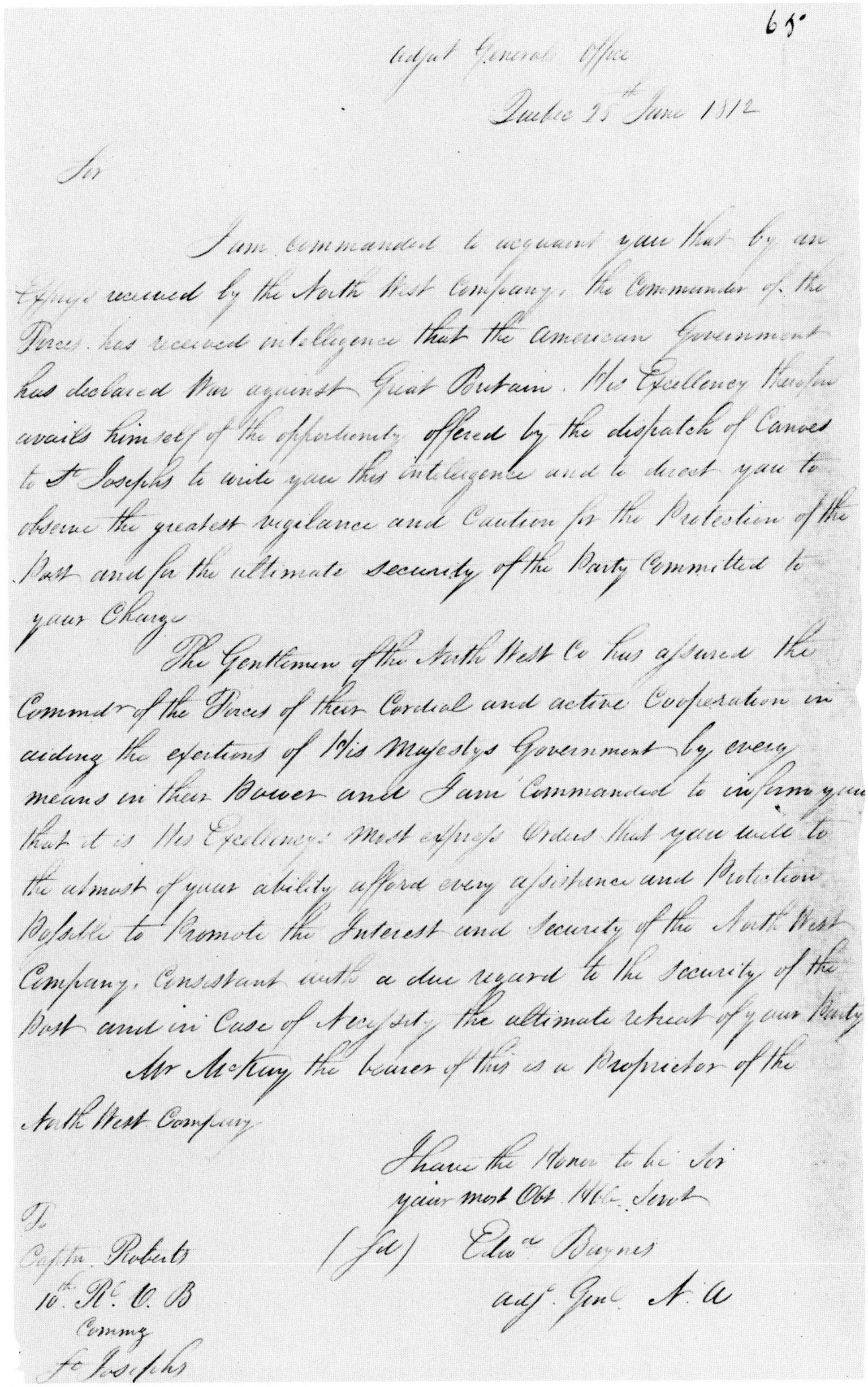

65

Adjut General's Office

Quebec 25th June 1812

Sir

I am commanded to acquaint you that by an Express received by the North West Company, the Commander of the Forces has received intelligence that the American Government has declared War against Great Britain. His Excellency therefore avails himself of the opportunity offered by the dispatch of Canoes to St Josephs to write you this intelligence and to direct you to observe the greatest vigilance and Caution for the Protection of the Post and for the ultimate security of the Party Committed to your Charge.

The Gentlemen of the North West Co has assured the Commdr of the Forces of their Cordial and active Cooperation in aiding the exertions of His Majestys Government by every means in their Power and I am Commanded to inform you that it is His Excellencys Most express Orders that you will to the utmost of your ability afford every assistance and Protection Possible to Promote the Interest and Security of the North West Company, Consistant with a due regard to the Security of the Post and in Case of Necessity the ultimate retreat of your Party.

Mr McKay the bearer of this is a Proprietor of the North West Company

I have the Honor to be Sir
your most Obt Hble Servt
(Sd) Edwd Baynes
Adjt Genl N.A

To
Captn Roberts
10th R.V.B
Commg
St Josephs

Letter, Edward Baynes, Adjutant General to Captain Charles Roberts, Quebec, 25 June 1812 [clerical copy].

National Archives of Canada: Manuscript Division, British Military and Naval Records Series, RG 8, C Series, vol. 688A, p. 65.

An Indian Ceremony to Mark the Death of Brock, 1812

Having lost in the far West, the Americans risked a second army at Queenston Heights near Niagara and lost again. The British took 925 prisoners, but at the cost of the life of their brilliant commander, Sir Isaac Brock (1769–1812).

Brock was buried in a formal but simple funeral at Fort George on 16 October 1812. On 6 November, the Indian allies of the British, chiefly Iroquois, gathered to hold a solemn council of condolence.

The Indians had played a vital role at Queenston Heights. After Brock's fall, they had recommended the circuitous path the British and Canadians used to gain the heights. Four hundred Indians, along with a platoon of black troops, served as forward skirmishers, striking terror and confusion into the American ranks while the British regulars and Canadian militia advanced to rout them.

In his address, here translated by William Claus, the Deputy Superintendent General of the Indian Department, Koseanegonte, Chief of the Cayugas, uses ritual and poetic language to offer consolation to his people's white allies who are "darkened with Grief, your Eyes dim with Tears, and your throat stopt with the force of your affliction."

This report of an Indian council comes from the British Military and Naval Records Series in the National Archives. Because, until at least the end of the War of 1812, native peoples were viewed by the government primarily as military allies, there is an extensive amount of material on Indian affairs in this series. The National Archives also holds the records of the Department of Indian Affairs and its predecessors, covering all regions of the country and dating from 1677 to the present. The records presently fill a massive 2,600 metres of shelf space.

At a General Council of Condolence held at the Council house Fort George 6th November 1812 with the Six Nations, Hurons Chippawas. Potawatamies &c.

194

C-256

Present. William Claus Esqr. Dep. Supt. General
Captain Norton
Captain J. B. Rousseaux and
several other Officers of the Indian Departmt.

Kodeaneyonte. Little Cayuga Chief Speaker

Brother. The Americans have long threatened to strike us. and in the beginning of the Summer they declared War against us. and lately they commenced Hostility by invading the Country at Queenstown in this contest which with the help of God terminated in our favor your much lamented Commander General Brock his Aid de Camp Colonel McDonell and several Warriors have fallen.

Brother. We therefore now seeing you darkened with Grief your Eyes dim with Tears, and your throat stopt with the force of your affliction. With these strings of Wampum we wipe away your Tears. that you may view clearly the surrounding objects. We clear the Passage in your throat that you may have free utterance for your thoughts. and we wipe clean from Blood the place of your abode. that you may sit there in comfort without having renewed the

remembrance

A General Council of Condolence Held at the Council House at Fort George on the Death of Brock, 6 November 1812.

National Archives of Canada: Manuscript Division, British Military and Naval Records Series, RG 8, C Series, vol. 256, p. 194.

XI

French Canada Supports the War, 1813

In contrast to its uneasy neutrality in the American Revolution, French Canada united in a whole-hearted support of the War of 1812. This *mandement* of the Bishop of Quebec in 1813 not only criticized the United States for attacking Canada, despite Britain's attempt to avoid shedding blood and to maintain the long-standing relationship of peace, friendship and commerce with Americans, but also expresses deep pride in the support French Canadians had given the war. The clergy militantly opposed the American aggression as giving aid to their mortal enemy, revolutionary France. The French Canadian aristocracy saw in the war a chance to revive their faded military glory. All of society resisted what to them was an attempt by Anglo-Saxons to subjugate and absorb French Canada.

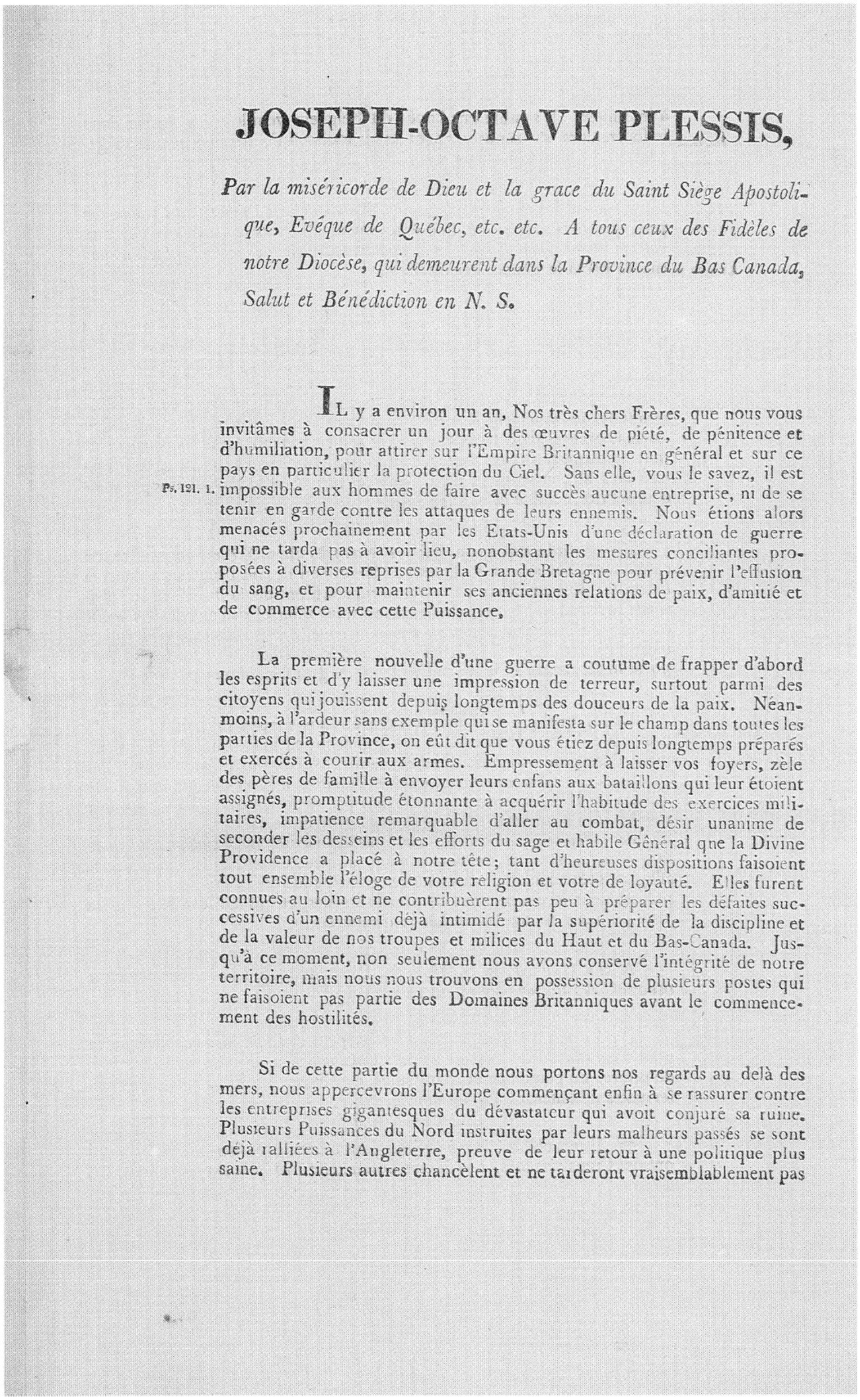

JOSEPH-OCTAVE PLESSIS,

Par la miséricorde de Dieu et la grace du Saint Siège Apostolique, Evéque de Québec, etc. etc. A tous ceux des Fidèles de notre Diocèse, qui demeurent dans la Province du Bas Canada, Salut et Bénédiction en N. S.

IL y a environ un an, Nos très chers Frères, que nous vous invitâmes à consacrer un jour à des œuvres de piété, de pénitence et d'humiliation, pour attirer sur l'Empire Britannique en général et sur ce pays en particulier la protection du Ciel. Sans elle, vous le savez, il est
Ps. 121. 1. impossible aux hommes de faire avec succès aucune entreprise, ni de se tenir en garde contre les attaques de leurs ennemis. Nous étions alors menacés prochainement par les Etats-Unis d'une déclaration de guerre qui ne tarda pas à avoir lieu, nonobstant les mesures conciliantes proposées à diverses reprises par la Grande Bretagne pour prévenir l'effusion du sang, et pour maintenir ses anciennes relations de paix, d'amitié et de commerce avec cette Puissance.

La première nouvelle d'une guerre a coutume de frapper d'abord les esprits et d'y laisser une impression de terreur, surtout parmi des citoyens qui jouissent depuis longtemps des douceurs de la paix. Néanmoins, à l'ardeur sans exemple qui se manifesta sur le champ dans toutes les parties de la Province, on eût dit que vous étiez depuis longtemps préparés et exercés à courir aux armes. Empressement à laisser vos foyers, zèle des pères de famille à envoyer leurs enfans aux bataillons qui leur étoient assignés, promptitude étonnante à acquérir l'habitude des exercices militaires, impatience remarquable d'aller au combat, désir unanime de seconder les desseins et les efforts du sage et habile Général que la Divine Providence a placé à notre tête; tant d'heureuses dispositions faisoient tout ensemble l'éloge de votre religion et votre de loyauté. Elles furent connues au loin et ne contribuèrent pas peu à préparer les défaites successives d'un ennemi déjà intimidé par la supériorité de la discipline et de la valeur de nos troupes et milices du Haut et du Bas-Canada. Jusqu'à ce moment, non seulement nous avons conservé l'intégrité de notre territoire, mais nous nous trouvons en possession de plusieurs postes qui ne faisoient pas partie des Domaines Britanniques avant le commencement des hostilités.

Si de cette partie du monde nous portons nos regards au delà des mers, nous appercevrons l'Europe commençant enfin à se rassurer contre les entreprises gigantesques du dévastateur qui avoit conjuré sa ruine. Plusieurs Puissances du Nord instruites par leurs malheurs passés se sont déjà ralliées à l'Angleterre, preuve de leur retour à une politique plus saine. Plusieurs autres chancèlent et ne tarderont vraisemblablement pas

Mandement of Bishop Plessis, 22 April 1813. Pamphlet.

National Archives of Canada: Library (Negative no. C-130549).

Châteauguay, 1813: A Key French-Canadian Victory

The year 1813 was a dark one for Canada: the Americans won major victories in the west; burned York (Toronto) and carried out intensive, if finally unsuccessful, attacks in the Niagara Peninsula. Late in the fall, the Americans launched a two-pronged attack on Montreal. One force of 4,000 regular troops advanced up the Châteauguay River to within 15 miles of the St. Lawrence River. There they were met by a small force — only about 500 of them actually engaged in the battle — consisting of French Canadian militia and some Upper Canadian Scots. The core of the force was the Canadian Voltigeurs, who had been drilled all the previous winter by their leader, Lieutenant-Colonel Charles de Salaberry (1778–1829), a French Canadian career officer in the British army with wide experience in the Napoleonic Wars.

As this map shows, de Salaberry chose carefully the position where he would meet the Americans — the spot where the road on which they were advancing veered near the river and was bordered on the other side by swamp. After prolonged skirmishing in which de Salaberry cleverly deployed his men to suggest a much larger force, the Americans lost their nerve and withdrew. The second American army was later defeated at Crysler's Farm.

Châteauguay was a small battle, but a handful of Canadian militia, some only partially trained, resisted and turned back an attack by American regulars. Montreal was saved, and its loss could well have cost the war.

This plan was prepared in August 1814 by the British military for its own reference from a sketch done by de Salaberry himself.

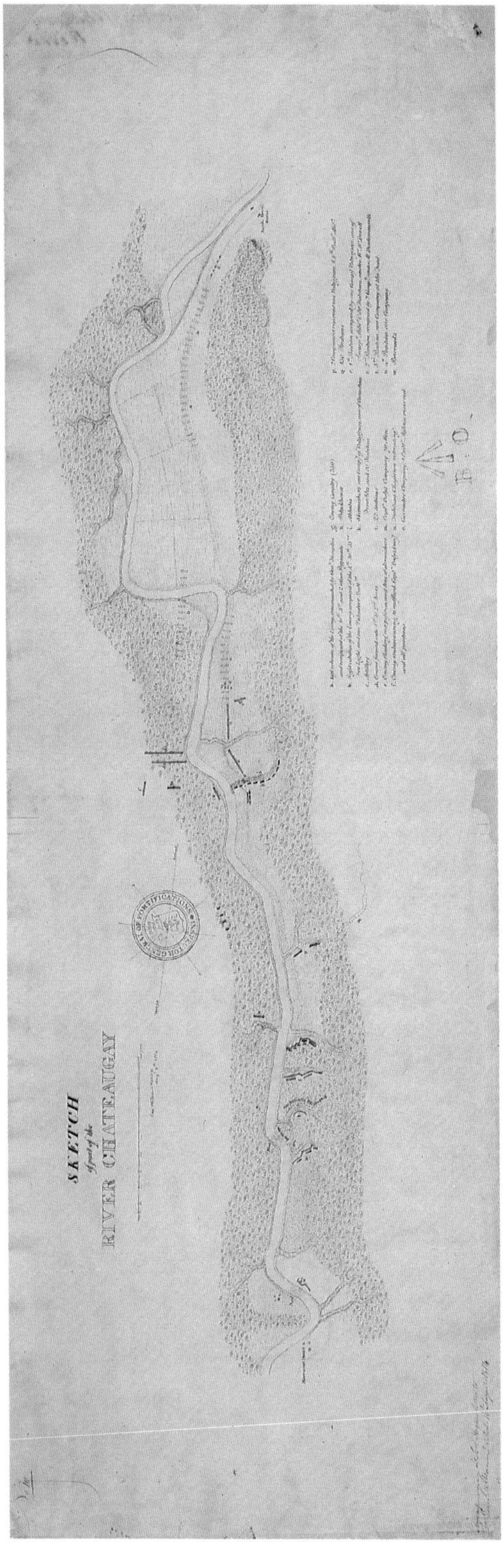

Sketch of Part of the River Châteauguay.
George Williams, R.M.S.D. Map:
manuscript, 9 August 1814.
101.1 × 33.3 cm.

National Archives of Canada:
Cartographic and Architectural Archives
Division (NMC 19176).

Attack on Fort Oswego, 1814

Control of the Great Lakes was very important in the War of 1812. With limited land communications, the lakes were vital for moving men and supplies. The Americans gained and held control of Lake Erie from 1813, while the balance on Lake Ontario see-sawed between the two sides.

In early 1814, the completion of the *Prince Regent* (seen here on the left, close to shore) and the *Princess Charlotte* (centre of the view) gave the British a temporary advantage, which they exploited to attack Fort Oswego at the eastern end of Lake Ontario. The battle is seen in its early stages, with Swiss mercenaries, Upper Canadian militia, and marines storming ashore on the left and forming ranks, while seamen and marines armed with pikes are disembarking from the ships to land immediately below the fort on the right. The British took the fort, capturing large quantities of supplies. If they had pressed further inland to the Oswego Falls, they could have captured a major equipment cache and perhaps would have kept the American fleet out of action for the summer.

Lieutenant John Hewett (fl. 1806–1869), a Royal Marine upon whose drawing this aquatint was based, was in the thick of the fighting. According to a letter in the National Archives, he rushed the fort's flagstaff, climbed it under heavy fire and ripped down the American flag — which perhaps explains why the flag and flagstaff occupy a disproportionately large position in this view.

Attack on Fort Oswego, Lake Ontario, N. America, May 6th, 1814, Noon. John Hewett (fl. 1806–1869). Etched by Robert Hovell. London, 1 May 1815. Hand-coloured aquatint. 47.8 × 61.0 cm.

National Archives of Canada: Documentary Art and Photography Division (Negative no. C-41207).

Carnage at Fort Erie, 1814

Later in 1814, the Americans again crossed the Niagara River, taking Fort Erie. After a victory at Chippewa and a bloody draw at Lundy's Lane, they withdrew to the fort. The British army set up camp and constructed gun batteries, while the Americans extended the fort's defences, all of which can be seen on this plan.

After insufficient shelling of the fort, the British regulars on 15 August attempted a complicated night attack that the explosion of an ammunition magazine turned from defeat to disaster. The British casualties were an appalling 900 men.

On 15 September, an American sortie, for which the British were inexcusably ill-prepared, spiked three of the six British siege guns. Losses were heavy on both sides, and neither could claim a clear victory. The British withdrew to Chippewa and the Americans eventually re-crossed to Buffalo, blowing up Fort Erie on 5 November. The war in the Niagara peninsula had become increasingly bloody and senseless.

This contemporary manuscript copy was prepared by George D. Cranfield, Deputy Assistant Quarter Master General at Kingston in 1815, for future reference from an original done on the spot by Lieutenant W.A. Nesfield. It passed out of the military's hands and came to the National Archives as part of a private collection.

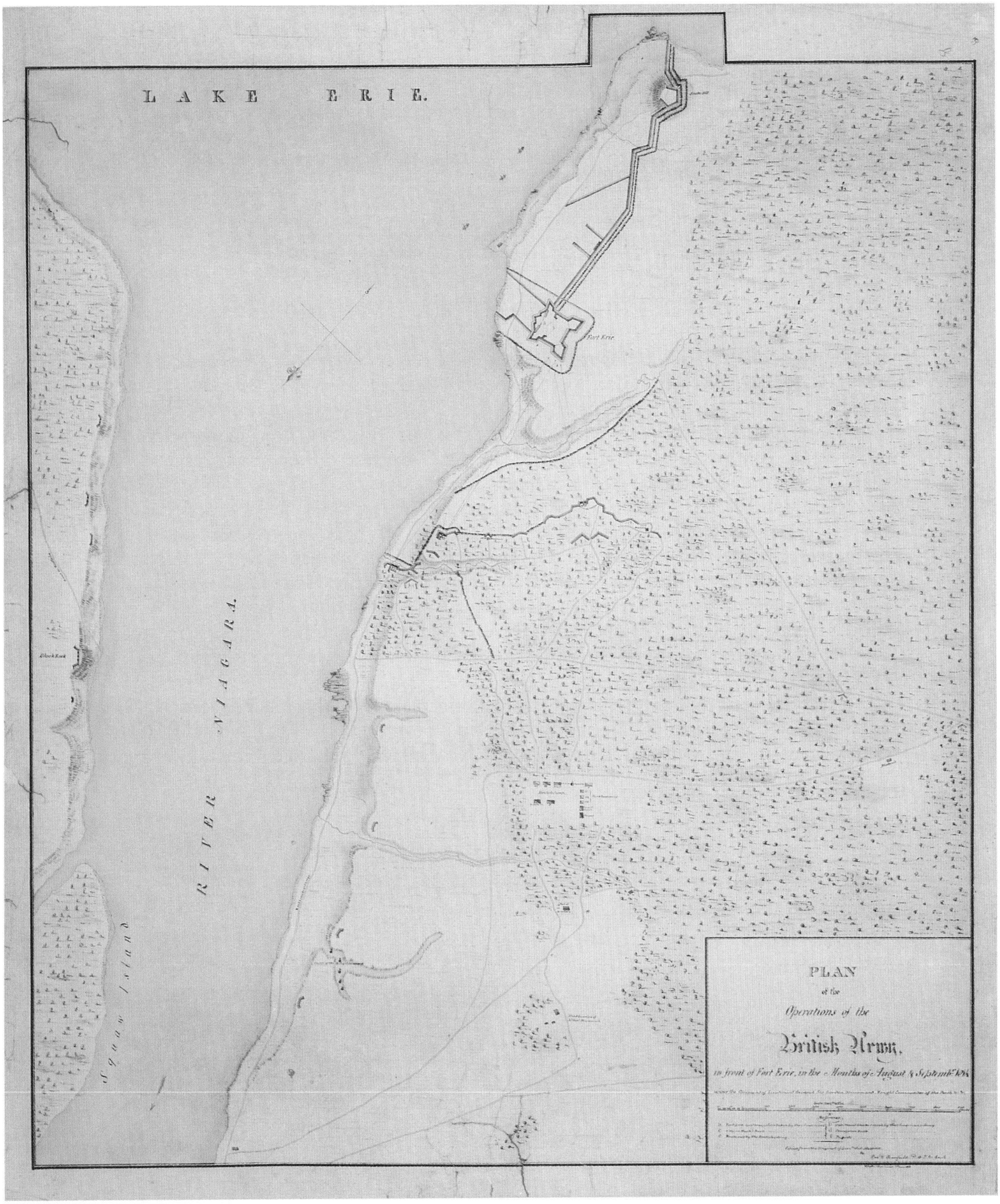

"Plan of the Operations of the British Army in front of Fort Erie, in the Months of August & September, 1814." George D. Cranfield, Deputy Assistant Quarter Master General, after Lt. W. A. Nesfield. Map: manuscript, hand-coloured, 3 May 1815. 58.4×49.4 cm.

National Archives of Canada: Cartographic and Architectural Archives Division (NMC 22341).

A Woman's View of the War, 1814

Surviving letters, diaries and journals that record the everyday thoughts and concerns of people are not very common for this period, and those by women are especially rare.

The "Mrs. Gordon" who wrote this letter is possibly the wife of James Gordon, an assistant commissary during the War of 1812. Catharine Prendergast, the recipient, was living at this date in the United States.

Through the letter, a reader gets some sense of the stress the war was causing Mrs. Gordon. She laments that "this fine country is all most laid in wast" and longs for peace. Despite the fact she has a one-year-old child, she had twice accompanied her husband as the British army in 1813 retreated up the Niagara peninsula. She had not expected to see her parents, who had stayed behind, alive again, but is touchingly grateful that her entire family survived to be together on Christmas day. Her fervent wish concerning the conflict is "I hope and trust this year will put an end to it."

This letter comes from the Merritt Family papers. Catharine Prendergast was the fiancée of William Hamilton Merritt, later builder of the Welland Canal. The papers contain rare personal letters dating back to the American Revolution and before.

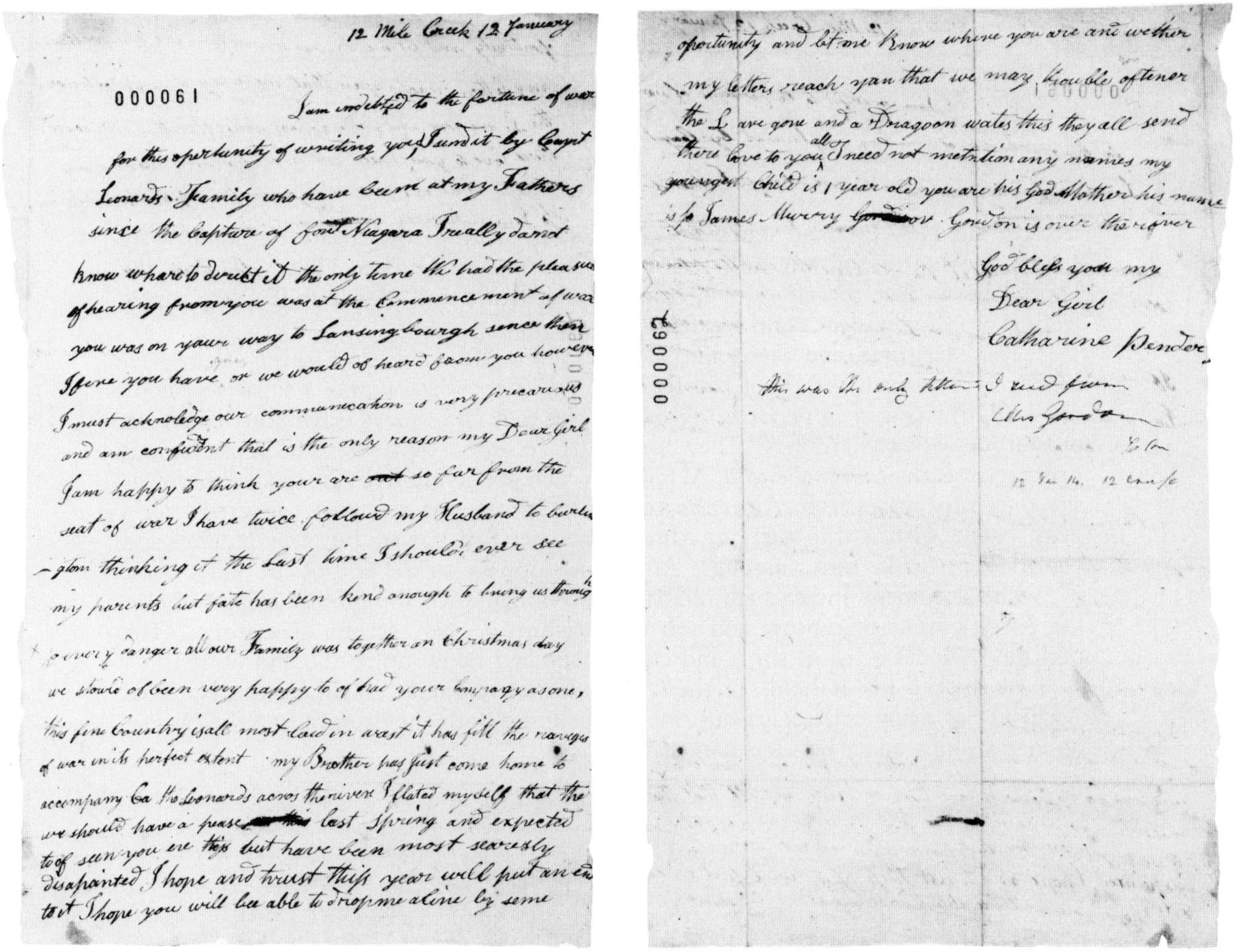

12 Mile Creek 12 January

000061

I am indebted to the fortune of war for this opertunity of writing you I send it by Capt Leonards Family who have been at my Fathers since the capture of fort Niagara I really dare not know where to direct it the only time we had the pleasure of hearing from you was at the Commencement of war you was on your way to Lansingbourgh since then I fere you have gone or we would of heard from you however I must acknoledge our communication is very precarious and am confident that is the only reason my Dear Girl I am happy to think your are ~~not~~ so far from the seat of war I have twice followed my Husband to Burlington thinking it the last time I should ever see my parents but fate has been kind enough to bring us through every danger all our Family was together on Christmas day we should of been very happy to of had your company as one, this fine Country is all most laid in wast it has felt the ravages of war in its perfect extent my Brother has just come home to accompany Ca the Leonards acros the river I flated myself that the we should have a pease [illegible] last Spring and expected to of seen you ere this but have been most severely disapointed I hope and trust this year will put an end to it I hope you will be able to drop me a line by some

opertunity and let me Know where you are and wether my letters reach you that we may trouble oftener the L are gone and a Dragoon wates this they all send there love to you all I need not mention any names my youngest Child is 1 year old you are his God Mother his name is Jas James Murray ~~Gordon~~ Gordon is over the river

God bless you my
Dear Girl
Catharine Pender

000062

This was the only letter I recd from Mrs Gordon

12 Jan 14. 12 Creek

Letter, Mrs. Gordon to Catharine Prendergast, 12 Mile Creek, 12 January [1814].

National Archives of Canada: Manuscript Division, Merritt Family papers, MG 24, E 1, vol. 3, pp. 61–62.

XI

Canada's Most Famous Privateer, the *Liverpool Packet*, 1813

Because the New England states remained largely neutral, the Atlantic colonies were spared the horrors of war inflicted upon Ontario and Quebec. The war with the United States had the effect of lifting the Maritimes and Newfoundland to a new feeling of self-confidence and local pride.

The Maritimes and Newfoundland, however, did more than cheer others' victories. Thirty-seven vessels of the five colonies (Cape Breton was a separate colony until 1820) engaged in privateering during the war, and twelve others carried letters of marque as armed traders. They made 207 recorded captures. The most famous privateer was the *Liverpool Packet*. Manned by a crew of forty-five Liverpool fishermen, she took fifty prizes from American coastal shipping. She was once captured after a grim battle with a ship carrying three times her fire power, but was retaken and continued to strike terror amongst American shipping to the end of the war.

The document shown here relates to a problem with the official recognition of the *Packet*'s right to capture and sell enemy ships — her "letters of marque." The petition includes a list of ships and cargoes she had taken up to the end of 1812.

In the records it holds of the Vice Admirality Court, Halifax, the National Archives has many prize court documents outlining both the capture and the cargoes of enemy ships taken by Canadian privateers.

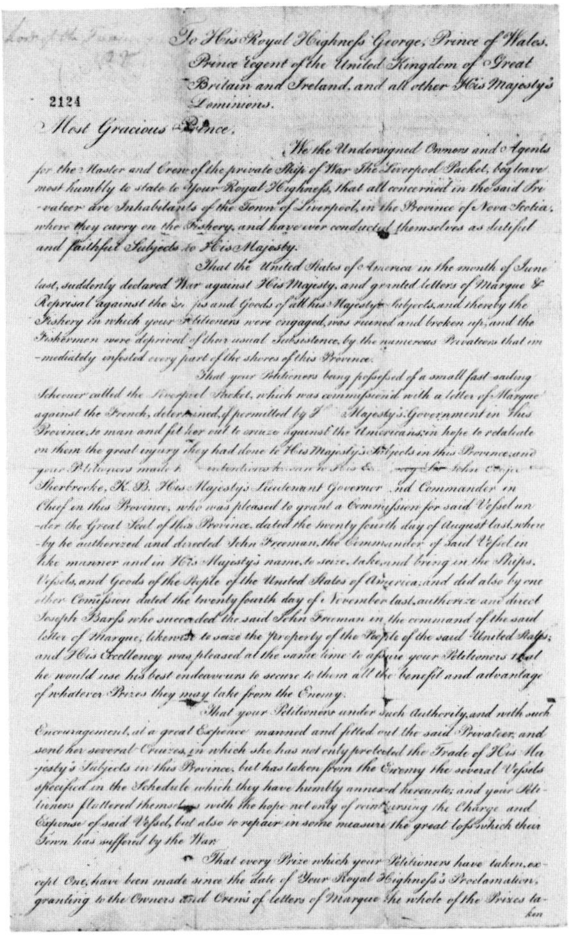

2124

To His Royal Highness George, Prince of Wales. Prince Regent of the United Kingdom of Great Britain and Ireland, and all other His Majesty's Dominions.

Most Gracious Prince,

We the Undersigned Owners and Agents for the Master and Crew of the private Ship of War The Liverpool Packet, beg leave most humbly to state to Your Royal Highness, that all concerned in the said Privateer are Inhabitants of the Town of Liverpool, in the Province of Nova Scotia; where they carry on the Fishery, and have ever conducted themselves as dutiful and faithful Subjects to His Majesty.

That the United States of America in the month of June last, suddenly declared War against His Majesty, and granted letters of Marque & Reprisal against the [illegible] and Goods of all his Majesty's Subjects, and thereby the Fishery in which your Petitioners were engaged, was ruined and broken up, and the Fishermen were deprived of their usual Subsistence, by the numerous Privateers that immediately infested every part of the shores of this Province.

That your Petitioners being possessed of a small fast sailing Schooner called the Liverpool Packet, which was commission'd with a letter of Marque against the French, determined, if permitted by [illegible] Majesty's Government in this Province, to man and fit her out to cruize against the Americans, in hope to retaliate on them the great injury they had done to His Majesty's Subjects in this Province, and your Petitioners made [illegible] intentions known to His E[illegible] Sir John Coape Sherbrooke, K. B. His Majesty's Lieutenant Governor and Commander in Chief in this Province, who was pleased to grant a Commission for said Vessel under the Great Seal of this Province, dated the twenty fourth day of August last, whereby he authorized and directed John Freeman, the Commander of said Vessel in like manner and in His Majesty's name, to seize, take, and bring in the Ships, Vessels, and Goods of the People of the United States of America; and did also by one other Commission dated the twenty fourth day of November last, authorize and direct Joseph Barss who succeeded the said John Freeman in the command of the said letter of Marque, likewise to seize the Property of the People of the said United States; and His Excellency was pleased at the same time to assure your Petitioners that he would use his best endeavours to secure to them all the benefit and advantage of whatever Prizes they may take from the Enemy.

That your Petitioners under such Authority, and with such Encouragement, at a great Expence manned and fitted out the said Privateer, and sent her several Cruizes, in which she has not only protected the Trade of His Majesty's Subjects in this Province, but has taken from the Enemy the several Vessels specified in the Schedule which they have humbly annexed hereunto; and your Petitioners flattered themselves with the hope not only of reimbursing the Charge and Expense of said Vessel, but also to repair in some measure the great loss which their Town has suffered by the War.

That every Prize which your Petitioners have taken, except One, have been made since the date of Your Royal Highness's Proclamation, granting to the Owners and Crews of letters of Marque the whole of the Prizes taken

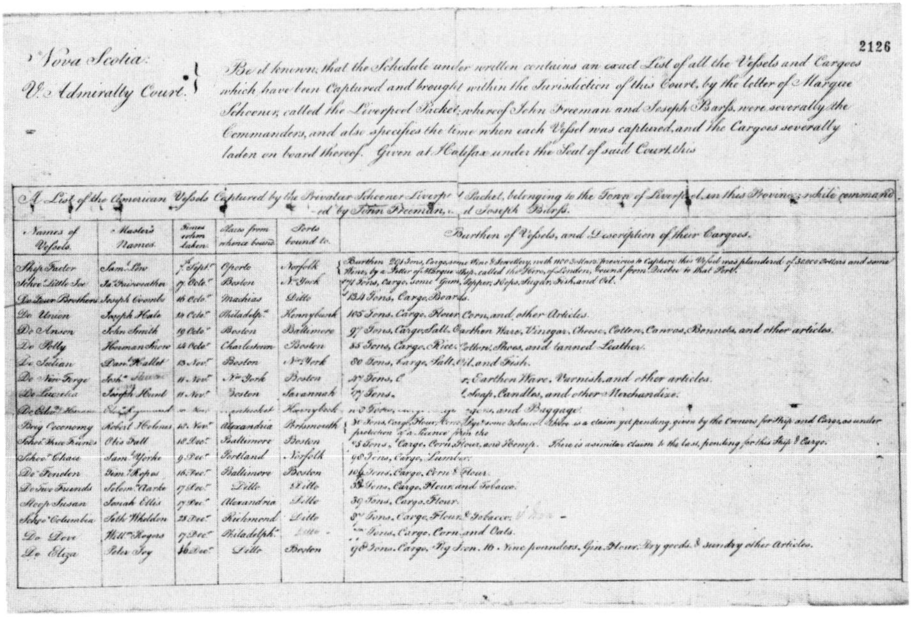

2126

Nova Scotia.
V. Admiralty Court.

Be it known, that the Schedule under written contains an exact List of all the Vessels and Cargoes which have been Captured and brought within the Jurisdiction of this Court, by the letter of Marque Schooner, called the Liverpool Packet, whereof John Freeman and Joseph Barss, were severally the Commanders, and also specifies the time when each Vessel was captured, and the Cargoes severally laden on board thereof. Given at Halifax under the Seal of said Court, this

A List of the American Vessels Captured by the Privateer Schooner Liverpool Packet, belonging to the Town of Liverpool, in this Province, while commanded by John Freeman, and Joseph Barss.

Names of Vessels.	Master's Names.	Times when taken.	Place from whence bound.	Ports bound to.	Burthen of Vessels, and Description of their Cargoes.
Ship Factor	Saml. Low	7th Sept.	Oporto	Norfolk	Burthen 201 Tons, Cargo, some Wine & Jewellery, with 1100 Dollars; previous to Capture this Vessel was plundered of 32000 Dollars and some Wine, by a letter of Marque Ship, called the Hero, of London, bound from Quebec to that Port.
Schr. Little Joe	Jas. Fairweather	7 Octr.	Boston	Nw. York	171 Tons, Cargo, some Gum, Pepper, Hops, Sugar, Fish, and Oil.
Do. Four Brothers	Joseph Coombs	16 Octr.	Machias	Ditto	134 Tons, Cargo, Boards.
Do. Union	Joseph Hale	14 Octr.	Philadelpa.	Kennybunk	105 Tons, Cargo, Flour, Corn, and other Articles.
Do. Anson	John Smith	19 Octr.	Boston	Baltimore	97 Tons, Cargo, Salt, Earthen Ware, Vinegar, Cheese, Cotton, Canvas, Bonnets, and other articles.
Do. Polly	Herman Snow	24 Octr.	Charlestown	Boston	85 Tons, Cargo, Rice, Cotton, Shoes, and tanned Leather.
Do. Julian	Danl. Hallet	13 Novr.	Boston	Nw. York	80 Tons, Cargo, Salt, Oil, and Fish.
Do. New Forge	Josha. [illegible]	11 Novr.	Nw. York	Boston	[illegible] Tons, C[illegible] r, Earthen Ware, Varnish, and other articles.
Do. Lucretia	Joseph Hunt	11 Novr.	Boston	Savannah	[illegible] Tons, [illegible] Soap, Candles, and other Merchandize.
Do. Eliza [illegible]	[illegible]	[illegible] Novr.	[illegible]antucket	Kennybunk	[illegible] Tons, [illegible] and Baggage.
Brig Economy	Robert Holmes	10 Novr.	Alexandria	Portsmouth	30 Tons, Cargo, Flour, Corn, [illegible] some Tobacco. There is a claim yet pending, given by the Owners for Ship and Cargo, as under protection of a Licence from the
Schr. Three Friends	Otis Hall	18 Decr.	Baltimore	Boston	[illegible]5 Tons, Cargo, Corn, Flour, and Hemp. There is a similar claim to the last, pending for this Ship & Cargo.
Schr. Chase	Saml. Yorke	9 Decr.	Portland	Norfolk	98 Tons, Cargo, Lumber.
Do. Fenelon	Jam. Rogers	16 Decr.	Baltimore	Boston	10[illegible] Tons, Cargo, Corn & Flour.
Do. Two Friends	Solom. Clarke	17 Decr.	Ditto	Ditto	5[illegible] Tons, Cargo, Flour and Tobacco.
Sloop Susan	Josiah Ellis	17 Decr.	Alexandria	Ditto	39 Tons, Cargo, Flour.
Schr. Columbia	Seth Whelden	28 Decr.	Richmond	Ditto	8[illegible] Tons, Cargo, Flour & Tobacco.
Do. Dove	Willm. Rogers	17 Decr.	Philadelph.	Ditto	[illegible] Tons, Cargo, Corn and Oats.
Do. Eliza	Peter Joy	16 Decr.	Ditto	Boston	98 Tons, Cargo, Pig Iron, 16 Nine pounders, Gin, Flour, Dry goods & sundry other Articles.

Petition to George, Prince Regent, by the Master and Crew of the *Liverpool Packet*, 1813 [copy].

National Archives of Canada: Manuscript Division, MG 24, I 182, vol. 4, pp. 2124 and 2126.

The Upper Canada Preserved Medal, 1813

The War of 1812 ended in a stalemate; the Treaty of Ghent re-established the status quo before the war. Canadians, however, could be proud of their role in fighting a powerful enemy to a stand-off in a war they had had no wish to incur.

A number of medals were issued by the British authorities relevant to the War of 1812 "in commemoration of the brilliant and distinguished events in which the success of His Majesty's arms has received the royal approbation." It was decided to honour the engagements at Fort Detroit, Chateauguay and Crysler's Farm.

In addition, a special medal was struck by a colonial organization, the Loyal and Patriotic Society of Upper Canada, formed in the early months of the war to relieve wartime distress and commemorate conspicuous bravery. The obverse of the medal showed, as the directors described it in 1813:

> A streight between two lakes, on the north side a Beaver (emblem of peaceful industry), the ancient armorial bearing of Canada. In the background an English lion slumbering. On the south side of the streight, the American eagle planeing in the air, as if checked from seizing the Beaver by the presence of the Lion. . . .

Recipients were to be recommended by officers of the militia. Because of the large number of recipients recommended and because of controversy over the authority to award the medals, all the extant ones — 62 gold and 550 silver — were eventually melted down. This medal is a modern re-strike, made from the original moulds.

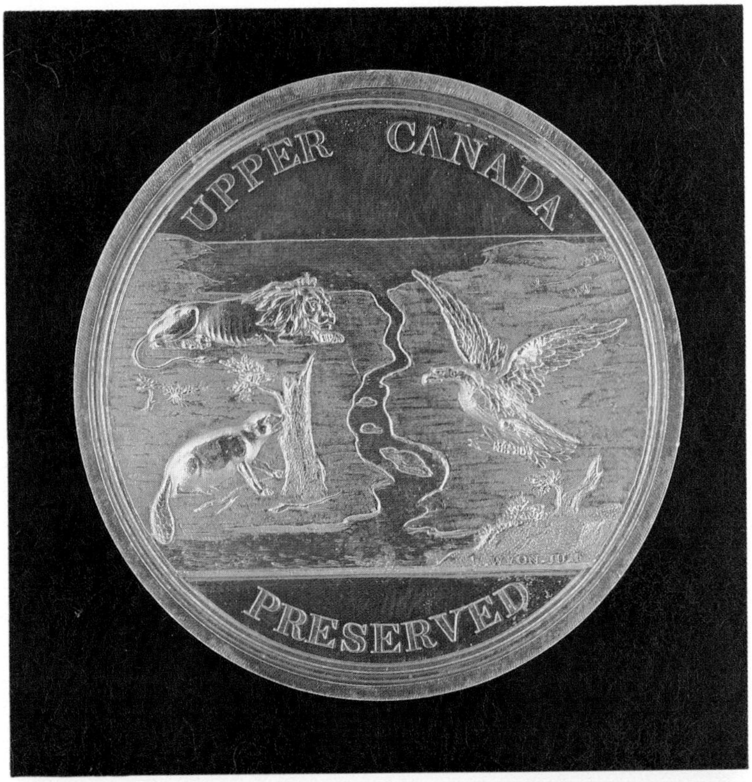

Obverse and reverse of "Upper Canada Preserved" medal, 1813 (modern re-strike). Struck in silver. Diameter 51 mm.

National Archives of Canada: Documentary Art and Photography Division.

Index